Erotic Transference and Countertransference

C000298035

Erotic Transference and Countertransference brings together, for the first time, contemporary views on how psychotherapists and analysts work with and think about the erotic in therapeutic practice.

Representing a broad spectrum of psychoanalytic perspectives, including object relations, Kleinian, Jungian, self psychology and Lacanian thought, the contributors highlight similarities and differences in their approaches to the erotic in transference and countertransference, ranging from love and sexual desire to perverse and psychotic manifestations.

Erotic Transference and Countertransference offers ways of understanding the erotic which should prove both useful and thought-provoking.

David Mann is a psychoanalytic psychotherapist and a member of the London Centre for Psychotherapy. He works in private practice and primary care. His previous book *Psychotherapy: An Erotic Relationship – Transference and Countertransference Passions* is published by Routledge.

Contributors include Marco Chiesa, Ronald Doctor, Nathan Field, Fiona Gardner, Jackie Gerrard, Sheila Gordon, David Mann, Andrew Samuels, Martin Stanton and Jean Thomson.

Erotic Transference and Countertransference

Clinical practice in psychotherapy

Edited and introduced by
David Mann

Routledge
Taylor & Francis Group

LONDON AND NEW YORK

First published 1999
by Routledge
27 Church Road, Hove, East Sussex BN3 2FA

Simultaneously published in the USA and Canada
by Routledge
711 Third Avenue, New York NY 10017

Reprinted 2003, 2005, 2007

Transferred to digital printing 2010

Routledge is an imprint of the Taylor & Francis Group, an Informa business

©1999 David Mann for the collection as a whole,
the authors for individual chapters

Typeset in Garamond by
BC Typesetting, Bristol
Printed and bound in Great Britain by
TJI Digital, Padstow, Cornwall

British Library Cataloguing in Publication Data
A catalogue record for this book is available from the British Library

Library of Congress Cataloging in Publication Data
Clinical approaches to the erotic transference and countertransference
    /edited by David Mann.
        p. cm
    Includes bibliographical references and index.
    1. Psychotherapy–Erotic aspects.   2. Transference (Psychology)
    3. Countertransference (Psychology)   I. Mann, David
    RC489.E75C58   1999
    616.89'14–dc21   98–30535

ISBN 978–0–415–18453–3 (pbk)

For Michelle and our sons Mark and Peter

Contents

Acknowledgements

I would like to thank Michelle MacGrath for her patience and interest during the progress of this book. As always, she is the most valuable muse and resource.

Thanks are also due to Drs Estela Welldon and Cleo Van Velsen for their assistance during the early stages of the book. I would like to thank the staff at the Crown Dale Medical Centre for their interest and support and, in particular, Dr Patrick White for our discussions and his stimulating 'otherness'; also to John Lees for his thoughtful comments on my ideas. I would further extend my thanks to my editor, Kate Hawes, and all at Routledge for their assistance.

Chapters 4 and 6 were first read at the Institute of Psychotherapy and Counselling (WPF) 1997 Summer Conference on 'What is this thing called love? Should therapists love their patients?' Chapter 1 is a revised version of an article that first appeared in the *British Journal of Psychotherapy* 13(2), 1996. Chapter 10 is a revised version of an article that first appeared in *Psychoanalytic Dialogues* 6(3), 1996. Acknowledgement and thanks are also due to Faber & Faber for permission to quote W. H. Auden in Chapter 6.

List of contributors

Marco Chiesa MD, MRCPsych. is a member of the British Psychoanalytical Society and Consultant Psychiatrist in Psychotherapy at the Cassel Hospital, Richmond, Surrey. He is also Senior Tutor in Psychotherapy at the Institute of Psychiatry, London and Honorary Consultant Psychotherapist with the Maudsley and Bethlem NHS Mental Health Trust, London.

Ronald Doctor MBBCh., MMed. Psych., MRCPsych. is Consultant Psychiatrist in Psychotherapy and College Tutor at West Middlesex and Ashford Hospital, Hounslow and Spelthorne CMH NHS Trust. He is a supervisor on the Forensic Psychotherapy Course, Tavistock and Portman NHS Trust. He is also an Associate Member of the British Psychoanalytical Society and in private practice.

Nathan Field is a Fellow of the London Centre for Psychotherapy and a full Member of the British Association of Psychotherapists. He has worked in private practice as an analytical psychotherapist for nearly thirty years. In addition, he teaches, supervises and lectures. He has published a number of papers linking analysis, healing and unconscious communication. These themes have been brought together in his book *Breakdown and Breakthrough* published in 1996 by Routledge.

Fiona Gardner is a psychoanalytic psychotherapist currently working with young people for Bath Mental Health Care Trust, and in private practice. She was a founder member of the Avon Counselling and Psychotherapy Service in Bristol, is a Member of the Severnside Institute for Psychotherapy and is on the Editorial Board of the *British Journal of Psychotherapy*. She has published on gender and mental health, child sexual abuse and psychotherapy training.

Jackie Gerrard had a background in social work before training as a psychoanalytic psychotherapist in 1978. She is a Full Member, Training Therapist and Supervisor at the London Centre for Psychotherapy and a Full Member of the Lincoln Centre. She works in private practice and also supervises at the Westminster Pastoral Foundation.

Sheila Gordon read History at University College London and worked as a teacher and educational writer off and on for twenty-five years. She decided to switch careers and trained as an analytic psychotherapist. She set up in private practice in 1982 and is still working in South London as an individual and group therapist. She is particularly interested in the history of psychoanalytic thought and in bringing psychoanalytic psychotherapy 'down to earth'. She is an Associate Member of the London Centre for Psychotherapy.

David Mann is a psychoanalytic psychotherapist and a member of the London Centre for Psychotherapy. He works in private practice and primary care and lectures, teaches and runs workshops around the country on 'Working with the erotic transference and countertransference'. He has published extensively in leading national and international psychotherapy journals. He is author of *Psychotherapy: An Erotic Relationship – Transference and Countertransference Passions* (Routledge, 1997) and is the editor of this present book.

Andrew Samuels is Professor of Analytical Psychology at the University of Essex and a Training Analyst of the Society of Analytical Psychology, London. He also works as a political consultant. His books for Routledge are *Jung and the Post-Jungians* (1985), *A Critical Dictionary of Jungian Analysis* (1986), *The Plural Psyche* (1989) and *The Political Psyche* (1993).

Martin Stanton is a psychoanalytic psychotherapist in private practice in Peckham, London. He is a clinical staff member of the Tavistock Marital Studies Institute, founder and director of the Centre for Psychoanalytic Studies at the University of Kent, council member of the London Centre for Psychotherapy and chair of the Universities Association for Psychoanalytic Studies. He is the author of *Outside the Dream* (Routledge, 1983), *Sandor Ferenczi* (Aronson/ FAB, 1991), *Sandor Ferenczi et la Technique Active* (PUF, 1996), *Out of Order: Clinical Work and Unconscious Process* (Rebus, 1997), and editor of *Jean Laplanche: Seduction, Translation, Drives* (ICA, 1989) and *Teaching Transference: On the Foundations of Psychoanalytic Studies* (Rebus, 1996).

Jean Thomson is a professional member of the Society of Analytical Psychology. Previously, as a Psychiatric Social Worker, she worked in psychiatric hospitals and for several years in the Adolescent Department of the Tavistock Clinic and as a tutor on the psychodynamic counselling course for student counsellors at the Department of Extra-Mural Studies, University of London. For a time she was Principal Lecturer in Social Work at the former North East London Polytechnic. She is now in private practice as a Jungian analyst.

Erotic narratives in psychoanalytic practice

An introduction

David Mann

How do I love thee? Let me count the ways.
Elizabeth Barrett Browning, Sonnets from the Portuguese, XLIII

THE SHADOW OF THE EROTIC IN THE PSYCHOANALYTIC NARRATIVE

In the beginning the ancient Judaic thinkers who conceived the Book of Genesis realised that knowledge and sexual awareness went hand in hand: when Adam and Eve ate the apple from the Tree of Knowledge they became aware of their own and each other's sexuality. The acquisition of knowledge and awareness of sexuality are thus pivotal to consciousness. In the biblical context, they feel shame and incur the father's wrath for concealing their nakedness, are thus banished from paradise, and henceforth, we are told, childbirth will be painful. The ancients astutely observed that real knowledge about oneself is intimately linked to sexual curiosity and that there is a price to pay for consciousness; losing peace of mind might seem like a poor swap for a piece of apple but the development of consciousness is the only way to individuate. Put another way, we might say that erotic thoughts about ourselves and others are a major, if not the most important, way we have to separate from our parents.

Of course erotic thoughts are not that simple. The recipient of our adult erotic desires is never entirely free from incestuous influence. Individuals acquire their capacity for erotic desire or love in the context of their own familial experience. We learn the language of love by conscious and unconscious experience, becoming aware of its possibilities and prohibitions (and perversions) through our relationship with both parents. Although the eroticism of childhood finds its culmination in adult sexual experience there is no hiatus here: it is all one life. In the arena of the erotic we find the most intense mingling of infantile and adult passions. The ancients missed that connection: while the erotic leads us away from our parents its incestuous foundations bind us to our mother and father. Our experience as infants and children will flesh out how we manage our erotic relations (both love and sex) as adults. The erotic is primarily object related. Since any two people will have an erotic transference to each other this brings their mutual need for object relating into an erotic bond: related and connected at the point of their most intense unconscious erotic desires. The purpose of the erotic bond is that it deepens the individual's capacity for connection and relatedness to others as well as to him or herself. The erotic bond therefore highlights issues of intrusiveness and intimacy. The erotic entails the breaching of boundaries always psychological and, as far as mothers and babies and adult lovers are concerned, physical as well. In that manner, the erotic challenges our sense of self and other, when somebody gets under our skin, whether this is experienced as enhancing and intimate or intrusive and threatening.

The erotic subjectivity of the individual is thus inextricable from his or her psyche. There is exemption out from this erotic subjectivity: the analytic rule of abstinence will stop neither erotic fantasy life nor the erotic nature of the unconscious. The analysand and the analyst have that much in common: they are connected by their erotic bond at deep layers of the unconscious.

The erotic has a paradoxical status in psychoanalysis. There is general agreement that it is a universal experience and, therefore, probably part of every therapeutic transaction. Yet such a ubiquitous phenomenon is scarcely reported in the literature and is excluded from most training programmes. The prevalence of the erotic is thus acknowledged as a universal feature that is rarely discussed.

But the paucity of discussion is not the same as an absence from discourse. The erotic has dominated psychoanalytic theory and practice since its inception: from the therapeutic débâcle between Breuer and Anna O which floundered on the erotic transference and countertransference, via Jung's sexual misconduct with Sabina Spielrein and Ferenczi's experimental love techniques and misconduct right through to the present day and the public horror at the sexual exploitation of patients. Freud (1915) could only recommend repression as a way of dealing with the erotic countertransference (his own understanding of psychoanalysis failed to inform him of the futility of that tactic). Jung was so unable to work with the erotic transference and countertransference that, in my view, he took flight into a desexualised theory of Eros.

What the patient, therapist and public are worried about is sexual misconduct. The general public is now alert to sexually abusive therapists. A number of publications have directly looked at this issue (Rutter 1989, Jehu 1994, McNamara 1994). In fact, there is sexual abuse among all professions: social workers, solicitors, lawyers, teachers, priests, businessmen and women, doctors, etc. Yet a particular horror grips the public when it is perpetrated by psychotherapists and counsellors. Perhaps this is because there is a dim awareness of the incestuous transference issues involved with vulnerable patients. The positive side of this public outcry is to break the silence about malpractice that has followed psychoanalysis in every step of its history.

The veil that has been unconsciously drawn around the erotic transference and countertransference merely draws attention to its fantastical importance. The presence and influence of the erotic are felt by their lack of discussion and draw attention to themselves by being almost unspeakable. For example, the British School of Object Relations has explored every conceivable aspect of aggression – up and down, left and right, inside and outside – but barely a word has been said about the erotic. This is defended by apologists saying that aggression is the underlying issue behind the erotic. But it could equally be said, and indeed I am saying, that the erotic is often the underlying issue behind aggression. By not forming part of analytic discussion the erotic transference and countertransference thus become the dominating influence in analytic discourse: a subject to be bypassed, avoided, circumvented. By requiring avoidance, the erotic has exerted a structuring influence over the formation of psychoanalytic theory and practice: everything constellates around the erotic and what is discussed is framed by what has to be left in silence; the path of circumvention is defined by what is being side-stepped. I am not describing a conscious conspiracy here. Rather, I am drawing attention to the unconscious processes in the psychoanalytic research programme itself.[1]

Since about 1985 the erotic transference and countertransference has achieved much more open discussion. This has to be seen in the context that this same period has brought unprecedented public awareness of some patients being sexually taken advantage of by their analysts and therapists. (Concomitant with this is an awareness of sexual abuse in other domains: actual incest in the family, sexual abuse in teaching and social services, exposure of organised paedophile gangs, etc.) This has not only led some therapists to discuss malpractice openly but, equally importantly, has also provoked a flurry of books and articles reevaluating the erotic transference. Two processes have come together here: the realisation that the erotic nature of therapy cannot be foreclosed by silence and the admission that, historically, psychoanalysis has not dealt with this subject effectively. These dynamics have propelled therapists to come to terms with the erotic nature of the unconscious and its effect on the transference and countertransference. One hundred years after the sorry state of relations between Breuer and Anna O, therapists are now realising that perhaps the erotic might be more than merely a problematic resistance to the analytic dyad.

THE REGRESSIVE AND PROGRESSIVE DUALITY OF THE EROTIC NARRATIVE

The subject of this book is how the universal experience of eroticism impacts on the therapeutic adventure. There is, in fact, a remarkable degree of agreement between various analytic schools in that Freudians and Jungians alike prioritise the status of Eros in therapeutic practice, though for seemingly different reasons. For Freud (1915) the erotic or love transference led back to the infantile origins of the Oedipal triangle; through the erotic, childhood experience or memories could be rediscovered. Jung (1911) saw Eros as a need to return to an earlier state from which to grow and progress. Despite the difference in interpretation, at least they could agree about the importance of Eros. However, the point I wish to make at this stage is that classical psychoanalytic thinking sees the role of the erotic as central to therapeutic process.

In my opinion, the split in the views between Freud and Jung replicates the split found in the narrative of love first outlined by Plato. In *The Symposium*, Plato had seen love as either a backward glance (searching for our lost and missing other half of a hermaphroditic whole) or a forward motion, a progressing along stages in a hierarchy (the ladder of love). In making such a division Plato split the nature of love and divided its regressive and progressive elements, love being one or the other rather than both. The difference in approaches between Freud and Jung might be viewed as a continuation of that platonic split. We can see the Freud/Jung split (quite apart from all the other issues between them) as representing two sides of a schism arising from the duality in the nature of the erotic; Freud and Jung become the bicephalous mouthpieces on the erotic body of knowledge. In effect, I am proposing that Freud and Jung are representatives of two ways of thinking about the erotic, providing two accounts, two descriptions, two ways of reading the story of the erotics, the bifurcation of the erotic narrative. In that sense, the progressive and regressive sides of the erotic narratives are thoughts in search of speakers, Freud and Jung can be seen as representing the two strands of this narrative, the division having been ushered in by Plato in ancient Greece. The narrative of the erotic transference and countertransference has tended to emphasise one of the two sides of the erotic in therapeutic practice. As a gross simplification of these views, we may call them the progressive or regressive narratives. In the model I am suggesting it is not a matter of 'either/or': the erotic is both backward-looking to infantile origins and components and forward-looking, seeking a developmental progression which allows the individual to be transformed into something different from the past. It is both things simultaneously, though one or the other may be stronger at any one time.[2]

As in so many things, this duality in the erotic narration is more apparent than real. Let us take an example from another discipline, quantum physics. At different times over the last three hundred years physicists have thought that light was made of either waves or particles and each description had its own supporters and evidence. The contemporary view is that light is made of both waves and particles: that under certain conditions of measurement light behaves as though it were made of particles while under other conditions it appears to exist as a wave. In viewing the narration of the erotic in psychoanalytic practice we find a similar dichotomy: the erotic can appear very backward-looking, a form of resistance, essentially infantile in nature. Under other conditions the erotic appears progressive and innovative. It incites and excites growth and development and leads to higher and deeper and more intricate forms of relationships; it is transformational. Depending on the relative position of the viewer, either strand can seem paramount. It is only latterly that some psychoanalytic thinkers have come to the conclusion that these disparate observations are actually part of the same thing.

It may reasonably be objected at this point that the erotic transference and countertransference cannot be simply reduced to two narratives: there are as many narratives as there are analytic couples. Actually this is also my view. The bifurcation I am describing for the moment is best understood as an umbrella concept like other bipolar opposites: body/mind, masculine/feminine, mother/father, heterosexual/homosexual. Any of these terms are not fixed but are capable of being lived, described, illustrated or understood in a variety of ways. To acknowledge the plurality of such dualities it might be more accurate to delineate bipolar opposites differently: bodies/minds, masculinities/femininities, mothers/fathers, heterosexualities/homosexualities, etc. Using such a broad bipolar continuum it might be more accurate to make my terms plural: 'progressions' and 'regressions'. Of course, there is an additional issue that bipolar opposites describe extremes with a considerable amount of grey area in between. My point is, however, that they are linked and inseparable.

This book takes the centrality of eroticism and explores its significance on the transference and countertransference. There are two immediate rationales behind this current volume. The first is that the book emphasises clinical practice with authors focusing on how analysts and psychotherapists work with erotic material rather than just writing a theoretical treatise on Eros. In that regard, it is intended that this book will have useful insights for the analytic practitioner. The second aim of the book is to present, in a single text, a variety of analytic views illustrating how therapists from various schools of thought have come to think about the erotic in therapy. In that respect I have attempted to represent as wide a range of perspectives as possible from mainstream analytic practice. By including authors from a variety of analytic traditions the reader may compare and contrast the similarities and differences between schools as they resonate on a single subject: the erotic in therapeutic practice. The discerning reader will also realise that authors of a similar school do not necessarily think in the same way, and such divergences and similarities of thought within a single school may also be teased out as they cluster around the subject of the erotic transference and countertransference.

EROTIC TRANSFERENCE AND COUNTERTRANSFERENCE LITERATURE: HISTORICAL DEVELOPMENT OF THE EROTIC NARRATIVE

The erotic transference and countertransference needs to be viewed in the context of the development of the psychoanalytic understanding of transference and countertransference. This is not the place to review the extensive literature on these twin subjects, but a useful summary of the pattern of development might be made.

Wolstein (1988) highlights three major trends in the development of understanding the countertransference (and I would add that these also significantly influenced the understanding of the transference). The first begins with Freud himself. Freud's view (1910) was that the direct consideration of the countertransference would threaten the analytic endeavour (and this theory was despite the evidence from his own case studies which showed him exercising his personal imagination to the fullest) and should be repressed. Many of the classical analysts attempted to follow his formula that the analyst acts like a mirror or a surgeon, an uninvolved expert.

This view of the countertransference remained largely fixed until a new approach emerged in the 1950s when analysts realised the inescapability of countertransference. The impetus came from changing views about resistance, shifting from the absolutism of the single universal perspective to a pluralism of perspectives based on direct experience. Wolstein cites Anna Freud, Reich and Sullivan as instrumental in this change. The 1950s also saw a shift in the understanding of the interpretation. The development of reality-testing skills in patients meant they tested these skills on the analyst, thus enlarging the scope of awareness of self and other. Patients were now observing unconscious and dissociated aspects of the therapist. Wolstein writes: 'If adaptive or consensual observation moved psychoanalysts into closer relational proximity to their patients, it also moved patients into closer relational proximity to their psychoanalysts' (1988: 11). Patients and analysts were now seen as both participants and observers.

Gradually this trend in psychoanalysis came to a dead end, unable to reach the generative roots of counter anxiety. The third wave of developments in understanding the countertransference (and transference) occurred during the 1970s with the formulations of the psychology of the self. This provided for a reflective activity in the personal and interpersonal experience of analysis. Thus every psychoanalytic inquiry had its own personal stamp. This embraced such ideas as self–object psychology and self–subject where the transference/ countertransference flows in the experiential field of therapy.

It is useful to map the bifurcated strands of thinking about the erotic in therapeutic practice on to the schema outlined by Wolstein. In this way we can perhaps see more clearly how investigation into the erotic transference and countertransference has not only paralleled the general movement within psychoanalysis but in many ways also highlights the changing picture during the twentieth century. In a manner of speaking, how psychoanalysis has thought about the erotic transference and countertransference can be seen as a gauge of how psychoanalysis has thought about transference and countertransference generally. In that sense, because current analytic thought sees the analytic process as a personal, interactive process between two participants we can make two observations. First, the bifurcated strands of erotic desire have come together in recent analytic thinking in a way that parallels the general understanding of the analytic process of how the analytic dyad comes together. Secondly, with the current preoccupation with the relationship between the analytic dyad, we may describe this as a return to the origins, how two people affect each other or, in my terms, find an erotic bond at the deepest layers of the psyche. The erotic bond brings people into relationship. As psychoanalytic thinking has been able to contemplate the deep layers of relationship between analyst and analysand so the question of unconscious eroticism has needed to be addressed by more and more authors as the century progresses. This brings analytic thinking back full circle to its origins in contemplation of the erotic, psychoanalysis being born from Freud's understanding of the erotic countertransference and erotic transference between his mentor Breuer and Anna O. The gap between the patient and therapist that classical analysts saw has not been sustained over the last hundred years. As our understanding of their overlap has come together, so too have the two strands of thinking about the erotic, the regressive and progressive, converged. But to state as much now I jump ahead of the path I wish to trace.

It would be tempting to say that as the nature of the transference and countertransference changed with greater understanding, so the erotic transference and countertransference accordingly evolved as part of the general flux, perhaps, a good barometer of general change. In fact, I think it could be argued just as strongly in the other direction. The erotic connects people at deeply unconscious levels, driving them into relationships at least at the level of fantasy. The erotic bond forms links between individuals. Because the erotic was never going to go away in analysis this propelled analysts into a greater realisation of their connection and closeness to the patient, into understanding that there is a connection between the transference and countertransference. From that point of view the underlying erotic unconscious of the analytic couple can be seen as an instigator that energised and compelled greater awareness and investigation of the transference and countertransference generally. Indeed, it is probably a chicken-and-egg argument to wonder which came first, developments in the transference and countertransference or the erotic bond. More likely the two influenced each other in a dynamic relationship and stimulated development.

Wolstein's description of the first phase of understanding countertransference, dominated by Freud's thinking that it should be repressed, is neatly illustrated by looking specifically at erotic processes in therapy until the 1950s. As Tower (1956) noted, virtually every previous writer on the subject of countertransference had stated unequivocally that no erotic reaction to the patient by the analyst was to be tolerated.

As analysts began to think differently about the countertransference we see a change in the view of the erotic transference and countertransference, though bifurcation of regressive and progressive notions remained. By the 1950s, some analysts now saw countertransference as inevitable and that the analyst and analysand were more involved with each other than the classical model of the detached expert had foreseen. On the one hand there is the view derived from Freud's classic paper of 1915 that the erotic distorts perceptions, is unreal and is a resistance to the therapeutic process. Rappaport (1956, 1959) discusses this particular manifestation in terms of the erotised transference, which he considers a particularly tenacious resistance of a psychotic nature that inhibits the patient's capacity to form real relationships. Similarities between the analyst and the patient's parent may perpetuate such an erotised distortion. Essentially the therapist must remain unstirred by the patient's feelings if the latter is to continue therapeutic progress.

Saul (1962) also takes up the idea of resistance qualities, though he does not consider the erotic to be necessarily psychotic. He describes the erotic transference as a negative therapeutic reaction in therapy with young women in 'full sexual vigour' who use sexuality as a major channel for expression. He acknowledges that this makes it hard for the therapist to keep a 'modulated countertransference'. Only by the analyst staying aloof can the treatment progress: the analyst's task is to remove inner blocks, not to give love.

Writing around the same period are a number of analysts I would group together in the progressive strand. Tower (1956) notes that various forms of erotic fantasy and countertransference are normal, though she thought it was aim-inhibited and without impulse to seek expression. She describes falling in love as a state between the biological and psychological and relates two cases, one therapeutically successful the other not. The difference resided in her countertransference: she felt 'connected' and affection towards the patient who was successful and this was unconsciously communicated between them.

Searles (1959) was also articulating the progressive strand of thinking. He saw the development of Oedipal love as a maturational milestone arising towards the end of analysis and signifying progression from a more infantile phase. From his perspective ego impairment arises if the child cannot experience him or herself as erotically desirable by the beloved parent of the opposite sex. If a little girl cannot win the heart of her father how can she have confidence in her womanliness as an adult? In another paper Searles (1958) saw that the greatest threat to the therapeutic process was not the presence of sexual desires, but the analyst's inability to own them consciously, when the patient's unconscious is receptive to disassociated states in the therapist.

The third wave of development in understanding the countertransference that Wolstein describes begins in the 1970s. Every therapy was seen to have its own personal stamp and the demarcation between what the analyst and patient experiences to some extent fades. Regarding the erotic transference and countertransference particularly, we now begin to see a convergence of the bifurcated strands of regressive and progressive aspects of the erotic. They began to appear less clear cut, with more ambiguity and overlap and less polarisation of views about the erotic transference and countertransference. A number of writers seemed to reflect this change of thinking. Previous writers had generally spoken for or against, seldom integrating both points of view. In the writing of the 1970s onwards, we can see that analysts are still predominately at one end of the progressive or regressive spectrum, but there are more grey areas emerging, particularly after the 1980s. Psychoanalysis generally began a greater trend towards pluralism with more agreement over what were previously seemingly disparate views. It is quite striking that, as the patient and analyst were seen in ever deeper relational proximity, so the progressive and regressive strands of the erotic narrative also come closer together. I do not think this is coincidental. I would not suggest that one led to the other but that, clearly, there is a dynamic relationship between the coming together of the previously polarised views on the erotic in confluence and with the perception of a closer connection between analyst and analysand. The closer people become the greater the activation of erotic material in the unconscious. By the same token, we see this working the other way: the greater the activation of erotic material in the unconscious the closer people become and an erotic bond is established; the erotic draws people together and binds them in what I have termed an 'erotic bond' (Mann 1994, 1997a).

For example, Blum (1973) essentially saw the erotic transference as a form of resistance, indicative of the 'intractable love addicts'. These patients flood the analysis with erotic material and hope the analyst feels similarly. Blum noted that this was often the case if the patient had been sexually abused as a child or had parents whose sexual exhibitionism had intruded into their children's privacy. Blum considered that the therapist's role was not to be a mirror but to differentiate past from present, fantasy from reality. It is striking to note that, though Blum considered the erotised transference as a resistance, he also saw it as 'relatively universal' and that the infantile yearnings were susceptible to integration into adult awareness. In his view, it is not surprising that a disturbed or disappointed patient should want to be loved and fulfilled.

If Blum takes a position that sees the erotic transference primarily as resistance but also considers its transformational opportunities, Gorkin (1985) takes the reverse view: it is primarily useful but can also be a resistance. Gorkin suggests that if the therapist has a distaste for the erotised transference this is best understood as counter-resistance, where resistance is mutual hostility denied. Patients using projective identification will inevitably get the therapist involved at an emotional level as their projections find a chord with which to resonate in the analyst. He lists four types of characters that elicit an erotic countertransference: one exhibiting the erotised transference; the female hysteric; the female masochist; and the male and female phallic characters. Each of these tend to produce a different response from the analyst. The optimal solution is for the therapist to be aware of his or her erotic feelings as this will diminish the danger of acting them out. He stresses, though, that any sexual material that emerges offers optimal occasion for transformation.

Among contemporary French writers Kristeva (1983) has been one of the more articulate thinkers about the erotic transference. In her view, the analyst interprets his or her desire and love and this sets him or her apart from being either a seducer or zealously virtuous. By being the 'loving Other to the patient' the analyst becomes a living, loving father, not a dead father. Specifically the therapist represents the 'father of personal pre-history', that is, the pre-Oedipal father, which is understood as the mother's desire for the father's phallus. At the same time, the analyst lets it be known that he or she is a fleeting subject of desire: 'He will then trigger within the psychic space his love has allowed the tragicomedy of life and death drives' (1983: 31). Concentrating on love within analysis leads not to narcissistic merger with the maternal container 'but to emergence of a metaphorical object, the very splitting that establishes the psyche . . . bends the drive towards the symbolic of an other'. A loving mother is somebody who has an object of desire, an Other with relation to whom the child serves as a go-between. Statements like 'Isn't he beautiful?' or 'I am proud of you' are addressed to a third party. The negation of the Oedipal father is linked to the inability to love. Psychoanalysis is thus 'an infinite quest for rebirths through the experience of love' (p. 1). In the analysis, transference love allows the patient some subjectivity, to become a 'subject-in-process' in the symbolic order.

Spector-Person (1985: 163) emphasises that, though the erotic transference is universal, its expression is variable. She felt that women patients use the erotic as a resistance while men, on the other hand, resist the awareness of the erotic because they fear dependency. This latter results in the relative absence of reports of erotic transference by male patients towards female therapists. Person notes that the erotic transference tends to have an unsavoury reputation. In her view, though, it has unique qualities. She conjures up her own metaphor for the bifurcated strands by stating: 'It remains both a goldmine and minefield'. The erotic is a resistance only in so far as it is not fully analysed.

The Jungian analyst Samuels (1985) following Searles (1959) saw that the child needs 'erotic playback' from the opposite-sex parent, and he particularly emphasised the role of the father here. In his view, the incestuous taboo is linked to the strength of incestuous desire. The desire is linked to the need for psychological growth, not sexual satisfaction, arising from the parent and child intensely interested in each other. The erotic is therefore transformational, the absence of the erotic indicating that perhaps a transformation cannot take place.

Weinstein (1988: 194) highlights the point that the more powerful the therapist's feelings are towards a patient, the more potential for therapeutic success, a point previously made by Tower (1956). The inner awareness of the therapist directs emotional communication towards the unconscious 'reciprocal emotional state' in the patient. Moreover, the bipolar aspect of the erotic transference is discussed by Kavaler-Adler (1992: 527) as it relates specifically to mourning. She argues that the erotic transference is a resistance when it 'fails to be a conduit for unconscious desires'. When it is a conduit for these desires it allows the chance for them to be understood, thereby reducing all forms of resistance. The critical factor in this transformation is the clinical mourning process whereby pre-Oedipal and Oedipal objects are grieved for, thus allowing movement into the depressive position.

The most thorough discussion and, in my opinion, one of the most important works on this subject is by Wrye and Welles (1994). They take the view that classical object relations theory emphasises the nurturing side of the mother and infant relation while ignoring the erotic aspect. They argue that the basis for eroticism forms a 'body loveprinting' from the mother dealing with the infant's bodily fluids. The 'maternal erotic transference' and the 'maternal erotic countertransference' recreate the sensual erotic contact between the mother and baby. They see this as a positive and necessary transforming process in psychoanalytic treatments. They distinguish four narrative processes in particular: birth of desire (body-based aspects of self); anal eroticism (making something special, cloacal birth or sense of self-worthlessness); the sensual matrix in the formation of object relations (reworking a primitive fractured narrative into a living whole object); the solidification of gender identity through erotic experience (the oscillation between pre-Oedipal and Oedipal phenomena). Such primitive mother and baby object relating may often find non-verbal ways of entering the transference.

As with Gorkin, Wrye and Welles see that the greatest danger to the therapeutic process is the therapist defending him or herself from participation with the patient at very deep levels. In their words (1994: 87), the therapist needs to 'tolerate the heat without fanning the flames' of the erotic transference. In their view, analysts are prone to four defensive constellations when faced with such primitive erotic material: grandiose fantasies (analysts collude with the 'magical breast' desires of the patient); anaclitic-depressive tendencies (keeping the patient as a needy infant); erotic horror/schizoid distancing (a reluctance to deal with erotic material); the therapist's gender (male therapists may find it difficult tolerating regression and bodily longings of the pre-Oedipal mother, female therapists may find it easier to identify with the nurturing not the seductive mother).

While seeing that resistance can emerge in either the patient or the analyst, Wrye and Welles emphasise the positive, progressive movement that the erotic transference and countertransference can signify.

Bolognini (1994: 82) explores the progressive and regressive side of the erotic. He considers the erotic transference in four forms: (1) erotised: essentially psychotic; (2) erotic: essentially a neurotic modality; (3) loving and (4) affectionate, both of which correspond to normal development. He highlights that the evolutionary potential is more important than the defensive aspects. In a rather poetic image he concludes:

> *every good father should at least dance a waltz with his daughter* and thereby show himself moved and honoured . . . so that she can feel appreciated, valued and admired, enabling her to stay serenely

aloft when eventually confronted with the inevitable pain of oedipal disillusionment.

In turn, the analyst must also go through a natural waning of the loving transference so the patient can succeed in finding a new object in reality.

Covington (1996: 347) takes the view that the strength and weakness of the erotic transference stems from the infant's primitive need to feel wanted. In this manner, part of the aim of the erotic transference is to elicit the spontaneous response from the analyst in order to experience the possibility of expressing loving feelings safely: 'Without this there can be no freedom to think or to symbolise because fantasy has to be continually blocked and controlled'. The patient's desire for sex with the analyst is thus dual edged: a form of repetition compulsion and its 'purposive aspect', to 'find a loving breast and an empathic father' (1996: 339) and this is achieved by internalising a new primal scene.

In some of my own writing (Mann 1989, 1994, 1995a, 1997a, 1997b and Chapter 4 of this book) I have sought to place the erotic transference and countertransference within the universal context of humanity: that is to say, the erotic is ubiquitous and at the heart of unconscious experience. As such it is a structuring dynamic in all two-person interaction (whether this is mother–baby, father–baby, two lovers or the analytic couple). Because the erotic is frequently the basis for the most transformational experiences in ordinary life (e.g. between mother and baby or adult lovers) it is, potentially, the most transformational opportunity in the analytic process. The erotic transference is simultaneously two things. First, it is an expression of the patient's infantile experience and in that sense can be a form of resistance through the compulsion to repeat. Secondly, it is progressive since the patient is also looking for a different outcome to his or her previous erotic encounters (be it with mother, father or adult lovers); in that respect the patient is searching for a 'new transformational object' whereby infantile patterns can be relinquished in favour of a more mature erotic attachment less dependent on incestuous repetitions. The therapist, because of his or her own erotic subjectivity, is outside the patient's script and, thereby, the erotic countertransference can enable the patient to experience a different reaction, a new transformational object, that facilitates change and development.

What I have attempted to demonstrate in this section is the broad trend, the pattern that has emerged during the twentieth century concerning changes and developments to an understanding of the erotic transference and erotic countertransference. This needs to be seen in the context of how the understanding of the transference and countertransference has influenced our view of the relationship between the patient and the analyst.

Hamilton (1996) points out that, in the early decades of psychoanalysis, both the transference and countertransference were viewed as symmetrical: both were seen as erotic and viewed with suspicion. He, however, considers that precisely because eroticism was publicly excluded from the analyst's countertransference repertoire this allowed the concept of the counter-transference to take off. My view is that this is probably the case in the decades between the late 1940s and late 1970s. Since the 1980s the situation is less clear cut: major advances in the understanding of the countertransference have occurred simultaneously with the growth in literature about the erotic transference and countertransference. I would argue that these are connected. I am not saying that all advances were solely about the erotic transference for clearly this is not the case; what I am saying is that neither the transference nor the countertransference could be fully understood until the erotic could find a place in the process. Not everything is erotic, of course, but even non-erotic issues could not be fully explored until the erotic could be taken into the equation. Quite simply, the erotic is too fundamental and pervasive to allow much creative investigation if the areas under observation are defined by circumventing and avoiding it. Once the erotic transference and counter-transference can be more creatively placed in the discourse, then non-erotic areas can also be more fruitfully mined.

THE EROTIC NARRATIVE OF GENDER DIFFERENCE

In the years following the end of the Second World War there was a sudden reconsideration of ideas about the countertransference. Simultaneously and with seemingly little or no cross-fertilisation of ideas a number of writers began to reevaluate the therapist's response to the patient. At first there was no gender difference as male and female writers seemed to make an equal contribution. We may note Jung (1946), Winnicott (1947), Heimann (1950) and Little (1950). However, female writers seemed to be slower at exploring aspects of the erotic transference and countertransference and most, but not all, of the contributions until the 1980s were by men. In addi-tion, until the end of the 1970s therapists writing about the erotic transfer-ence had tended to assume a kind of androgyny: it was taken for granted that descriptions, usually of a male therapist with a female patient, applied to all gender combinations in therapy. Since the 1980s, female therapists have been telling us how it is for them: a number of female writers have begun to discuss whether the sex of the therapist influences the erotic transference and counter-transference and, if so, in what ways.

Not surprisingly, opinion seems divided. As well as the bipolarisation of the regressive and progressive bifurcation a further split has emerged about whether female therapists receive an erotic transference, especially with male patients. Lester (1985) considers that female therapists were more likely to evoke powerful pre-Oedipal mother issues and this would threaten and inhibit the expression of strong erotic fantasies in male patients. There may also be sociocultural reasons why female analysts do not explore erotic issues with male patients, fearing to appear seductive or vulnerable to seduc-tion. Spector-Person (1985) and Kulish (1986) seem to concur with this view.

A number of other female writers have taken a contrary view. I have already mentioned Tower (1956), Kristeva (1983), Kavaler-Adler (1992), Covington (1996) and Wrye and Welles (1994). The latter see the erotic as pervasive in what they call the 'maternal erotic transference' and the 'maternal erotic countertransference'. Chasseguet-Smirgel (1986) considers that male patients do not fall in love with female analysts in the way Freud described. She argues that the male patient retreats from love to sex. The sexualised transference is, therefore, more aggressive than loving, lacks affectionate elements and is closer to perversion. The analyst is idealised and any erotic aspects are repressed. Maguire (1995) takes a similar view. She considers that the maternal erotic transference of a male patient to a female therapist is likely to be overt and arouses, for cultural and psychic reasons, particular countertransference anxieties. These include the female dread of sadistic male violence. Maguire goes on to suggest that the female patient retreats into love transferences as resistance but male patients may attach sadism and cruelty to the erotic transference as a defence against incestuous merger with the mother. On the other hand, Kavaler-Adler (1992) thinks the erotic transference is as primary in the female analyst–male patient scenario as vice versa. Schaverien (1995) proposes that sexual arousal is common in all gender combinations and that the erotic transference is directed towards the female therapist but that the countertransference danger is that it will be viewed as infantile and reduced to a maternal frame of reference. Silverman (1988: 179) shares the view that the erotic transference contains both a repetition of the previous wounds encountered in love (both pre-Oedipal and Oedipal in nature) and the hopes 'attached to treatment for cure, reparation and redemption'. By and large, these female writers are divided about the relative weight they give to the regressive or progressive side of the spectrum, though in common with their male colleagues since the 1980s they hold a tension between these two poles, seeing the mix but favouring one or other side of the argument. Interestingly, though female analysts have discussed and recorded less about the erotic transference than their male colleagues, they have generally been more positive about it, seeing the more progressive, transformational side of the erotic, and giving less weight of the male analyst's insistence that the erotic transference and countertransference is merely operating as a defensive resistance.

It would be highly presumptuous of me, as a male psychotherapist, to intervene too much in this discussion between female writers about whether they receive erotic transference or not and, if they do, whether this is essentially aggressive or loving. I will say a few words though. In my workshops on 'Working with the erotic transference and countertransference' which run around the UK, female therapists do report overt erotic transference of all kinds. Furthermore, I am aware that evidence about male and female erotic fantasies tends to show they are fairly similar for both sexes. My impression is that the views of Silverman (1988) and Wrye and Welles (1994) are, therefore, generally correct in this matter.

THE ENCAPSULATED EROTIC NARRATIVE

In some respects, what I have described as a convergence of the regressive and progressive elements of the erotic can be seen as an oversimplification. I consider that this has certainly been the general trend during the twentieth century and this model has evolved in relation to the reevaluation of the countertransference and transference. This has entailed a perception of the connection between the analyst and analysand, which is now seen as more intimate, deeper and closer than Freud could possibly have imagined. The more the analytic couple have been seen as a single unit the greater the trend to shift the bipolar strands of the erotic into a single, unified understanding. As I stated previously, in my view, the erotic has, directly and indirectly, been the driving force behind the reevaluation of the transference and countertransference. There has been a dynamic interaction and convergence of the bifurcated strands of the erotic and the closer relational proximity between the analyst and analysand. There are, it must be admitted, numerous authors who do not fit this trend in bringing together the progressive and regressive stands of the erotic. Because they stand outside this developmental process I describe their contributions to the understanding of the erotic transference and countertransference as encapsulated, split off and detached from the development of transference and countertransference theory. I shall elaborate this point below.

A number of authors, while not writing specifically about the erotic transference have expressed their thoughts on the subject. For example, Greenson (1967) saw psychoanalytic procedures as unable to influence the erotised transference. Under the subheading of 'Special problems in analyzing transference reactions' (a categorisation of the erotic as a 'special problem' tells us everything about Greenson's perception here), he describes a patient who just wanted physical proximity, not interpretations. Sandler *et al.* (1970) see the erotised transference as a special form of transference linked to psychotic loss of reality-testing, therefore, serving a malignant purpose. Meltzer (1974) saw an erotic state of excitement as related to earlier masturbatory excitement.

More extensive books and articles have taken a similar view about the destructive nature of the erotic in therapy. Stoller (1979, 1985) proposes that hostility is the essential ingredient in the erotic. It is the desire to harm that generates and enhances sexual excitement. In the transference, hostility in sexual excitement becomes the enemy of insight and understanding, leaving the patient feeling at the mercy of his or her passions. In that way, the erotic is destructive to the therapeutic process (Stoller, 1985).

The term 'erotic horror' was introduced by Kumin (1985) to describe the impending awareness and discomfort felt as the patient experiences the erotic transference. The erotic transference is experienced as uncomfortable and unpleasurable and is, therefore, seen as a resistance and a negative transference. This may also affect the therapist as the rule of abstinence frustrates and excites both analyst and analysand. The way out is for the analyst to have an appreciation of what both he or she and the patient desire. The greatest threat to the treatment is the therapist's unrecognised erotic countertransference. Kumin sees the erotic as an inevitable feature of any therapy, but one which works primarily as an obstacle to therapeutic progress.

A collection of articles (Spector-Person 1993) explores Freud's (1915) paper on transference love. All the papers end in agreement that Freud was right: the erotic transference is a defensive resistance in therapy. Most of the papers add little that is new since Freud's article. I have given a more extended and critical review of this book elsewhere (Mann 1995b and 1997a: 49–52). We may note, however, four authors of particular interest: Schafer, Gill, Canesti and Stern.

Schafer makes what he calls five 'readings' of Freud's article of 1915 on transference love. He highlights the contradictions in the paper and Freud's failure to grasp his earlier insight in 'Remembering, repeating and working through' (Freud 1914) that repetition and acting out are forms of communication, ways of remembering. This same point is made by Stern. Schafer sees the countertransference as a way of monitoring enactments both from the analysand and the analyst as well as being a 're-edition'; the patient is looking for a new attachment. Even with this insight Schafer still sees the erotic transference and countertransference as a resistance, largely disguising underlying aggression or pre-Oedipal maternal issues.

Exploring the therapeutic process from 'one person to two person' perspectives Gill sees the therapist as inevitably a co-participant in the analytic situation and states that 'he participates whether he likes it or not' (Spector-Person 1993: 127). In Gill's view, the analyst should try to be aware of how the patient experiences his participation, in all the various shades of gratification and frustration. Gill recognises that the erotic contains positive ingredients, such as consideration for the beloved's wishes, but still sees that it can only be a resistance, following Freud's classical dictum that 'the resistance accompanies the treatment step by step' (Freud 1912).

Canestri highlights the contradictions in Freud's account of transference love. He concludes that transference love is genuine love and shows that Freud knew this, too, despite his attempts to prove the contrary. He notes that, if love is defined as unrealistic even if it is genuine, this leaves the criteria for reality in the hands of the analyst. He argues that transference love appears in most analytic dyads, whatever their sex, but returns to the view of the erotic transference as resistance by seeming to regard normal love as neurotic.

Finally in this book of papers we may note the work of Stern. Using research from infant–mother observations he shows how most of the major psychological, physical and behavioural patterns (except for genital contact) we associate with adult lovers have their beginning in infancy. For example, an exclusive focus on one specific individual, synchronised movements, psychic intimacy of intersubjectivity; prolonged silent eye contact, shared meaning of experiences, etc. Stern concludes that 'the experiences of falling in love and being in love have a rich early developmental history' (Spector-Person 1993: 180). Most of these are registered as motor memories rather than as symbolic knowledge. These psychic processes allow the parent and child continuously to re-fall in love with each other and are developmental milestones. However, when it comes to the therapeutic process, Stern does not seem to register the progressive function but rather sees the repetition as acted out memory and, therefore, the erotic transference is framed only as a resistance.

Essentially, without exception, all the authors I have just cited follow Freud's classical view that the erotic transference and countertransference are a form of resistance and act as a defence against therapeutic progress. One of the things I find striking, though, particularly with those writing in the 1980s and 1990s, is that they share at least one remarkable characteristic. It seems clear that these authors have kept abreast of developments in the understanding of the countertransference; indeed some of them have written influential papers or books that have advanced our understanding of the transference and countertransference. Yet the striking feature I find is that, though we now have such a rich and elaborate view of the countertransference compared to Freud, the developments in countertransference theory have not been extended to redefining or rethinking what bearing this has on the erotic transference and countertransference. It is almost as if, for some analysts, the erotic transference and countertransference have remained an island bypassed by the changing sea of theory about countertransference. To my mind, this indicates something of the exceptional nature of the erotic: it is not like other transference and countertransference material.

There is a seam of analytic thinking in which the erotic is isolated from the general developments in analytic theory about the transference and countertransference. In this seam the erotic, rather like Miss Haversham, has been frozen in a time bubble since Freud's paper of 1915. This suggests the hallmarks of encapsulation. Hopper (1991: 607) defines encapsulation as 'a defence against the fear of annihilation'. He is specifically looking at an individual's pathology in which annihilation anxiety is defended against by attempts to 'enclose, encase and to seal-off the sensations'. What is enclosed is not an empty space but an internal world full of intense feelings. Hopper is, of course, describing processes in some patients and we must be careful when generalising from this to larger numbers, to the workings of groups or broad trends in intellectual development. Yet even observing these cautions, I would suggest that the erotic transference and countertransference has sometimes been encapsulated in psychoanalytic thinking precisely because the intense sensations associated with it seems so annihilative, feeling like a threat to the therapist in particular, undermining the concept of neutrality. In my view, seeing the erotic transference and countertransference solely as a resistance indicates not only resistance in the individual therapist but also in some seams in the psychoanalytic research programme. What is resisted is the intense feelings of deep psychological connectedness with the patient:

in a word, intimacy in the analytic dyad. When intellectual currents and theoretical developments are subject to encapsulation this circumscribes creative thinking and inhibits the development of the theoretical programme. In my view, just such a case can be made to account for those aspects of our theory that have not kept pace with other areas of theoretical development and have thereby been sealed off, encased and isolated. This nowhere applies more strikingly than in the case of the erotic transference and countertransference.

It is in the nature of the erotic to bring us into deep and more intricate patterns of relationships with another, leading to greater ability to tolerate intimacy without intrusiveness. The erotic is thus instrumental in the process of developmental transformation and maturity. It is all the more surprising, then, that in psychoanalysis it should find itself so marginalised and only so partially revised from its Victorian origins and influence. My thoughts are very much along the lines of Tauber (quoted in Weinstein 1988: 192) when he writes:

> I have thought for a long time that what strongly blocks us is a profound unease in dealing with love, affection and tenderness in our work; we have acknowledged the need to deal with anxiety, hate, rage, etc. but are unclear about and evasive with love, affection and tenderness.

'Love, affection and tenderness', which I prefer to subsume under the umbrella of the erotic, have in some strands of analytic thinking been encapsulated and as a result discussion has been curtailed and the development of theoretical thinking limited.

EROTIC TRANSFERENCE AND COUNTERTRANSFERENCE: CLINICAL PRACTICE IN PSYCHOTHERAPY

This book represents another chapter in the psychoanalytic narrative of the erotic transference and countertransference resting upon the preceding narrative of the last hundred years of psychoanalysis. It is also the case that the narrative of the erotic transference and countertransference will move beyond the point currently reached in their development of theory: as one theory supersedes another, so the new theory eventually succumbs to a 'newer' theory.

Within this volume I have tried to bring together authors representing a wide variety of psychoanalytic perspectives. The sub-title, 'Clinical practice in psychotherapy' is a recognition of the plurality of perspectives that now occupy the term 'psychoanalytic'. Broadly speaking the representation of theoretical perspectives is as follows:

Kleinian: Chapters 5 and 8 by Doctor and Chiesa;
Lacanian: Chapter 7 by Stanton;

Jungian: Chapters 3, 6 and 10 by Thomson, Field and Samuels;
Kohutian: Chapter 2 by Gordon;
Independent group: Chapters 1, 4 and 9 by Gerrard, Mann and Gardner.

To an extent, such designations are misleading as many of the authors draw on ideas from more than one group. However, even such a rough category reveals how the erotic transference and countertransference continues to be a subject for inquiry within a wide range of psychoanalytic traditions.

All the authors were invited to write about the erotic transference and countertransference and each has interpreted the idea 'erotic' in diverse manners. The erotic has been applied as an umbrella term seeking to express, with different emphasis and combinations, passionate genital longings, deeply felt tenderness or sensuality and the gift of love. Even a cursory reading of this book reveals the diversity of interpretation. Eros has many faces, as McDougall (1995) notes in the title of one of her books. We might equally say that the erotic, as beauty, is in the eye of the beholder. Though these authors may envisage a different face on Eros, all recognise his features as essential in the therapeutic process. The erotic, like Eros himself, is enigmatic, difficult to pin down, but its presence demands that we try to cast a light upon its features.

The book is divided into three sections. Again, there is an arbitrary demarcation in this process: several chapters could fit neatly into two or more sections. The ultimate destination has been secured by where each author places emphasis.

Part I deals with 'Love and the erotic: developmental issues and their relevance to clinical practice'. Love in the developmental process is the focus for Gerrard (Chapter 1). She proposes two forms of love, primary and secondary. The former is the archaic, infantile love, 'to be able to love in peace' when the primary object, the mother, is gratifying. Secondary love is more mature and civilised, though elements of the more enmeshed and primitive primary love are always present. Most psychotherapy patients experience themselves as unlovable at a very deep level. Gerrard argues that, unless the therapist can feel moments of love for the patient, the latter is not able to develop fully. This love is genuinely felt as the therapist becomes the primary object. The therapist's love needs to be aroused by the patient before the patient can discover his or her own capacities to love and be lovable.

Gordon (Chapter 2), writing from a different perspective – Kohut's self-psychology – starts with the myth of Eros and Psyche. Gordon highlights the similarities between the early versions of the Eros myth in which the god is a 'primitive and powerful demonic force' with that of the 'vital energy' of the human infant. By the time these infants have become psychotherapy patients the vital energy has become trapped by their attempts to satisfy the longings of infancy rather than the realistic needs of their present adult lives. This is linked to Kohut's idea that such patients have failed to internalise a 'sufficiently idealised maternal imago' to be transformed into self–object representations. This leads away from healthy growth into a search for an idealised figure and the ego is weakened by narcissistically derived grandiosity. Therapeutic procedures allow for a reworking of the 'idealising transference' and, in effect, present the patient with a corrective emotional experience via the therapist's empathy. The experience of 'mutual empathy, enjoyment and concern' is then linked to the foundations of loving and erotic sexuality. Eros, the erotic, is reawakened like the mythical figure and reaches more maturity and enrichment.

Thomson (Chapter 3) also takes the myth of Eros and Psyche as her starting point. Love is seen as the 'integrating factor in Eros' bringing together the 'body/mind/emotional system'. For therapy to be effective the therapist and patient must engage with each other and sometimes these feelings can be so overwhelming that they lead to sexual consummation. The function of Eros is to find a way of understanding a problem that arises in the course of development. In this context the problem in the transference is not sex but love, where love means integration.

What is striking about the three chapters in Part I is that, though the authors are writing from different theoretical traditions – object relations, self-psychology and Jungian – all three have seen love in its various erotic disguises as integral to the therapeutic process; all three stress the authenticity of the therapist's own reactions in response to the unfolding erotic therapeutic process.

Part II consists of five chapters dealing with the erotic transference and countertransference as they variously offer opportunities for transformation or resistance. My chapter (Mann, Chapter 4) takes an object relations view and explores the erotic transference and countertransference from the position of their unconscious incestuous manifestations. This is first described with reference to the Oedipal scenario. The patient and therapist are both seen as erotic subjects that also connect as each experiences the other as an erotic object. As with Chapter 3, the erotic is seen as what connects and unites. The 'erotic bond' is the unconscious erotic process that brings the patient and therapist into the deepest unconscious relationship and by that process offers the greatest opportunity for therapeutic growth. Both the patient and the therapist work through their unconscious issues into what is termed 'good enough incestuous desires'.

Field (Chapter 6) notes that the early psychoanalytic experience of the erotic transference, as encountered by Breuer and Freud, led to a restricted and negative view of transference love. The classical view proposed that love in the analytic encounter is considered an illusion, a defence against insight. Field concludes, in a similar fashion to Gerrard, that, on the contrary, 'without the therapist's love the therapy cannot succeed'. Therapeutic breakdowns can lead to a breakthrough if they can be contained and explored. The power of the erotic transference is that it takes the analytic couple, for brief moments, into a 'four-dimensional relationship': profoundly united yet with a singular sense of themselves. Field, a Jungian, and Mann, using an object relations perspective, are very similar in this conclusion.

A Kleinian perspective is presented in Chapters 5 and 8 by Doctor and Chiesa. Doctor (Chapter 5) sees the transference as essentially an erotic phenomenon and this is stratified along a continuum from a neurotic (erotic) to a psychotic (eroticised) pole. He explores why the erotic is such a form of resistance in analysis but also why for that reason it 'augurs well' for therapeutic processes: the resistance is an aspect of the patient's love and the appearance of the erotic is a way of 'exhuming ancient psychic relics' from the past.

Chiesa (Chapter 8) notes that the literature demonstrates there is no universally agreed definition of what constitutes erotic transference. He draws attention to the fact that transference and countertransference difficulties have specific features between a particular patient and a particular therapist. The erotic transference may have a marked impact on the therapist's emotional state generating anxiety, fear, confusion, gratification, attraction, disgust, etc. Chiesa, like Mann and Gardner (Chapters 4 and 9) also considers that the therapist will experience a full range of difficult internal reactions but that he or she needs to be ready to analyse these in order to be in 'the right frame of mind' to maintain a non-judgmental position of technical neutrality. Chiesa looks specifically at how the erotic may find either overt expression or may be denied in the transference. Along with most of the authors in this volume, he concludes that, if properly handled, the erotic transference has a restorative and generative therapeutic potential.

A Lacanian reading of the erotic is offered by Stanton (Chapter 7). He proposes that Freud had indicated two processes when describing transference: (1) 'the carriage of something from one place to another' (e.g. the patient transferring psychic material); and (2) transferral of something from one language to another (e.g. of visual (dream) material to verbal form). This latter poses problems of 'untranslatability' in psychotherapy. The 'residual unconscious nature of the transference' places limits on interpretation. Transference will intrude at the points of untranslatability between primary and secondary registers. The erotic transference adds a further difficulty to translating. Following Lacan, Stanton places emphasis on 'desire' which cannot be mastered by knowledge: desire returns us to all that we repress in order to maintain primary identifications with the other. The erotic transference, therefore, might 'stall' identifications so the other appears alien or it might create a dissociation between primary sensory processes and their symbolisations, thus creating undigested material. The erotic becomes an 'enigmatic power' that resists symbolisation but renders desired objects so precious and full of enhanced potential. Stanton seems to imply that the erotic, therefore, highlights difference. In this respect, his chapter appears to have a different emphasis from other writers who prioritise erotic connection. It is important to bear in mind, though, that 'connection' does not mean 'sameness' or similarity and difference does not foreclose relatedness.

Considering these five chapters in this section together, all seem to recognise that the erotic can be both regressive and progressive, a resistance or a form of transformation. The difference seems to be where the therapeutic emphasis is placed. Mann and Field emphasise the transformative nature of the erotic as this leads to greater authenticity and intimacy, expanding the patient's capacity for love and loving. Doctor, Chiesa and Stanton emphasise how the erotic is employed to avoid therapeutic change, although a working through of the resistance can lead to greater transformational opportunities.

Part III deals with the impact of sexual abuse on the practice of psychotherapy. Gardner (Chapter 9) examines this in relation to the erotic transference and countertransference when working with patients who were sexually abused as children. She suggests that this entails the patient and the therapist getting in touch with all aspects of the human condition, including the 'most depraved' and 'perverse aspects'. It is only through reaching such an understanding that the patient and therapist can find a path for healing and transformation. All the chapters in this book draw attention to how the erotic transference and countertransference in the therapeutic setting seek to heal past difficulties about love and loving. Gardner, along with Gerrard, Gordon and Mann (Chapters 1, 2 and 4) explicitly sees the patient seeking a new experience that is mediated by a new kind of relationship with the therapist. Gardner, along with Chiesa and Mann, also implies that the way of finding this new kind of relationship entails going through a process in which the patient and therapist get caught in each other's world and that this world also contains experiences and feelings of the more 'dreadful' kinds as well as more desirable and positive emotions.

The theme of sexual misconduct by therapists is explored in Chapter 10. Samuels, Field and Mann all indicate how much psychoanalysis has tended to respond defensively to the erotic energies in the consulting room. Samuels goes on to suggest that the one thing all psychotherapists agree about is that sexual activity between therapists and their patients is an abuse of power. The subject has caused great concern to the profession and the public. In Samuels' view this has led to a growing practice of 'safe' analysis. This is exemplified in the difficulty of translating a physical sexual excitement into a metaphorical and symbolic representation. In 'safe' analysis there 'is no sexual prima materia' which is foreclosed from symbolic work in analytic therapy. One way around these difficulties is to broaden the theoretical base of sexual desire in analysis and this is done via a fresh look at the theme of incestuous fantasy and by reconsidering the role of the father in terms of the 'good enough father of whatever sex'.

The chapters in this book have not been brought together to be fully representative of this extensive topic. Rather, it is the intention to illustrate how erotic narratives may be understood in many tongues. Hopefully this does not lead to a babble, a confusion of tongues, but rather casts light on how practising therapists and analysts 'translate' the erotic narrative. In the Epilogue of this book, 'Cupid's Myriad Arrows' (pages 172–5) I have attempted to draw attention to broader convergencies and differences amongst the ten authors who have contributed chapters here. In my opinion, the erotic narrative can lead to many unexpected paths. At the end of this collection of chapters I hope to indicate more of the unifying and diverging erotic themes.

The erotic is so pervasive, so fundamental to psychological life, that it causes more dispute, as well as paradoxically agreement, than any other subject in psychoanalysis. That should not surprise us. As clinicians and theoreticians, it behoves the psychoanalytic practitioner to face unconscious fantasies and to maintain the tension but to do so in the full knowledge that detached objectivity is not an option in the midst of the deepest passions. Understanding the erotic transference and countertransference means accepting the push and pull to progressive and regressive elements of erotic desire, and tolerating unsettling fantasies and physical sensations. Like Cupid, it is easily possible for the clinician and the patient to feel blinded by the erotic. However, in finding ways of thinking about the erotic unconscious fantasy life of the analytic couple at least we can begin to peek under the blindfold.

NOTES

1 By 'research programme' I refer to Lakatos' (1974) idea that a research programme involves hard core basic assumptions around which auxiliary hypotheses form a 'protective belt'. This structure then provides guidance for research both in positive and negative ways.
2 Terms like 'progressive' and 'regressive' lend themselves to being misunderstood. Let me be clear here: I am not implying that one kind of thinking is revolutionary or reactionary or any similar moral judgment of these modes of thought. I use these terms merely descriptively. I am not saying Freudian thinking is backward or Jungian thinking is more advanced. In fact, on this particular issue I do not consider either by themselves to be sufficient. Only a creative intercourse between the two will push our imaginative thinking developmentally forward.

REFERENCES

Blum, H.B. (1973) 'The concept of the erotized transference', *Journal of the American Association* 21: 61–76.
Bolognini, S. (1994) 'Transference: erotised, erotic, loving, affectionate', *International Journal of Psychoanalysis* 75: 73–86.
Chasseguet-Smirgel, J. (1986) *Sexuality and Mind*, New York: New York University Press.
Covington, C. (1996) 'Purposive aspects of the erotic transference', *Journal of Analytical Psychology* 41: 339–52.
Freud, S. (1910) 'The future prospects of psychoanalytic therapy', *Standard Edition* 11, London: Hogarth Press.
—— (1912) 'The dynamics of the transference', *Standard Edition* 12, London: Hogarth Press.

—— (1914) 'Remembering, repeating and working through', *Standard Edition* 12, London: Hogarth Press.

—— (1915) 'Observations on transference love', *Standard Edition* 12, London: Hogarth Press.

Gorkin, M. (1985) 'Varieties of sexualised countertransference', *Psychoanalytic Review* 72(3): 421–40.

Greenson, R.R. (1967) *The Technique and Practice of Psychoanalysis* (1985), London: Hogarth Press.

Hamilton, V. (1996) *The Analyst's Preconscious*, Hillsdale, NJ/London: Analytic Press.

Heimann, P. (1950) 'On countertransference', *International Journal of Psychoanalysis* 31: 81–4.

Hopper, E. (1991) 'Encapsulation as a defence against the fear of annihilation', *International Journal of Psychoanalysis* 72(4): 607–24.

Jehu, D. (1994) *Patients as Victims: Sexual Abuse in Psychotherapy and Counselling*, London: John Wiley & Sons.

Jung, C.G. (1911) 'Symbols of transformation', *Collected Works* 5, London: Routledge.

—— (1946) 'The psychology of the transference', *Collected Works* 16, London: Routledge.

Kavaler-Adler, S. (1992) 'Mourning and erotic transference', *International Journal of Psychoanalysis* 73: 527–39.

Kristeva, J. (1983) *Tales of Love* (1987), New York: Columbia University Press.

Kulish, N.M. (1986) 'Gender and transference: the screen of the phallic mother', *International Review of Psychoanalysis* 13: 393–404.

Kumin, I. (1985) 'Erotic horror: desire and resistance in the psychoanalytic setting', *International Journal of Psychoanalytic Psychotherapy* 11: 3–20.

Lakatos, I. (1974) 'Falsification and the methodology of scientific research programmes', in I. Lakatos and A. Musgrave (eds), *Criticism and Growth of Knowledge*, Cambridge: Cambridge University Press.

Lester, E. (1985) 'The female analyst and the erotized transference', *International Journal of Psychoanalysis* 66: 283–93.

Little, M. (1950) 'The analyst's total response to his patient's needs', in *Towards Basic Unity*, London: Free Association Press.

Maguire, M. (1995) *Men, Women, Passion and Power*, London: Routledge.

Mann, D. (1989) 'Incest: the father and the male therapist', *British Journal of Psychotherapy* 6: 143–53.

—— (1994) 'The psychotherapist's erotic subjectivity', *British Journal of Psychotherapy* 10(3): 344–54.

—— (1995a) 'Transference and countertransference issues with sexually abused patients', *Psychodynamic Counselling* 1(4): 542–59.

—— (1995b) 'Book review of *On Freud's Observations on Transference Love* by E. Spector-Person', *Free Associations* 5(4) (no. 36): 571–4.

—— (1997a) *Psychotherapy: An Erotic Relationship – Transference and Countertransference Passions*, London: Routledge.

—— (1997b) 'Masturbation and painting', in K. Killick and J. Schaverien (eds), *Art, Psychotherapy and Psychosis*, London: Routledge.

McDougall, J. (1995) *The Many Faces of Eros: A Psychoanalytic Exploration of Human Sexuality*, London: Free Association Press.

McNamara, E. (1994) *Breakdown: Sex, Suicide and the Harvard Psychiatrist*, New York: Simon and Schuster.

Meltzer, D. (1974) 'Narcissistic foundation of the erotic transference', *Contemporary Psychoanalysis* 10: 311–16.

Rappaport, E.A. (1956) 'The management of an erotized transference', *Psychoanalytic Quarterly* 25: 515–29.

—— (1959) 'The first dream in an erotized transference', *International Journal of Psychoanalysis* 40: 240–5.

Rutter, M.P. (1989) *Sex in the Forbidden Zone*, London: Mandala, 1990.

Samuels, A. (1985) 'Symbolic dimensions of Eros in transference–countertransference: some clinical uses of Jung's alchemical metaphor', *International Review of Psychoanalysis* 12: 199–214.

Sandler, J. *et al.* (1970) 'Basic psychoanalytic concepts: eight special forms of transference', *British Journal of Psychiatry* 117: 561–8.

Saul, L.J. (1962) 'The erotic transference', *Psychoanalytic Quarterly* 31: 54–61.

Schaverien, J. (1995) *Desire and the Female Therapist: Engendered Gazes in Psychotherapy and Art Therapy*, London: Routledge.

Searles, H. (1958) 'The schizophrenic's vulnerability to the analyst's unconscious process', in *Collected Papers on Schizophrenia and Related Subjects* (1965), London: Hogarth Press.

—— (1959) 'Oedipal love in the countertransference', in *Collected Papers on Schizophrenia and Related Subjects* (1965), London: Hogarth Press.

Silverman, H.W. (1988) 'Aspects of the erotic transference', in H.W. Silverman and J.F. Lasky (eds), *Love: Psychoanalytic Perspectives*, New York: New York University Press.

Spector-Person, E. (1985) 'The erotic transference in women and men: differences and consequences', *Journal of the American Academy of Psychoanalysis* 13: 159–80.

—— (ed.) (1993) *On Freud's Observations on Transference Love*, New Haven, CT: Yale University Press.

Stoller, R. (1979) *Sexual Excitement: Dynamics of Erotic Life* (1986), London: Maresfield Library.

—— (1985) *Observing the Erotic Imagination*, New Haven, CT: Yale University Press.

Tauber, E.S. (1979) 'Countertransference re-examined', in L. Epstein and A.H. Feiner (eds), *Countertransference*, New York: Aronson.

Tower, L. (1956) 'Countertransference', *Journal of the American Psychoanalytic Association* 4: 224–55.

Weinstein, R. (1988) 'Should analysts love their patients? The resolution of transference resistance through countertransferencial explorations', in J. Lasky and H. Silverman (eds), *Love: Psychoanalytic Perspectives*, New York: New York University Press.

Winnicott, D.W. (1947) 'Hate in the countertransference', in *Through Paediatrics to Psychoanalysis* (1987), London: Hogarth Press.

Wolstein, B. (ed.) (1988) *Essential Papers on Countertransference*, London: New York University Press.

Wrye, H.K. and Welles, J.K. (1994) *The Narration of Desire: Erotic Transferences and Countertransferences*, Hillsdale, NJ: Analytic Press.

Part I

Love and the erotic

Developmental issues and their relevance to clinical practice

1 Love in the time of psychotherapy

Jackie Gerrard

It is the physician's love that heals the patient.

Attributed to Ferenczi

It has long seemed to me that 'love' in our work as psychoanalytical psychotherapists has been much neglected. I believe that most patients who present for analysis or psychotherapy feel themselves quite unlovable at some very deep level. My hypothesis in this chapter is that until and unless there can be felt moments of love for the patient by the therapist, the patient is not able to develop fully. I think it is only when a patient can arouse our deepest loving feelings (not empathy) that we can really hope for a truly positive outcome from our work.

At times when I have questioned changes in patients, I have asked myself: 'Do I love X because he/she is making use of me and starting to change?' (my narcissism); or, indeed, 'Is it because I have found myself able to love him/her that growth and a sense of lovableness are now possible?' (allowing his/her healthy narcissism to develop). Paradoxically, I may discover my loving feelings when a patient is finally able to vent his/her rage and hate towards me, or when a patient is struggling or has managed to reach feelings of pain, loss, despair, joy, etc., either towards me or towards some significant other. I may find my loving feelings when a very 'concrete' patient shows some capacity for play and symbolization. In other words, those moments, not of compassion, pity or empathy, but of an unspoken rush of feeling of 'I really love you' for a patient, can arise at various times and within many scenarios.

In my first analysis, when I felt unlovable very often even though I had many loving relationships in my life, I wanted urgently to know if my analyst loved me. Her wise response was something like 'When you come to feel loved by me, then you will know'. It was very true. It happened again in my second analysis. In hindsight, although many years of hard work and interpretation were undergone by both of us, what mattered most to me was that I reached a deeply felt sense of being lovable.

First, I shall endeavour to say what I mean by love, then to trace the various historical theories regarding love and finally to give some clinical material for illustration. Coltart (1992: 118–19) speaks of love as a mystery, indefinable by the language of psychological theory. She also writes of qualities such as 'patience, endurance, humour, kindness and courage', then adds 'detachment' and states that they can 'all be subsumed under the name of love'. 'Loss or lack of it brings about depression, alienation, feelings of emptiness, and False-Self manifestations'.

Suttie (1935: 31) emphasized that the love bond comes from an emotion of tenderness; 'more a mental sympathy than a genital relationship'. It is this emotion of tenderness that I am referring to in this chapter, although I would almost wish to call it 'extreme tenderness' to distinguish it from a milder feeling. Suttie stressed the point that tender feelings and affection are not based on libido theory and sexual desire, but on the 'pre-oedipal, emotional and fondling relationship with the mother and upon the instinctual need for companionship'. In other words, Suttie saw these tender feelings arising out of a similar but discrete instinctual need 'characteristic of all animals which pass through a phase of nurtured infancy' (p. 86). Tender love, which is the descendant or derivative of infantile need combines with (oral or genital) appetite in a state he describes as the 'complete passion of love' (p. 72). Suttie is quite clear that tenderness operates alongside sexual desires.

I believe my patients need to experience (or re-experience) the therapist as a loving mother. This would encompass Coltart's qualities listed above, although I feel that 'detachment' is not present in more primitive loving states. To these qualities mentioned by Coltart, I would add containment and reverie (Bion) and the oft-missing ingredients referred to by Suttie – tenderness and affection. However, these tender loving feelings must emanate from one's most authentic self – there is no place for sentimentality here.

As I demonstrate, love is initially experienced through an 'oceanic' feeling (Freud) or a 'harmonious, interpenetrating mix-up' (Balint 1968) but later matures into a separated-out activity, with recognition of the other's subjectivity ('detachment'). Perhaps these earlier feelings are part of Coltart's 'mystery'. In any case, I believe that more mature, object related love is a derivative from the earlier oceanic feelings and primary love. I assume that both are present in my countertransference feelings, and are significantly linked to mother love. Unlike most mothers, however, I am unlikely to begin a new therapy 'loving' a patient, though I may like him/her. Thus, I shall also be exploring what happens in the therapy to arouse my love, without which I am suggesting my patients cannot reach their capacity for loving and a sense of lovableness.

Moving now to history and Freud's statement in his 'Three essays on the theory of sexuality', 'a child sucking at his mother's breast has become the prototype of every relation of love' (Freud 1905: 145). Coltart called this first stage of Freud's theory on love the 'genetic'. The second stage she termed the 'narcissistic', referring to his 1914 paper 'On narcissism', regarding the conditions for falling in love, and the third stage (the nucleus of object relations theory) 'the expression of the whole sexual current of feeling; of the relation of the total ego to its object' (Coltart 1992: 114). By 1923 in 'The Ego and the Id', Freud had replaced the topographic model with the structural model, incorporating the Ego Ideal and thus the importance of the object began to be emphasized further. In his 1930 paper, 'Civilization and its discontents', Freud refers to 'falling in love' and 'oceanic feelings' (undifferentiated love) and later to 'aim inhibited love' and 'genital love' (differentiated love). The latter two imply more mature object related love and would therefore develop out of the former.

Since 1920 in 'Beyond the pleasure principle', Freud struggled with the antithesis between death and life instincts – the need to overcome hate with love. Later, Klein too was strongly influenced by Freud's ideas on libidinal and death instincts. Meira Likierman (1993) considers these ideas in her article, 'Primitive object love in Melanie Klein's thinking'. She has noted that most Kleinian papers, while emphasizing destructiveness and sadism, pay little attention to primitive loving feelings. Indeed, there is a current tendency to confuse loving feelings with a state of idealization, as opposed to an acceptance of an early object love arising 'in response to the love and care of the mother' (Klein 1937: 65).

Likierman identified two separate states in Kleinian thinking: that of 'a normal primary experience of an ideal nature', and another where it is 'defensively transfixed in a boundless, all-giving form' (1993: 251). She states that it would be quite erroneous to think that Klein believed the infant to experience only a defensive form of idealization. Ferenczi (1933: 166) became convinced that it was necessary to separate out early feelings of 'tenderness' from a later, more mature, partly sexual love of passion, thus seeing love as having its own developmental phases from the beginnings of life. Klein, however, believed 'the infant to experience love of an ideal, boundless quality from the beginning of post-natal life' (Likierman 1993: 251). I feel my term of 'extreme tenderness' to some extent combines the tenderness referred to by Ferenczi and Suttie with these feelings referred to by Klein and by Balint (primary love). I shall return later to ideas of the infant's love 'in response to' the love and care of the mother.

Ferenczi's ideas, focusing on the role of the mother's loving feelings for the infant as vital for healthy growth, were a strong influence on Klein, and began to place an emphasis on the role of the mother that had to a large extent been overlooked by Freud. Alice Balint's (1949) paper, 'Love for the mother and mother-love', describes the archaic love that exists from the beginning in both child and mother. What the infant demands is absolute unselfishness from the mother – that she should 'be there' or 'not be there' as needed. 'The ideal mother has no interests of her own' (p. 252) and the infant has a complete lack of reality sense in regard to the interests of its love object.

This fundamental archaic love implies a mental state where there is a 'complete harmony of interests' (p. 254).

Balint (1949: 255–9) then goes on to examine the mother's archaic love for her infant and sees in it the same lack of reality sense because 'one's child is indeed not the external world'. For the child, the mother is an object of gratification and so is the child for the mother who looks upon her child as a part of herself. She calls this early relationship 'instinctive maternity' as opposed to later 'civilized maternity' and goes on to say: 'The real capacity for loving in the social sense . . . (tact, insight, consideration, sympathy, gratitude, tenderness) . . . is a secondary formation' governed by the reality principle. She stresses the essential difference between maternal love and love for the mother in that 'the mother is unique and irreplaceable, the child can be replaced by another' and 'We experience the repetition of this conflict in every transference neurosis'. So, in this archaic love, there is no reality sense towards the love object but 'what we are wont to call love' develops directly under the influence of reality.

Alice Balint has written about a patient who had within her 'the deep conviction that it belongs to the duties of a loving mother to let herself be killed for the well-being of her children' and quotes a warm feeling – something like: 'How kind of you that you did die, how much I love you for that' (1949: 251). This is most reminiscent of Winnicott's statement in 'The use of an object' where the subject says: 'Hullo Object!' 'I destroyed you', 'I love you', 'You have value for me because of your survival of my destruction of you', 'While I am loving you I am all the time destroying you in (unconscious) fantasy' (Winnicott 1971: 105). This, then, also leads on to the idea that archaic love demanding the life of the other is what has to pre-date civilized love – love occurring within the reality principle – within the real world of objects.

In contrast to this destructive, devouring, archaic love, Michael Balint (1968: 65) takes a gentler approach to primitive love and puts forward his theory of 'primary love' as a more apt and useful concept than 'primary narcissism'. He likens it to 'an all embracing harmony with one's environment, to be able to love in peace'. So, while Freud (1930) saw this feeling of fusion ('oceanic feeling') as a pathological phenomenon, being a regression to an early state of narcissism and an inability to relate to objects in the real world, Balint saw it as an essential stage of early development. He also felt that regression to this state would occur in important moments in analysis.

Balint stresses the point that aggressiveness and even violence 'may be used and even enjoyed, well into the states immediately preceding the desired harmony, *but not during the state of harmony itself*' (1949: 65, my italics). Winnicott (1950: 205) also says 'aggression is part of the primitive expression of love'. In 'Hate in the countertransference', he says 'if the patient seeks objective or justified hate, he must be able to reach it, else he cannot feel he can reach objective love' (1947: 199). He also tells us 'that the mother hates the baby before the baby hates the mother, and before the baby can know his mother hates him' and that the 'patient cannot see that the analyst's hate is often engendered by the very things the patient does in his crude way of loving' (pp. 200, 203).

Here, I am trying to make the point that our emotions, particularly those of love and hate, are extremely closely connected but, at the moment of loving harmony, hate takes a back seat. So that, in writing of love, I am not ignoring hate, rage, violence and destructiveness but I want to place the emphasis on love for the purposes of this chapter. I take a position akin to that of Michael Balint – that sadism and hate are secondary phenomena – consequences of inevitable frustrations. This is, of course, a very different approach from that of Melanie Klein who focused on the innateness of sadism.

Balint (1968: 67) feels the individual is born 'in a state of intense related-ness to his environment'. The primary objects that prove to be gratifying are normally, first of all, one's mother. During certain stages of analysis or psychotherapy, the therapist or analyst also becomes this primary object.

> In this harmonious two-person relationship only one partner may have wishes, interests and demands of his own . . . it is taken for granted that the other partner, the object or the friendly expanse, will automatically have the same wishes, interests and expectations.
>
> (Balint 1968: 70)

This is like the 'archaic love' that Alice Balint postulates, in the sense of the 'harmony of interests'. I have pondered whether Michael Balint is talking of dependency or love here. I suspect he sees this as the most primitive form of love: the harmonious environment is the all-embracing love object and the infant can, according to Klein too, respond lovingly to this love and care. Because there is a relatedness, however primitive, Balint rejects the term 'primary narcissism'.

Fromm (1976) distinguishes between infantile love and mature love. Infantile love says, 'I love because I am loved' and 'I love you because I need you'. Mature love says, 'I am loved because I love' and 'I need you because I love you'. 'I love because I am loved' is a responsive love (Klein) while 'I love you because I need you' would seem to be more in line with Alice Balint's ideas on archaic love and the 'harmony of interests'. Fromm's statements regarding mature love imply a sense of self and other – an adult, separated-out state of being.

I return now to Freud whose paper, 'Observations on transference love', warns the analyst to resist any tendency towards countertransference feelings of love. Freud (1915: 166) states that it is dangerous to let oneself have tender feelings for the patient and it is imperative not to give up the neutrality acquired by keeping the countertransference in check. He goes as far as to say, 'the love-relationship in fact destroys the patient's susceptibility to influ-ence from analytic treatment'. It would seem, therefore, that Freud felt that tender love, a feeling of fusion, and erotic love on the part of the analyst were all equally threatening to a successful outcome from analytic work. These views did not modify over time.

Searles (1959), in total contrast to Freud, wrote a most frank and illuminating paper on 'Oedipal love in the countertransference' and, indeed, is of the opinion, which I share, that the analyst's work has to realize within the patient both 'the capacity for feeling loved' (p. 289) and the recognition of one's capability for being able to achieve mature love. He says later that the 'patient's self-esteem benefits greatly from his sensing that he is capable of arousing such responses in his analyst', and feels that the degree to which a patient is able to arouse these loving feelings in the analyst will affect the 'depth of maturation which the patient achieves in the analysis' (p. 291).

It might seem, therefore, that what I am trying to convey was said most lucidly and movingly by Searles in this paper where he talks about the analyst's countertransference to the patient as 'a deeply beloved, and desired, figure' (p. 286). I am making a similar point to Searles', except that throughout his paper, love is Oedipal and not pre-Oedipal. In addition, Searles is referring to the therapist as *responding* to the patient's love and longing; or to the analyst's narcissism when the patient gratifyingly improves; or else to the likeable adult the patient becomes in the termination phase of analysis. Other love responses are attributed to the therapist's unanalysed transference feelings carried over from his own past.

My point, therefore, is somewhat different in that I am stating that for many patients (particularly those with schizoid and narcissistic personalities), the therapist's love (not just his/her unanalysed transference feelings) will need to be aroused by the patient *before* the patient is able to discover his/her own capacities to love and feel lovable. This was Klein's point – the infant finding its loving feelings *in response* to the love and care of the mother. So I believe we are trying to work towards our patients reaching a state of lovableness within, and a capacity to love (out of intimacy and gratitude) their therapists truly – rather than all kinds of feelings which could be misconstrued as love, such as idealization, worship, clinging and defences against hate. Indeed, if this does not happen, then I believe that the state of being here described by Klein (1937: 63) remains unchanged: 'an unconscious fear of being incapable of loving others sufficiently or truly, and particularly of not being able to master aggressive impulses towards others; they dread being a danger to the loved one'.

Before leaving this theoretical section, I hope I have made it clear that I have been referring to two kinds of love – archaic and civilized, infantile and mature, primary and secondary. Whilst Freud considered the first kind somewhat pathological, feeling that it was a regression and not object related, others since have disagreed seeing primitive love as a vital state of being which is at times re-felt in life generally as well as in the consulting room. The capacity for secondary, civilized, mature love arises out of the more enmeshed and primitive but the latter is always present. Indeed, the analyst may not always be aware at the time how primitive or otherwise are the feelings of love engendered by patients. It is possible that if I were to ask myself 'Why did I feel I loved my patient at that moment?', I would find it difficult to define whether it was because I felt a 'harmony of interests' or whether I felt a more separate, realistic caring, sympathy or tenderness towards the patient. (Hopefully, if I do momentarily lose my reality sense, this would be promptly regained!) And I believe the same is the case for a patient. Whether he/she loves the therapist because of a sense of 'absolute unselfishness' on the therapist's part, or whether there is a deeply felt gratitude towards another for their insight, concern, etc. might be difficult to identify.

I would like now to turn to some clinical illustrations of my point of view. All the patients had been in therapy with me for several years.

John (aged 32) came into therapy able to verbalize that he wanted to feel loved, and thought that he could achieve this with me by giving me a 'brilliant' time with him and his being my 'best' patient. His two fears were of being found to be mad, and that the extent of his neediness might be seen and hated. He was also struggling hard to control his sadistic feelings – felt, in particular, towards his mother, though later experienced also towards a younger sibling and towards his father, who reportedly told John that he was 'shit' without him. John had come to believe this, and previous failed marriages and failed businesses seemed to prove to him that he was incapable of being successful on any front.

About one year into the therapy, he brought into the session the book *Love's Executioner* and, on exploration, one reason he wanted me to read this was that in it the therapist talked about finding something to like in the patient. At the end of the session, when I was coughing, he said that I might have accepted cough-drops from him.

Thinking about possible meanings in this material, I saw that John was preoccupied with loving feelings in one way or another. The book title seemed highly significant: who will be the executioner of the feelings? If he could get me to love him, would he then attack/destroy this love (shadows of past relationships), or was he trying to find something to love in me – which he was finding difficult, particularly with an impending break and the risk of my rejection of his loving feelings. I certainly had a sense that he experienced rejected, hateful and destructive feelings towards me, which may have led unconsciously to my coughing. I could not be allowed to know about them, however, because cough-drops were suggested by way of reparation. It could also be possible that he felt he was choking me with his material – both wanting yet fearing to do so. Perhaps he carried cough-drops through a fear that I would be choking him with my interpretations.

Shortly afterwards, in the session prior to the break, he told a story about Noddy and Big Ears:

> Noddy wakes up happy, feeling 'it's a lovely day and I'm going to see my friend Big Ears'. On the way he comments to people what a lovely

day it is and how he's off to see his friend. However, when he arrives,
Big Ears opens the door and says, 'Fuck off, Noddy'.

From this I understood that there was an inner configuration of a Big Ears
person who is telling the other (who is trying to be loving and friendly) to
fuck off, and a Noddy person who wants a loving, friendly relationship and
does not see the aggression coming. Just who is who in this picture may
change from time to time. There is certainly an issue of hurt rejection. I see
these feelings of hurt, rage and rejection as secondary feelings (as Balint
describes) – a response to recent feelings of not being lovable and acceptable
to me.

In the earlier years a constantly felt rejection and humiliation was the time
boundary around the session. If he came early, he felt humiliated by waiting
and being seen to be needy; whereas if he came late, not only did he miss out
on his session time but his fury and sadism might be detected. If only, he felt,
I had a waiting-room, then somehow he would not be so exposed as to what he
was feeling both internally with himself and also towards me.

Much later in the therapy, I started to feeling loving towards John because,
although his behaviour was often seductive and devious, there were also glim-
merings of efforts to make contact with me and to work and to play. It became
clearer that many of his internal objects were cruel, uncaring, demanding and
sadistic, yet not all. I heard about a father who scooped him into bed when he
was scared in the night and a grandma who felt safe enough to run to. He
desperately wanted me to believe him and to trust him and I found he
began to work and play more creatively in the sessions, developing a genuine
interest in his dreams, instead of bringing them along to please me. Alongside
his increasingly felt need of me he became more openly attacking with voci-
ferous complaints about not affording the fees, my discharging him a minute
early, hating the time boundary, and a fantasy of leaving a pile of shit on my
carpet. Then, perhaps, just as he was with his dad, I would be 'shit' without
him too. I, as object, had to survive his destructive attacks: then I could be
used and also seen as loving – accepting him for who and what he was, not
what he was trying to be to win me over.

I probably began to love him as I was gradually allowed to know him, not
his collusive, seductive performance but a man who hated me because he had
come to need me. Much later he was also able to value me, and protests about
the fee ceased. As I discovered his real hate, rage, fear, neediness, playfulness
and willingness to struggle, not a pseudo-copy – I became aware of loving
him, and there were moments of a sense of harmony.

As he slowly realized his independence firstly from his family and later
from me, he found he could acknowledge and even value those times of dependence on me and others. He lessened an attachment to a girlfriend who had
been sexually but not emotionally gratifying, and he worked through some
hateful and rejecting feelings towards his young son who lived abroad.

During this time he freely admitted how much he had need of me. As I became both less denigrated and less idealized and he discovered some trust and safety, he ceased to feel so antagonistic and destructive towards his mother and found a way to re-establish a friendly relationship with her, after cutting her out of his life for some years. His relationships and his work life began to be handled with greater maturity and he often reported an inner dialogue he had with me during the gaps. He had internalized my loving attitude towards him and was in turn behaving in a more loving, less destructive and aggressive manner in his external life. As this was happening, it brought about some fear that he might be with me for ever. He wanted to fix an ending date: he thought six months, I thought another year. However, being able to hold an idea that he could, if he wished, leave in six months without incurring my retaliation enabled him to stay another year. In that year he achieved the significantly more mature relationships that I referred to. At the end of therapy he thanked me for 'giving me my life' and said the therapy had 'meant everything to me'. Follow-up appointments have shown that he has been able to consolidate his capacity to love and his feelings of being lovable. He has developed 'the capacity to be alone' (Winnicott 1958) and a sense of himself as lovable for who he is, not what he does (Fromm 1976). Importantly, once he could feel more lovable for who he was, what he did in terms of business achievements and emotional relationships became significantly more successful.

Jean (whom I have written about elsewhere (Gerrard 1994)) came to therapy telling me about the Hans Andersen fairy tale of *The Mermaid*. She identified with this mermaid who had given up her tongue to try and win love. Her tongue was the instrument that would have expressed her feelings, but to express her needs made her vulnerable, humiliated and, in her mind, would almost certainly end in rejection. She defended herself by contempt and superiority. I was never allowed to know that the sessions mattered to her or that I existed for her in any alive way. What she most desired was love, closeness and intimacy but these were greatly feared, mostly because she would become so vulnerable, but also because she imagined she would destroy them. We could say she came to me with a warning: 'If I ever find my tongue again, that would certainly mean that I should be unlovable'. Indeed, Jean was so often harsh and attacking that she was difficult to love. Yet when I saw her tears in relation to images of two people together in a symbiotic relationship (a harmonious, interpenetrating mix-up), thus revealing the full extent of her yearning, I did begin to love her. Her internal objects were disinterested and disconnected and so mostly I was made to feel as she felt as a child, trying very hard to make contact with another who seemed not to see me at all as the person I was. Her image of me changed gradually over time. Initially she painted two blocks, side by side, with no movement or connection to each other. Later she painted two blocks again but joined together.

Near the end of therapy, Jean's image of me changed again. She had imagined me for some months flailing helplessly in my chair behind a newspaper, which looked like a printed firescreen. From my right armpit a dagger pointed towards her. This meant that for her it seemed I was hiding behind a blur of printed words (the books and theories that she feared stopped me from seeing her). It also meant that she could not get close or my dagger would pierce her heart. After a session when she had felt cold and I had put the fire on, which seemed to have conveyed to her that I had her needs in mind, and perhaps even a loving attitude toward her, she told me that her image had changed. The whole picture had reduced to the size of a key-ring and the knife had become very tiny and made of plastic. In other words, no damage could be done and nothing dangerous stood between us. She then imagined that she could look across, see me and say with recognition: 'Hello, Jackie Gerrard'. We were both moved by the telling of this, and I felt very loving toward her, with a sense that she knew and even if she could not yet reciprocate, she could at least allow it and risk a greater intimacy. At the end of our final session she asked for a hug, which we had, and she left me with the words: 'I love you, Jackie Gerrard'. This mermaid had found her tongue.

Lastly, there is Jenny (an only child of 26), a more disturbed personality who has also found 'connecting' extremely difficult. She had felt unconnected to her mother as a small child and had an absent father who was away for long periods at a time. With me she was highly anxious, sometimes to the point of incoherence, and seemed almost unable to 'take in' from me in any way, although occasionally something I had said that seemed to be ignored at the time would be brought back by her. I was not allowed to know, at least not in the moment, that I was of any use to her at all, which created something of a hopelessness and frustration in me.

She seems to be the type of patient described in Giovacchini's paper, 'Absolute and not quite absolute dependence', where 'helplessness is central to their pathology' and they also show a fear of lack of consistency, 'so that their environment is perfectly predictable' (Giovacchini 1993: 242). This results in difficulties in exploration and play in the therapy:

> This places the therapist in a precarious position. He cannot deal directly with the patient's often conscious assertions of helplessness, and yet he cannot abandon his patient to terror. Furthermore, he is incapable of becoming the rigid character that the patient demands, and that he believes he needs.
>
> (Giovacchini 1993: 243)

Giovacchini emphasizes that the therapist must accept the patient's helplessness and rigidity, but at the same time maintain a foothold in his own reality. If the patient can tolerate this split, then treatment can proceed.

With my patient, Jenny, I became the useless mother she felt she had, and I felt as helpless in dealing with her as she felt in her dealings with the world. She seemed similar to Giovacchini's patient, who has no particular wish to understand herself but looks solely for nurture and support. When she felt she did not get this from me (which happened quite frequently), then I was no better than a waste of time and money. With Giovacchini's patient it was the shift from absolute to 'not quite absolute' demands within a holding environment that enabled some form of play: 'a not quite is gradually transformed into a transitional space' (p. 251). He says that the patient can begin to play with the paradoxes contained in her rigid reality.

However, some patients are unable to find a 'not quite' zone and thus never manage to play. Giovacchini suggests that perhaps in these cases the safety of the analytic setting does not overcome the catastrophic terror that blocks the ability to play. I do not yet know whether or not Jenny will find this zone. Our work and my thinking about it, however, have enabled me to find a link between play and love. Mostly, I am not able to find within me the loving feelings that I am sure Jenny needs, nor can she give or accept love with me or others. Thus, I find that my difficulty in loving her does not allow for any movement in her capacity to form loving relationships. She has spent a life-time as a hidden self where genuine love and genuine hate are both risky.

Riviere's (1936) paper, 'A contribution to the analysis of the negative therapeutic reaction' mentions the horrors within the internal world: 'the undying persecutors who can never be exterminated – the ghosts' (p. 144). Jenny resists becoming aware of what is within, insisting instead that she needs care, advice and support. 'Belief in better things is so weak; despair is so near', says Riviere (p. 146). There is barely a grain of hope and yet the patient clings to analysis as there is nothing else.

My struggle with Jenny is ongoing. I certainly do feel that I need to find an entrée into my loving feelings for her before she can safely dare to reach for her own. My difficulties centre around the problems in locating her true feelings and in establishing a 'not quite' zone where play could take place and with it a space for love and hate.

We have all moved a long way from Freud's ideas of 1915 that analysis should be carried out in the state of abstinence or privation. However, it is still difficult, I think, for the analysts and psychotherapists of today to think about tender feelings towards their patients. For instance, Kernberg's book *Love Relations* (1995: 115) refers only to the analyst's countertransference in terms of erotic responses, and writes of patients who experience

> erotic longings in connection with unrequited love. . . . Patients with borderline personality organization may manifest particularly intense wishes to be loved, erotic demands with strong efforts to control the therapist, and even suicide threats as an effort to extract love by force from the therapist.

Although Kernberg, following Freud, considers the importance of under-standing and interpretation of the patient's erotic longings, unfortunately he does not give himself space to consider how the patient's needs, wishes, and/or demands may be impacting on the therapist's emotional attitude towards the patient. Perhaps more importantly, however, these patients of whom he writes with 'intense wishes to be loved' may evoke emotions such as hate, rage, fear, exasperation or some form of defensiveness in the therapist, possibly making it harder still for the therapist's loving or tender feelings to be accessed. I think that something of this was demonstrated in the work of Jenny. When the therapist can find his/her loving feelings towards a patient who has so much need of them, then indeed there is a remarkable shift in the therapy, even a breakthrough.

Suttie (1935: 72) wrote of intercourse and sucking (which are alike) as needing to happen where there is no 'difference or conflict-of-interest between the partners'. In the analytic situation, when therapist and patient have worked through, in whatever ways, their 'conflict of interest', then the patient's need to be loved and the therapist's capacity for love will be free to meet each other.

Balint (1968: 136) could allow for his patient 'to live with him in a sort of harmonious interpenetrating mix-up' – in other words, offering the possi-bility of primary love. Searles allowed far more rein to his countertransference feelings and their vital importance, but he was, on the whole, referring to the developmental stage of Oedipal love (romantically and erotically involving the therapist), while I am wishing to state that (1) the love of the therapist for the patient can certainly be pre-Oedipal; and (2) more importantly still, that until and unless the therapist finds these loving feelings within him/herself, the patient will be prevented from making the developmental changes that need to occur in the psyche for the depressive position to be reached (Riviere). To my mind, genuineness, a wish for connectedness and a capacity for work and play in the patient are the principal ingredients which will engender loving feelings in the therapist.

Finally, I hope I have not conveyed that love is all that is necessary in a psychotherapeutic relationship, because that is far from what I intend. Interpretation (and other agents for psychic change – Stewart 1990) is vital to the work and to allow the patient to feel understood. Sometimes, however, especially for quite regressed patients or those with a very weak ego (Balint 1968; Klein 1990), interpretation is felt as unhelpful or even at times per-secutory to the patient. Love is certainly not enough but then again, in my view, neither is interpretation, containment, reverie or any other psycho-analytical activity without the backing of love.

REFERENCES

Balint, A. (1949) 'Love for the mother and mother-love', *International Journal of Psychoanalysis* 30: 251–9.

Balint, M. (1968) *The Basic Fault*, London: Tavistock Publications.

Coltart, N. (1992) 'What does it mean: "Love is not enough"?', in *Slouching Towards Bethlehem*, London: Free Association Press.

Ferenczi, S. (1933) 'Confusion of tongues between adults and the child', in *Final Contributions to Problems and Methods of Psycho-Analysis* (1955), London: Hogarth Press.

Freud, S. (1905) 'Three essays on the theory of sexuality', in *On Sexuality* (1977), London: Pelican.

—— (1914) 'On narcissism: an introduction', in *On Metapsychology* (1984), London: Pelican.

—— (1915) 'Observations on transference love', *Standard Edition* 12, London: Hogarth Press.

—— (1920) 'Beyond the pleasure principle', in *On Metapsychology* (1984), London: Pelican.

—— (1923) 'The Ego and the Id', in *On Metapsychology* (1984), London: Pelican.

—— (1930) 'Civilization and its discontents', in *Civilization, Society and Religion* (1985), London: Pelican.

Fromm, E. (1976) *The Art of Loving*, London: Unwin.

Gerrard, J. (1994) 'Spaces in between', *British Journal of Psychotherapy* 10(4): 557–67.

Giovacchini, P. (1993) 'Absolute and not quite absolute dependence', in D. Goldman (ed.), *In One's Bones*, New Jersey: Aronson.

Kernberg, O. (1995) *Love Relations*, New Haven, CT: Yale University Press.

Klein, J. (1990) 'Patients who are not ready for interpretations', in *Doubts and Certainties in the Practice of Psychotherapy* (1995), London: Karnac.

Klein, M. (1937) 'Love, guilt and reparation', in M. Klein and J. Riviere (eds), *Love, Hate and Reparation* (1964), New York: Norton Library.

Likierman, M. (1993) 'Primitive object love in Melanie Klein's thinking; early theoretical influences', *International Journal of Psycho-Analysis* 74: 241–53.

Riviere, J. (1936) 'A contribution to the analysis of the negative therapeutic reaction', in *The Inner World and Joan Riviere* (1991), London: Karnac.

Searles, H. (1959) 'Oedipal love in the countertransference', in *Collected Papers on Schizophrenia* (1965), London: Hogarth Press.

Stewart, H. (1990) 'Interpretation and other agents for psychic change', *International Journal of Psychoanalysis* 71: 61–70.

Suttie, I. (1935) *The Origins of Love and Hate* (1988), London: Free Association Press.

Winnicott, D.W. (1947) 'Hate in the countertransference', in *Through Paediatrics to Psychoanalysis* (1978), London: Hogarth Press.

—— (1950) 'Aggression in relation to emotional development', in *Through Paediatrics to Psychoanalysis* (1978), London: Hogarth Press.

—— (1958) 'The capacity to be alone', in *The Maturational Processes and the Facilitating Environment* (1965), London: Hogarth Press.

—— (1971) 'The use of an object', in *Playing and Reality* (1971), Harmondsworth: Penguin.

2 Bringing up Eros

A Kohutian perspective

Sheila Gordon

THE MYTH

As I started to work on this chapter I tried to find out what the figure of Eros had meant to the Classical world.

I discovered variety, continuous development and deepening complexity.

The unfolding and elaboration of the mythology put me very much in mind of the parallel evolution of the psychoanalytic world's thought about the nature and significance of the erotic in human relationships, and its struggle to encapsulate its developing ideas not in myths but in theory. For both worlds it was a dynamic process. Neither the mythical figure nor the theoretical concept of Eros have remained static but have expanded and deepened with the consciousness of the thinkers.

For the early centuries of classical culture Eros, the representation of Love, was a primitive and powerful demonic force, half way between god and man, whose function was to ensure the continuity of the species by the fuelling and manipulation of human sexual passions. This Eros was portrayed as an unceasingly energetic but dissatisfied figure, and these early Greeks, who could see that his activities were essential to their survival, put no faith in his good will towards individuals. For later poets he became the mischievous winged child, still indiscriminately using his arrows to provoke human passions – enjoying the mischief of it all in a more light-hearted way – but still with no concern for individual heartbreak.

I was interested to discover how these earlier figures were followed by a later Roman version of Eros, as found in the Metamorphoses of Apuleius, where he appears in the story of Cupid and Psyche. The depth and subtlety of this tale show how the character of Eros/Cupid was, over the centuries, enriched and amplified. We can see that, by this time, his character is capable of more than mere mischief. He enters into a relationship with Psyche that gives her great happiness, despite the command from the gods that she must never look at him. When, however, she is persuaded by her envious mother and sisters to defy the Olympian ban and dares at last to shine her lamp on her mysterious partner as he sleeps, the betrayed Cupid flees from her, and Psyche is condemned by the gods to a life of wandering and persecution.

Significantly, however, this pessimistic, resigned outcome is not allowed to be the end of the story. Apuleius, like Psyche, challenges the gods' omnipotence. He allows Eros to find Psyche again, as she lies overcome by the deep sleep that has befallen her after disobeying yet another command, this time from Persephone. In this version Eros is a much more developed character and is capable of a love that includes tenderness, pity and affection. He is able to overcome his initial feeling of betrayal, and ignoring the ruling of the gods, wakes his lost partner with a prick from one of his arrows. The lovers are reunited, and married with the full approval of Zeus. The combination of sexual passion with human tenderness and concern, as well as the tolerance of human disobedience, was given divine legitimacy!

This gradual, centuries-long evolution of the Cupid/Eros figure is, surely, an apt metaphor for the process of psychotherapy. In that work the energy, even the ruthlessness of the early representations, have to be integrated, providing the drive for the difficult journey to the maturity and depth at which the later heroic and loving Eros can be found. Only when the two aspects of the erotic symbolised by the 'sadder and wiser' figure and by the rebellious yet resilient Psyche are brought together can there be a real chance of forging relationships that are at once passionate and generous.

Anyone who has been engaged as therapist or patient, on that fascinating and laborious journey, can bear witness to the pitfalls and difficulties, and also to the dangers of *not* undertaking it. Certainly I find that by the time many of my patients come to see me, that vital energy of the Cupid-like infant has been trapped in a cul-de-sac. Their unavailing attempts to satisfy the longings of infancy in the adult present have thoroughly blunted their arrows and there is no sharpness left to prick the sleeping Psyche into life.

These patients know that something is wrong, but find the road to freedom and maturity deeply terrifying, even though it is the road they consciously seek. Their whole fantasy-life is preoccupied instead with the goal of finding a love object who will provide them not with the mutual intimacy to which they pay lip service, but with the unfailing physical tenderness and emotional nurturing that they have come to believe is essential for their wholeness. The pleasures of the erotic are, for these patients, imprisoned totally in the world-view of the inner child. Sadly their concern for others, as Guntrip (1969: 171) identified, 'is not a fully healthy objective concern arising out of appreciation of the worth and interest of the object. Fear in the ego for itself plays a big part'.

The therapeutic setting does, I believe, give the Eros in these patients a second chance for 'a gradual and lengthy process of regrowing' (Guntrip 1969: 171) and this time round to grow rather wiser, yet without unbearable depression. The therapist and the patient have to make sure that this time the gradually unblocked libidinal energy is *not* deflected towards unrealistically idealised and therefore unsatisfying objects, but is free to develop, like Cupid in the Roman myth, a capacity for intimacy and compassion that makes for successful adult relationships. These relationships may or may not be sexual ones, but I would describe them nevertheless as libidinal/erotic in that they are charged with enduring energy and pleasure.

Like optimal parenting the relationship between patient and therapist provides a setting where those infantile needs can be explored and identified with understanding, but without collusion or exploitation. It allows the transferences that have bedevilled the patient's former relationships to become apparent in the therapeutic relationship so that they can be gradually dissolved and replaced by the truly satisfactory pleasures of the therapeutic alliance – an alliance that will be enjoyable and rewarding to both therapist and patient, and which has been aptly described as the 'erotic bond' (Mann 1997).

As I began to work with an increasing number of patients presenting these problems and to be assailed by their demands for an omnipotent object, a number of writers helped me to keep my therapeutic feet on the ground. I had already been, as I continue to be, largely influenced by the work of Fairbairn, Guntrip and Winnicott. The concept of the mature love so many of my patients seemed to lack is well delineated in their writing; so are the obstacles to its development; and so is the nature of the therapeutic environment needed to overcome them and to foster the necessary regrowth.

I also found much helpful insight in the work of Kohut. There were of course considerable similarities between his thinking and that of the British School of Object Relations; but I found his particular ideas about the origins of the unsatisfied yearning which many of my patients brought, and about the function of the therapist in the therapeutic process, were not only clear to me but also made sense to my patients. I have continued to find his work highly relevant to the men and women who present with feelings of loneliness and dissatisfaction, and who have become exhausted by their disappointing search for a Prince to wake up the Sleeping Beauty within.

Kohut's ideas on narcissism also link very well with my thoughts at the beginning of this chapter regarding an *evolving* concept of Eros, in that he was quite clear that the libido of the infant's early narcissism *progresses and develops* into a mature capacity for object love, rather than being *replaced* by it (Kohut 1971). Although he himself rarely uses the word 'erotic' his descriptions of the 'expanded capacity for object love' that he sees as the goal of the therapeutic process have much in common with Mann's 'erotic bond'. He speaks, for instance, of a 'deepening and refinement of the patient's love experience, whether in the state of being in love, in his long term fondness of another human being, or in his devotion to cherished tasks and purposes'. Moreover his emphasis on the contribution of the freed idealising libido to 'the intensity and flavour of the patient's love experience' (Kohut 1971: 297) links with my idea that both the energies of the early infant Cupid and the wisdom of the mature version are needed for the real breakthough into the erotic dimension of relationship.

THEORETICAL FRAMEWORK

Kohut regards the type of patient I have previously described as having failed at some point in their early infancy to experience and internalise a sufficiently idealised maternal imago, and to transform it into the *selfobject representation* that he considers essential for their future development. (These are the patients whom Kohut (1971) classifies as narcissistic, in distinction from the psychotic and borderline patients who have suffered from serious maternal failure from the very beginning, and whose ability to form any kind of cohesive self is fundamentally impaired.)

In favourable circumstances the mother *is* able to bear her baby's idealisation and to foster it. She is able to attune her mothering empathically to the personality and particular needs of her baby. Such babies are then able to build up a picture of a benign and powerful figure who becomes part of their inner world. This 'selfobject representation', which is cathected with the babies' own narcissistic libido gives them the gratifying feeling that they are themselves partaking in this 'grandiose' environment, and that they are themselves esteemed and enjoyed. This 'mirroring' makes possible the emergence and organisation of their good feelings about themselves and their world and becomes the foundation for a strong ego development.

Just as important as the mother's early empathic attunement is the subsequent period of *bearable* ('non-traumatic') disappointments that must inevitably follow. These disappointments will be in themselves, as Kohut (1971) perceived, essential for the further development of the confident and resilient child. If this early disillusionment is of 'tolerable proportions, the infant will gradually modify the original boundlessness and blind confidence of his expectation of absolute perfection'. He will 'with each of the mother's minor empathic failures, misunderstandings and delays, withdraw narcissistic libido from the archaic imago of unconditional perfection (primary narcissism) and acquire instead a particle of inner psychological structure which takes over the mother's functions' (Kohut 1971: 64). I find it intriguing that in a lecture in 1951 (published in 1953) Winnicott had already stated: 'the mother's eventual task is gradually to disillusion the infant, but she has no hope of success unless at first she has been able to give sufficient opportunity for illusion' (Winnicott 1953). It was clear to both Winnicott and Kohut that an infant who has been lucky enough to benefit from such optimal frustration begins to stand more and more on its own feet and to relate to its parents and to the world in what Kohut calls a 'flesh and blood' way – what Winnicott would describe as 'good enough'.

Kohut claims that this 'optimal frustration' will partially consist of the varying defects in the parents, such as lack of empathic response, inability to provide soothing comfort and reassurance, overidentification, an inability to say 'No', or an inability to take appropriate pride in the child's achievements. In his view all these defects of the parents are not only tolerable but *useful* to the child as long as they are *occasional*. 'Indeed (as humans) we are equipped to respond to these shortcomings with that most valuable possession of human beings, the capacity to respond to optimal frustrations via transmuting internalizations and creative change' (Kohut 1984: 26–7). If, however, these parental failures are the result of serious parental pathology and are therefore unacknowledged and *constantly repeated*, the child is in trouble.

Kohut recognised that some infants have a good early experience followed by a sharp and dramatic 'let-down'. For example, there may be changes in economic circumstances, the loss of a parent, hospitalisation of the child or of a member of the family. Any of these can result in significant trauma, not because of the actual event but because of the lasting impairment of the family's psychological ambience that it has occasioned. The disappointment is then not helpful but traumatic, and again straightforward development is interrupted. Sometimes such patients retain in their present memory feelings of emptiness, of 'something wrong' that overcame their environment. The events that precipitated such a change may well be deduced and acknowledged consciously in adulthood, but, of course, in childhood the feelings of shock and let-down cannot be adequately expressed, particularly if they occur at a pre-verbal stage. The child, and the later adult, is left with a feeling of unspecified dissatisfaction and often with fantasies of a future miracle or rescuer.

I am reminded of a patient, Ruth, who came for therapy presenting with a feeling of 'not living life to the full' and a sense of being 'unrecognised and unappreciated' in her work. Outwardly she was an attractive, confident and notably successful woman with some good friends and her own home. She had the impression that her early childhood had been happy, but when she was 6 her mother had spent two weeks in hospital, and she had the sense that after that everything changed. Her mother remained tired and unwell for a long time after the operation, and the relationship between her parents developed an acerbity from which it never recovered. The mother felt impelled to go out to work to supplement the family income and Ruth found herself expected to take more and more responsibility for her younger brother. I realise that there may be many ways of interpreting these disclosures, but my experience of Ruth confirmed the likelihood that there had indeed been a reasonably beneficent period of mothering whose 'tolerable shortcomings' only became intolerable as they were sharpened by these later family vicissitudes. At one level Ruth's reasonably successful management of her life was able to continue, but always impeded by the need to cope with an underlying feeling of depression and disappointment in herself and her circumstances, particularly in the absence of a relationship that would, in her words 'work some necessary magic'.

In Kohut's view all these serious failures of the child's environment, at whatever stage, profoundly affect the child's experience of the parents and therefore of themselves. Their emerging self is weakened and fragmented, and Kohut sees them as thrown back on the defences of splitting and projection which affect their perception of their inner and external worlds. In his view of child development these paranoid defences are not part of the innate raw material of the human psyche, but are to be seen as a retreat into pathology occasioned by the chronic failure of the psychological environment (Kohut 1971).

The energies of such infants are diverted from further healthy growth into the search for an idealised figure who will transform their present experience and satisfy the longing with which they have been left. Their ego is weakened by still unmodified, narcissistically derived grandiosity, and by their over-investment in any significant other who comes along. The ensuing intense anxieties and disappointments provoke them into an attempt to control and manipulate their relationships, and this prevents a relaxed and playful intimacy. In Kohut's words, 'If the child suffers the traumatic loss of the idealized object . . . or a traumatic (severe and sudden or not phase-appropriate) disappointment in it, then optimal internalisation does not take place. The child does not acquire the needed internal structure, his psyche remains fixated on the archaic selfobject, and the personality will throughout life be dependent on certain objects in what seems to be an intense form of object hunger' (Kohut 1971: 45). I might add that the partners of such patients often present for psychotherapy themselves, worn down by demands that they cannot meet. As one man said to me, 'I feel I am being punished, but I cannot identify the crime!'

Certainly in such relationships, where the unconscious needs of the child rather than the desires of the adult are dominant, there is little space for the joys of the truly 'erotic'. Indeed in many of these patients the child's healthy sexual development has been impaired by problems encountered at the Oedipal stage: 'There is a lack of opportunities for the gradual decathexis of the child's preoedipal objects, a dearth of structure-building internalisations in the psyche, and thus the child's capacity to desexualise and otherwise neutralise his impulses and wishes remains incomplete' (Kohut 1971: 171–2). The way forward to the kind of erotic relationships that are infused by an elaborated sexual impulse and a desire to give as well as to receive pleasure are well and truly blocked. *The preoccupation with the archaic objects rather than the actual lover or friend has become too strong.*

I should like at this stage to introduce a vignette which is, I think, relevant to the theoretical framework I have described. June came to see me because she had recently managed to end a ten-year-old relationship that had become increasingly unsatisfactory to her, and she feared the chaos and un-certainty of the next few months when she would be establishing herself as a single woman. Her partner, Stephen, to whom she was not married, was 'intelligent and interesting' but she had experienced him as constantly critical and undermining. Any forgetfulness or mistakes on her part were met with outbursts of anger and denigration, and she had found it increasingly difficult to stand up for herself. The realisation that his reproaches flooded her with feelings of fear and inadequacy had driven her in the end to make the break away from him. In her professional life she presented a very different picture – here she was successful and well respected for her original and creative ideas. In our sessions she presented as a warm, lively personality, with whom I found it easy to communicate. She did, however, complain of a general lack of energy, and although she had many lively and interesting independent friendships, she could sense that the edge of real enjoyment had been blunted.

As her story unfolded it became clear that her mother, because of her own lack of warm and empathic mothering, had not been able to feel motherly to the baby June, whose arrival had been neither planned nor welcomed. A bond had only sprung up between them when June at around a year old had been able to make her mother laugh. Even so their mother–daughter relationship had never become really close (although they now have a friendly and enjoyable adult relationship of several years' standing). The mother of June's childhood and adolescence remains in June's memory as a somewhat distant and cool figure, but it is interesting to note that June later learned both from her mother and other family members that when June had been seriously ill in hospital after a difficult tonsillectomy her mother had been stricken with anxiety and concern about her. But none of this distress and concern appears to have lent any warmth to her communications with her small daughter at that time. As Kohut, among other writers, has pointed out, it is not enough for the mother to have the feeling; it has to be communicated and experienced to be available for the baby's internalisation.

June was quite clear that it was her father, a benevolent and lively figure, who had 'done the mothering', and his death when June was 21 left her bereft and isolated. Devoid of a good experience of early mothering, June's idealisation of her motherly father had persisted into maturity. She had not been able to let him gradually down to earth, and the loss of the figure in whom she had invested so much of herself, but whose masculinity and firmness she had been unable to internalise, was consequently devastating. As Freud succinctly put it, 'an object loss was transformed into an ego loss' (Freud 1917). Not surprisingly her unconscious solution to her dilemma was to find a man apparently strong enough to bolster her impaired ego strength and this is where Stephen came into the picture.

I must draw attention at this point to the phenomenon that Kohut remarks upon in his seminal paper 'The two analyses of Mr Z' (Kohut 1979). In patients like June a considerable part of the personality is able to benefit sufficiently from the many good experiences of their otherwise difficult early life, and possibly from their genetic traits, to develop not only talents and ambitions but some capacity for enjoyable relationships. It seems in these instances that only a part of the personality is drawn into the temptation of a replacement relationship, leaving another part to function confidently and well.

This more resilient side of June which was well to the fore in her work with me was nothing like developed enough to cope successfully with her relationship with Stephen. Although it looked as if Cupid's arrows had done their work there was too much of the inner child's agenda around for the truly erotic to grow in their relationship. The small child still wanted protection and nurture from Stephen, who was infuriated although, I suspect, at the same time reassured by her demands; and June's lack of internalised masculinity made her unable to stand on her own feet and meet Stephen's outbursts with firmness and determination. In this respect she in her turn failed as a useful selfobject for him. I suspect that Stephen too had his own hidden infantile agenda and wished to keep captive this collusive partner, who provided not only a safe target for his rage but also assured gratification and support. How could the pleasurable passions of the mature Eros find a foothold in the battleground of these two infants dressed in adult clothes?

A revealing incident in the therapy took place when June was gazing at the bookshelves which face the end of the couch. 'I can see', she said, 'that you must share this room with someone else'. When asked to say why she had come to this conclusion she readily answered, 'Well, I know a man must use this room too because he keeps his books here'. It turned out that 'his books' were the ones on history and politics! It was a very useful piece of material because, of course, all the books were mine, and she was confronted with the extraordinary degree to which she had blocked out a whole section of interest and knowledge, and handed it over to the man.

Despite the vividness of this insight there was still a long way to go, as the unconscious child firmly resisted the consciousness of the powerful adult self. The frequency with which Stephen kept turning up in her dreams and associations revealed the degree to which her inner world was still affected by this male figure whose bad temper was for June's infantile self inextricably mixed up with power. As we explored the world of that inner child we realised that it was this 'power' in Stephen, with its promise of safety and protection as well as hostility, that was so difficult for her to relinquish. Better that the devil you knew should look after you than risk the terror of untried autonomy.

This powerful male figure was inevitably an element of the transference to me. Despite the strength of our emerging alliance and the lively and enjoyable tone of many of our sessions, much material emerged to reveal the other side of the picture. I too could easily became the powerful figure whose skill and initiative would obviate the necesssity for June to 'do the work'. She at one stage confessed that she had never exerted herself much in social gatherings – she had relied on Stephen to talk for them both, which he was quite happy to do.

Another unconscious strategy to keep me securely in a feeding role was to bring me the occasional poem she had written, inviting my comments. I went along with this for a few sessions – and indeed there were many genuinely revealing and creative insights to be gained from June's work – but I noted that I suddenly got very bored with one of these offerings. I immediately challenged her on the possible defensive function of bringing a poem at this particular juncture, and indeed this proved to be an accurate comment. The effect of the challenge was quite dramatic. At this stage of our work such an intervention was appropriate, and it was received with both an appreciation of its accuracy and with great relief at the palpable feeling of energy that returned to the session, an energy which June had sensed was lacking but had no clue as to its cause. The material that was then revealed was the still persisting preoccupation with Stephen's 'strength' and her resistance to the assumption of her own autonomy and exercise of her talents, a situation which she could see had been acted out in our session. She now found herself able to recognise and value the potency of my accurate if somewhat delayed intervention and to see it as a fair exchange for the protective and rescuing omnipotence she had unconsciously hoped to discover in me.

This case study obviously exemplifies certain issues of therapeutic technique as well as theory, and I should now like to comment on the degree to which Kohut's theoretical framework has affected my own practice and has helped me to facilitate the growth of 'the erotic bond' with my patients.

CONSIDERATIONS OF TECHNIQUE

When I was first invited to contribute a chapter to this book, I demurred. I felt that my experience of notable manifestations of the eroticised transference and countertransference was infrequent and had never been particularly troublesome. I accepted that this state of affairs might well be partly due to my own unanalysed material. But on reflection I have concluded that the therapeutic style both implicit and explicit in the works that had most influenced me, especially in that of Winnicott and Kohut, had helped me to evolve techniques that gave a particularly safe containment for the unfolding of the transference including its eroticised aspects. I believe that these techniques do not stop the achievement of the 'erotic bond', but that they do minimise the chance of *gross* idealisation of the therapist and of *gross* sexualisation of the narcissistic transference. My patients may have eroticised fantasies about me from time to time, but they are in no way disturbing or uncomfortable for them, or me, nor is there any expressed wish to act them out.

Paradoxically Kohut himself gives us at a somewhat early stage in his thinking a vignette which, though quoted with approval, actually offers an excellent example of the very dangers that the further development of his theory was to make less likely. I refer to the case of 'Mr B' cited in Chapter 8 of *The Analysis of the Self* (Kohut 1971: 233–5).

Mr B had been in analysis with a female analyst for nearly a year and had begun to speculate about the unsatisfied infantile needs which seemed to be at the root of his unbearable feelings of loneliness. The analyst, in response, commented that because of his mother's own problems he had not been able to experience himself as 'loving, lovable and touchable'. This turned out to be an acute observation. 'Crash! Bang! You've hit it', shouted the patient. The problem (not fully understood or admitted by Kohut at the time) was that though the empathic perception of the patient's problem was accurate, there was no corresponding empathic understanding of the fragility of his ego. In Winnicottian terms this patient still needed the analytic setting to be entirely holding and reflective. He was not yet at the stage where he could safely receive and use the word 'touchable', which after all came from the analyst not from him and was, I believe, likely to be experienced at this stage as a disturbing and overstimulating intrusion. The patient did indeed arrive the following day in 'a dishevelled and deeply troubled condition: and he remained excitedly and profoundly disturbed for the ensuing week'. The analyst, at first puzzled by the degree of his disturbance, by the sudden access of grossly sexual fantasies about her, and by his feeling of 'being like a radio with the wires all tangled', concluded that the patient's infantile long-ings had been intensely stimulated by her use of the words 'lovable and touch-able'. As Kohut described it, 'the suddenly intensely stimulated narcissistic libidinal tensions led to a frantic acceleration of psychic activity and to a gross sexualisation of the narcissistic transference' (Kohut 1971: 233–5).

It is interesting to note that at this point Kohut appears to accept such dis-turbance as an inevitable consequence of 'successful' interpretation. In his later work he makes a much clearer distinction between the empathy that enables the therapist to provide sensitive holding in the early stages of therapy and that of the 'explaining phase' of empathy which though indispensable for the permanent success of the process is dependent on the foundation of the early holding. As he was to acknowledge, 'In some analyses . . . the analyst will even have to realise that a patient whose childhood self-object had failed traumatically in this area will require long periods of "only" under-standing before the second step – interpretation, the dymamic-genetic expla-nations given by the analyst – can be usefully and acceptably taken' (Kohut 1977: 88). I would further stress that this kind of sensitive holding back by the therapist of premature ill-matched responses and the intense awareness of the level of comment that is helpful to the patient at a particular stage is a useful model for patients in their own relationships. I think this experience of being treated both with care and restraint can be a deeply satisfying and safely erotic experience whether as a child or a patient – an essential building-block in the development of the mature capacity for loving that the Cupid/Psyche relationship exemplifies.

Kohut identified this first phase of analytical therapy as a crucial one, in which the idealising transference must be allowed to establish itself sponta-neously and without active encouragement from the therapist (Kohut 1971: 164–6). I found, as he had done, that patients presenting with dis-appointment in themselves, in their love objects and their lives, seemed to benefit in even a few sessions from this fairly 'low-key' approach. They often began to look physically better, appeared more attractively dressed and seemed relieved at having found somewhere safe to come and talk. For the time being they seemed content to accept me and the setting I offered as the answer for which they had been searching. (I also noted as Kohut did that their newly found equilibrium could easily be toppled by upsets of any kind, whether it was my saying 'the wrong thing', cancelled sessions, holidays or unexpected window cleaners) (Kohut 1971: 90–1)!

Instead of dismissing these early signs of improvement as temporary 'transference cures' I began to understand the value of this early idealisation. I realised how important it was to take seriously patients' difficulties with interruptions to routine of any kind, and to avoid unnecessary comments. I could accept that during this period patients were getting a second chance to experience the feelings of mutual attunement that had in their cases been insufficiently present in their infancy. I noted, as I still do, that my countertransference in these circumstances did not contain the feelings of protectiveness and the wish to nourish that are traditionally associated with the maternal response. What I was aware of was an intense concern to understand what was going on and to respond appropriately. I also found that I was aware of the atmosphere between us as much as the words that were spoken. These feelings on my part seem to me very reminiscent of the feelings of a reasonable, relaxed mother during the early infancy of her baby – not overly emotional but intensely yet calmly preoccupied, and conscious of a deep and ruthless bond that already contains that gratification and pleasure I have already cited as the foundation for future erotic sophistication.

Kohut himself made no bones about psychotherapy being a corrective experience and stressed the need for an 'orientation that acknowledges and then examines the analyst's influence in principle as an intrinsically significant human presence, not his influence via distorting countertransferences (Kohut 1984: 37). It is the therapist's capacity to be consistently, though undemandingly and unseductively, *present* with the patient that provides the thoughtful and well-intentioned ambience that fosters the repair of deficient ego structures and the release of blocked energies. 'The patient', in Christopher Bollas' words, 'appreciates the analyst's fundamental unintrusiveness, not because it leads to freedom of association, but because it feels like the special kind of relating that is needed to become well' (Bollas 1987: 23).

This early phase of idealisation can of course be a delicate one, and although I do not consciously find it difficult, I must confess that on more than one occasion I have been guilty of serious slip-ups with patients' appointments during this stage. I would suggest that this is an indication of how easily that phase can tip into resentment and even fear on the part of the mother or therapist as they experience the ruthless intensity of the infant's/patient's focus. I suspect that such feelings may well be a sign that the acceptance of the idealisation has been unduly prolonged and is therefore inappropriate.

The most painful memory is of my forgetting to notify one young woman, one of whose bi-weekly sessions was early on Friday morning, that I would not be able to keep our appointment. I was, in fact, going to be away from home for a long weekend. She arrived to find a dark, locked up house and had recourse only to my answerphone, on which she left increasingly distressed messages conveying her rising panic and fears that something disastrous had happened to me.

It was a gruelling experience on my return to have to listen to her frightened voice. The knowledge that she was re-experiencing the early vicissitudes of her original childhood, and that this was 'supercharging' the inconvenience caused by my own shortcomings consoled me not at all. The only comfort I could draw was that her last recorded message conveyed the voice of someone who had 'come through'. It was as if she had reached the very depth of her panic and despair and had found a surprisingly secure landing in the resources of her own self. Her last message was delivered in a calm strong voice and assumed that there had been a miscommunication and that I had gone away for the weekend.

This experience, despite its pain, proved to be the basis of much useful work in subsequent sessions. It certainly gave me a much greater fellow-feeling with her mother, who had no doubt forgotten her baby quite often when she had felt burdened, not only by her needs but by her intense idealisation. Most important of all, the alliance between us, already strong enough to survive her despair and anger and my shame, became rock-like! We were both honest enough for a real repair to be made and the relationship was able to bear the light of reality. Unlike the relationship between Psyche and Cupid in the myth, our already developing erotic bond did not run away even temporally from the light of Psyche's torch but rather faced it and ultimately flourished. Nevertheless her disillusionment in my omnipotence and never-failing goodness was undesirably sudden and I must say that I believe that our ability to survive this experience owed something to the therapeutic milieu in which we worked.

For me, as for many therapists working at home, that therapeutic milieu inevitably lacks the complete neutrality that might theoretically be found in a hospital or specialised consulting room. Although boundaries regarding times and payment are rigorously kept, and evidence of other occupants and my external concerns kept to a minimum, it must be quite obvious that I live in the real world, and have responsibilities and interests other than my patients. Some may say that this state of affairs, together with a somewhat down-to-earth, idiomatic style, has disadvantages in that it prevents the uninterrupted development of the transferences. But as Ernest Wolf trenchantly observed, 'Ambiguous invisibility is not a necessary precondition for the emergence of intense transferences, nor does the presence of the analyst as a real person inhibit the transference relation' (Wolf 1988: 88).

I would further suggest that it is precisely because of the down-to-earth setting that those gross transferences which may become uncomfortable for both patient and therapist are much less likely to occur. It seems to me that such exaggeratedly intense transferences which can contain much bizarre erotic material, are often evidence of a pathology that is unconsciously developing in the therapeutic setting itself. This may be provoked by unnecessary even unconsciously sadistic withholding, by inaccurate and pushy interpretations, or by unconscious needs in the therapist or by the delusions of omnipotence to which we are all occasionally prone.

Even at the stage of the 'idealising transference' our 'ordinariness' and willingness to eschew a 'false self' enable that part of the patient which is already mature to take us 'with a pinch of salt' and set us in the real world. I believe that this is what happened to some extent with my Friday patient. Her underlying link with reality, though often masked by archaic material, had been an ongoing feature of the therapeutic alliance developing between us. It is my contention that when due attention is paid to this adult–adult relationship from the beginning, both patient and therapist are enabled to keep their bearings as the transferential phenomena develop. The idealising transference can then be accepted, but without being unnecessarily deepened or prolonged. The libidinal energy deriving naturally from the patient's early narcissism does not then get snarled up in a cul-de-sac with the therapist, but is available for further elaboration and development.

Crucial to the success of this further development is the ability of the therapist to discern the nature of the material the patient is presenting in each session, and the response they are unconsciously seeking. This will, of course, depend on the therapist's capacity for empathy, an aspect of therapeutic technique which Kohut placed firmly in the main body of his theory, making it the *sine qua non* of effective therapy and dignifying it as a concept by full discussion and repeated attempts at definition. He saw empathy as 'the mode by which one gathers psychological data about other people and, when they say what they think or feel, imagines their inner experience even though it is not open to direct observation' (Kohut 1979: I 450). Empathy is, then, not to be confused with compassion – indeed, in the wrong hands, it can be a powerfully destructive and manipulative tool (Kohut 1981). Used for the patient's benefit, however, it is a precision tool that can help the therapist to assess the tone of the session; whether, for instance, the patient is presenting material that requires the acceptance and clarification of the idealising phase, or the mirroring of his emerging assertiveness, or the cut and thrust of a more adversarial exchange. All these will need interpretation, but the tone and nuances of the interpretations must be differentiated if the patients are to feel understood, and, indeed, if they are to begin to understand themselves.

A short vignette may help to illustrate this. Claudette was a young and beautiful woman, rather overweight, who came complaining of general dissatisfaction with her life, with her mother and siblings, and with her lack of a partner. Her story was a sad one – a long break in childhood from her mother, bullying by her elder brother and sister from which she had felt unprotected, and an unreliable and occasionally sadistic father whom she no longer saw. At school she had been a bully as well as a victim of bullying, but after an indifferent record she appeared suddenly to have summoned up enough strength and determination to get into university and to graduate successfully.

I could sense in the first two sessions that she felt relieved to find me approachable and reasonably responsive. I expected that in view of the depressing and difficult situation she found herself in at home (she still lived with the family) the emergence of strong positive feelings for me would characterise the subsequent sessions, probably for some months, and that this would be a necessary basis for further work. I felt interested in her story and concerned to help her explore and understand it and the very painful feelings of distress and anger that had been aroused.

However, in the third session I was aware of a change in my response to her. She had told me of her difficult relationship with her elder brother, who also still lived in their mother's house. She had told me of his aggressive, competitive attitude to her, and her determination to have as little to do with him as possible. I could see and hear that despite her apparently adult intentions her manner and tone of voice were becoming sulky and aggressive. She went on to tell me that she had made him a short-term loan some weeks ago which he was refusing to pay back, and how aggrieved and upset she felt about it.

I *might* have said, 'I can see that you feel hurt and angry that your brother's behaviour is so disappointing'. This comment together with some exploration of the pain of her early situation might have suited the needy infant. I sensed, however, it was the sulky child resisting reality who had suddenly popped up; I put my money on my countertransference feeling of irritation and said instead, 'There seems to be a contradiction in what you're saying. Interesting, isn't it that you say you don't trust your brother and want to keep apart from him and yet you lend him money. What goes on?' At this she suddenly sat up straight, looked me in the eye, and replied in a much more 'adult' voice, 'You have a good point there!' I had gone from a nurturing self-object to an adversarial challenging self-object in a matter of minutes. Both experiences were necessary for her during that session and both could be accommodated.

The session, which I had been finding rather lacklustre, got a new infusion of energy, and we went on to a useful exploration of her difficulties in accepting the realities of her situation and her ever-present wish that somehow she could make her family into the ideally loving figures of her fantasies. Much of her energy had been diverted into this unproductive channel. She confessed that my comment had given her a profound sense of relief, although she also felt angry that she was not getting the 'patting and soothing' that she had hoped I would unfailingly provide.

I realised later that there were probably veiled references to me in her 'sulky' remarks. The fact that this did not occur to me in the session could be seen as a failure to take up the transference. It is possible, however, that my reply was rooted in my empathic response to the patient and attuned to the situation pertaining between us at the time. A more sophisticated interpretation might well have been appropriate at a much later stage or even if a more integrated mature self had appeared in that session. Given prematurely I believe it would have either 'wasted its sweetness on the desert air' or provoked Claudette's narcissistic rage, which would have looked impressively dramatic but been entirely unproductive and time-wasting (Kohut 1979: 395–446).

Authenticity, empathy and the willingness to be 'an intrinsically human presence' for the patient have, I am sure, always been the hallmark of effective psychotherapy. Kohut, of course, elevates these qualities to a primary role in his theoretical structure. They become the prerequisite for any significant improvement and growth. Certainly I have myself found that as the patient begins to enjoy the growing alliance with the therapist and to develop an interest in the work, the released energy in both of us drives the work forward and the increasing rapport emerging from the early idealisation presents a new focus for the patient's interest. I find that this shift of focus is often signalled by a decrease in patients' attempts to control the session by socialising it. Remarks about the weather, the difficult journey, inquiries about my health diminish, cheques are presented already written – the experience of the session has become gratifying in itself and too valuable to waste. Envy of the therapist's idealised 'goodness' gives way to an affectionate appreciation of the 'good enough'. Patients now begin to develop the courage to suffer frustration and disappointment and to bear to look at the reality of their situation. And they begin to understand the truth of Bion's quotation from Dr Johnson, that 'the consolation which is drawn from truth, if any there be, is solid and durable' (Bion 1970: 7).

However, even for those patients who have developed some ego strength the deepest and most necessary revelations of the truth are difficult to bear, and can go on provoking stubborn resistance at an unconscious level. I think, for instance, of a young woman who from the beginning appeared to participate willingly and energetically in her sessions, and began to 'feel much better' as our working relationship developed. Life outside the consulting room certainly improved for her but I could see that her apparent alliance with me was masking a deep, frightened compliance with a terrifying yet reassuring parental figure. It was to be many months before she could summon the strength to contemplate the full truth of her story.

It turned out that her relationship with her father, an eminent professional man, had been entirely marred by his unpredictability and sadism. Any attempt at self-assertion was met with ridicule and punishment and her mother, although basically sympathetic and loving, was herself too cowed to offer any protection. This interruption of normal Oedipal development resulted not only in a basic weakening of her ego, but also in an internalised confusion in which wishes for protective fatherly love were tinged with sado-masochism. Her subsequent lovers were the focus of intense infantile yearning for security and nurturing, but they were also unconsciously expected to be punitive and even delinquent, as these qualities had become inextricably linked in her mind with empowerment and authority.

Fortunately, enough of her self had remained intact to be aware that she was becoming increasingly imprisoned and exhausted, and that the sexual side of such relationships contained neither mutual pleasure nor genuine love-making. She had managed to summon up enough determination to escape from the last of these relationships which had already persisted for several years, and to seek therapeutic help. Her relief at finding someone to talk to was obvious, and the customary short-term improvement in her mood was clear. As her hopes of omnipotent solutions and injunctions from me were gradually replaced by a willingness to cooperate freely and to think for herself, nothing could prevent the gradual emergence of the painful truth about her father; the re-experiencing of her childhood terror and frustration (this time without defensive normalisation); the perception of her own sexually charged masochistic collusion with the brutality and delinquency of her most recent lover; and the awareness of how in the transference she had tried to turn me into a depersonalised source of narcissistic supply, controllable by her old 'little girl' strategies of compliance and 'niceness'.

Although much sexual material was acknowledged, put in perspective and, I hope, detoxified, I had no sense that the transferences to me were becoming eroticised. I would suggest, however, that as the working alliance progressed it became *libidinised*, in that it became energetic, interesting and dynamic, with an increasing capacity to see me as a person who could be perceived as a separate individual and who could in Winnicottian terms be 'played with' (Winnicott 1971).

When we reach this stage in the therapy, Eros has really begun to come of age and to infuse the work and the relationship with enjoyment and stimulus. I find that I begin to look forward positively to each session and the increasingly lively alliance provides the springboard for entry into the real world. The defences then become less rigid. Patients begin to feel able to bear enough reality to let go of their idealisations because there is now a new awareness of the deeper pleasure that comes from a relationship where separation and human failings can be tolerated. The erotic bond with its emphasis on mutual pleasure for two establishes its primacy over infantile self-gratifying sexual fantasies for one.

Surely it is the discovery in the therapeutic setting of this depth of object relationship, with its accompanying sense of achievement and joy, that enables the patient to find similar deeply enjoyable relationships in the world outside. As Fairbairn (1952: 32) stated,

> it is not correct to describe the libidinal attitude of the adult as characteristically genital. It should properly be described as 'mature'. This term must, however, be understood to imply that genital channels are available for a satisfactory libidinal relationship with the object. At the same time it must be stressed that it is not in virtue of the fact that the genital level has been reached that object

relationships are satisfactory. On the contrary, it is in virtue of the fact that satisfactory object relationships have been established that true genital sexuality is attained.

It is the non-intrusive, non-seductive nature of the therapy as well as the success of its interpretations and provision of insight that enable the process of gradual maturation to happen safely. It is the experience of mutual empathy, enjoyment and concern that provides the foundation for the loving and erotic sexuality that belongs ultimately not to the therapist or parent who may help to facilitate it but to the significant figures that will be encountered in the newly adult world.

So as Eros matures and becomes capable of the resilient and patient loving that in the myth resulted in the reawakening of the sleeping Psyche, he finds that the world is further enriched not only by the discovery of a sexual partner, but by many other sustaining and enjoyable relationships. These are the relationships Kohut (1984: 77) sees as the result of a process 'in which the analysand's formerly archaic needs for the responses of archaic selfobjects are superseded by the experience of the availability of empathic resonance, the major constituent of the sense of security in adult life'. It is these successful and lasting relationships and not a self-sufficient autonomy that he saw as the goal of psychotherapy and the reward for the long and painful struggle to human maturity.

REFERENCES

Bion, W. (1965) *Transformations*, London: William Heinemann.
—— (1970) *Attention and Interpretation*, London: Tavistock Publications.
Bollas, C. (1987) *The Shadow of the Object: Psychoanalysis of the Unthought Known*, London: Free Association Press.
Fairbairn, W.R.D. (1952) *Psychoanalytical Studies of the Personality*, London: Routledge & Kegan Paul.
Freud, S. (1917) 'Mourning and melancholia', *Standard Edition* 14, London: Hogarth Press.
Grimal, P. (1991) *Penguin Dictionary of Classical Mythology* (ed. S. Kershaw), London: Penguin.
Guntrip, H. (1969) *Schizoid Phenomena, Object Relations and the Self*, New York: International Universities Press.
Kohut, H. (1959) 'Introspection, empathy and psychoanalysis: an examination of the relationship between mode of observation and theory', in P. Ornstein (ed.), *The Search for Self vol. 1*, New York: International Universities Press.
—— (1966) 'Formations and transformations of narcissism', in P. Ornstein (ed.), *The Search for Self vol. 1*, New York: International Universities Press (1978).
—— (1971) *The Analysis of the Self*, New York: International Universities Press.
—— (1977) *Restoration of the Self*, New York: International Universities Press.
—— (1979) 'The two analyses of Mr Z', in P. Ornstein (ed.), *The Search for Self vol. 4*, New York: International Universities Press (1990).

—— 'On empathy', in P. Ornstein (ed.), *The Search for Self vol. 4* (1990), New York: International Universities Press.

—— (1984) *How Does Analysis Cure?*, A. Goldberg and P. Stepansky (eds), Chicago and London: Chicago University Press.

Mann, D. (1997) *Psychotherapy: An Erotic Relationship*, London: Routledge.

Winnicott, D. (1953) 'Transitional objects and transitional phenomena', *International Journal of Psychoanalysis* 34.

—— (1971) *Playing and Reality*, London: Tavistock Publications.

Wolf, E.S. (1988) *Treating the Self: Elements of Clinical Self Psychology*, New York: The Guilford Press.

3 Eros

The connecting principle (or the complexities of love and sexuality)

Jean Thomson

Why Eros? Eros was an ancient god – the god of love and lust. How can an archetypal figure help us with the very modern complexities of transference and countertransference, of resolving splits between creative and destructive defences? Surely analysis is a science? If science includes the 'Eureka!' principle, of knowledge carefully collated and sifted but then coming together in a flash of unconscious creativity, then psychoanalysis and analytical psychology are science, where Eros as the connecting principle in life provides the basis for such flashes of creativity by integrating the system which produces the energy. Eros, to the Greeks a god, and both child and man, was their way of defining and explaining connections of apparent opposites, including sex, composed as it is of love and lust, tenderness and aggression, relationship and loneliness, trust and paranoia. When we fear the sensations and emotions of the countertransference, if we are in the world of Eros, we can as Psyche in thrall to Eros or Eve tempted by the serpent, seek enlightenment through trying to know something about what is really going on. It could not have been carnal knowledge which Eve sought. She and Adam already had that. It may be that what was sought was consciousness about what was already part of their experience. Non-consciousness had been keeping them in a paradise which prevented them using their brainpower. In other words, sexual lust may be a diversion from the overall task. That which we have learned to call transference is an expression of the strange power of the *coniunctio* (Jung 1946), the instinct to become part of the other. In the containing ephemeral space which is the analytic hour, through the few transformative words which describe and acknowledge change, we try to find some understanding of what it is to be two separate beings. Where sexuality is not sufficiently recognised as a part of that transference, it can take over and prevent progress in the task.

Although love and lust may be differentiated, Jung's definition of Eros as the connecting principle recognises the curious fact that human beings, the human as part of a species, want to live together in groups yet each individual wants to feel that he or she is uniquely him or her self. (Psycho)analytic thinking has its roots in our cultural group norms and states that our repressions are in the cause of adaptation to the resulting beliefs. A return to the original Eros can free us from such concretised bonds belonging as it does to the infinite from which we can clutch some sense of what it is that we fear, what troubles us, what holds us from the fierce rage of a lifetime of grappling with inner and outer realities. What we fear may be derived from early developmental experiences and a desire to be socially acceptable beings, but imaginings and fantasies also have their origins in less explicable processes, the layer of the psyche Jung called the collective unconscious.

Here, I hope to weave the ancient lineage of Eros, as the origin of our capacity to make relationships, with that of transference and countertransference theory, built over the past hundred years on the discoveries of Freud and Jung and their successors. For most of that time science has been limited to determining causes and effects and to believing that matter and non-matter could not be part of each other. Only recently have we begun to relate analytic work to a newer science of quantum theory through which Jung's quest to understand the infinity of the human psyche can make sense, even when it includes the Greek myths where humans and gods share the same world of chaos and order. Through quantum physics (Bohm 1980; Zinkin 1987; Zohar 1990) it can be seen that we are part of a vast system of movement, of constantly changing matter and non-matter, in which parallel processes go on apparently related and without cause. Through these discoveries, Jung's descriptions of acausal connections such as synchronicity (Jung 1972) can be verified.

According to one of the earliest Greek creation myths, indeed, chaos and time met to produce earth and sky in a moment very similar to the Big Bang theory. Eros then was said to be around as the original impulse to connect 'heaven and earth', neither male nor female, before being embodied (cf. Hesiod). The *Oxford* and the *Chambers* dictionaries refer to 'erotic' merely as 'sexual excitation' – a definition in line with the difficulty of determining what 'love' can possibly be as a connecting principle other than having a reproductive purpose. Another dictionary (*Reader's Digest* 1996) on the other hand links the erotic with Eros and Greek mythology: Eros is defined as 'the sum of all self-preservative as contrasted with self-destructive instincts' (i.e. Thanatos). However, it sometimes seems that in contemporary life such links have been lost and that sexual excitation is feared more than any other physical response as if it had no connection with the rest of human feelings. Anxieties about sex have become focused on child abuse and paedophilia, subjects rendered almost impossible to discuss by the revulsion they cause. Love is totally denied. We forget that a few years ago homosexuality caused equal public revulsion and early in the century Freud was reviled for discussing heterosexuality. It still seems to be impossible to allow for desire and for problems of sexuality but still acknowledge the presence of love. In this chapter, love is regarded as the integrating factor in Eros. The quest in analysis and psychotherapy is for the patient to achieve a more effective personal integration. To do this therapist and patient must engage with each other.

In an original Greek creation myth, before anything else existed there was Eros (Hesiod 1988 writing c. 500 BC). The Greeks seemed to be trying to explain the physical world. Gradually, attributions of maleness and female-ness began to be made, no doubt out of observations of behaviour. Later the observations of behaviour were the result of the way everyday life became organised. At first there were a whole lot of gods and goddesses in no particular hierarchy and no particular morality. Eros became Aphrodite, goddess of love, and later emerged as son of Aphrodite and Ares (Mars). But Ares also represented the end of cowardice and the courage for peace. Aphrodite (Venus) was an extremely powerful, often vindictive goddess and a seducer. Eros, child and man, is a tricksterish god who, as Cupid, acts out the connecting principle by causing people to fall in love with each other and forget all else. In his commentary on Amor (Eros) and Psyche, Neumann (1973) says this is a myth of female development: Eros as an arche-type cannot develop, he just is. But Eros is both human and god and therefore the tale seems to be about human development towards acquiring godlike aspects (Psyche is eventually taken up into heaven to join the pantheon). 'Godlike', in this sense, means the emerging archetypes become conscious parts of the personality.

The story of Amor and Psyche is curiously akin to that which we have about Princess Diana. Psyche, the virgin, escapes being a sacrifice, is taken to the palace where she can have everything she wants as long as she doesn't ask questions or otherwise attempt to see what is happening to her. Eventually, she cannot bear to meet her lover only in the darkness and tries to see him by lighting her lamp (of understanding). She drops some burning oil on him and he flees. Then they are both in trouble and have many trials to undergo. Unlike Princess Diana, Amor and Psyche are eventually reunited – and join the gods (Neumann 1973).

Eros, more usually in the later pantheon, is a kind of Peter Pan figure with a rampant and undeveloped sexuality. He is the original hero. With the advent of monotheism, this older mythology of the diversity of human sexuality and its godlike qualities of love became lost in a morality which expressed itself as a hierarchy of power. God (Yaweh, Jehovah, Jove, Zeus) was the creator of everything and therefore the Lord and possessor of everything. This elimi-nates and does not give a place to much of human diversity. There was a con-flation of Zeus and Eros – Zeus, power; Eros love (connection) – which then becomes a division, when God's Son becomes the embodiment of (non-sexual) love and God himself retains the power and authority. The role of the father becomes confusing. Yet the original Eros, the connecting principle in creation, was neither male nor female and had no specific characteristics except that of bringing opposites together – air and matter, spirit and flesh – continually evolving.

Or notions, including those in psychotherapy, of love, sexuality and perver-sion are based on the censorship of ideas, usually unacknowledged, and the monotheistic legacy of our time and culture. Adaptation to societal beliefs, achieved as it is by repression, leaves us unconscious of what is rational and irrational. Useful messages from the collective unconscious, if they get through, for example in dreams, are generally scoffed at or at best often mis-interpreted according to 'where the therapist is coming from'. If, as I do, we regard societies as trying to achieve a balance between destructive and posi-tively creative forces, in the way that each individual member of the society does, it becomes necessary to try to work out why conscious rules are so often sabotaged by powerful emotional beliefs. Group relations theory states that the shared cultural unconscious is an unconscious underlay for such sabotage (Bion 1965). But the Jungian notion of the collective unconscious takes this further into the shared phenomenon of our phylogenetic inheritance expressed through archetypes. This accords with the amorality of the original Greek gods and goddesses, playing out human attributes. Later, when these had been contained in a hierarchy, Greek drama enlisted the pantheon to argue out human ethical codes and a social organisation with power allocated to men and moral codes which emphasised gender and power relations in an increasingly rigid way. They reflected the social order, but through the original gods and goddesses it is possible to see how in ancient times people sought ways of explaining not only the unknowable and inexplicable but ways of describing how human beings feel and think. The vast number of gods and goddesses reflect the vast possibilities in each human.

Had quantum physics existed when Jung was writing his thoughts about acausal connections his ideas would have seemed less bizarre to the scienti-cally minded of the time (including himself!). Or had DNA been discovered with the complex blueprints possible in our genetic structures, where, so it is said, a single hair follicle holds all the information about an individual, arche-type theory might have been more accepted. Had Jung himself cared to apply his anthropological studies or his views about collective unconscious to present-day political organisation, his contribution to the recognition that the individual exists only in the context of the environment might have been more influential in studies of group dynamics. As it is, I am writing as a Jungian analyst trained in the Society of Analytical Psychology, influ-enced as much by Kleinian psychoanalysis as by Jung. My own experiences, including an interest in social and organisational life fostered during ten years of working at the Tavistock Clinic in London, lead me to regard developmental theory as the basis for understanding in the analytic hour, which I see as rather like expressionist art. The exchange can only happen in that space, at that time with the two people involved, in the Now which cannot be codified or quantified. But still it is necessary to concep-tualise about the palette, the context and how connections are made. 'Eros' emphasises that development is continuous, past, present, future, and enables us to put 'love' as a definition of the integrative understanding required in the task of analysis.

SEXUALITY AND LOVE IN THE TRANSFERENCE

The problem is not so much sex as love, taking love to mean integration. If the aim of psychotherapy is a rebalancing of internal complexes, erotic feelings obviously are part of what has to be integrated. Yet erotic feelings can be so overwhelming that therapist and patient feel compelled to consummate them. How then can the therapist regain a sense of the task of psychotherapy? At the level of the collective unconscious, the couple are drawn to deny all difference and merge together, everything belongs to everything else. In reductionist terms of developmental psychology, they are drawn to regress to the original mother-and-baby, the object in its environment. From a more teleological standpoint, the future beckons as well as the past, the desire to be part of the infinite again, thus fulfilling the task of life. In prosaic terms, if the couple can just have sex together, they think they will fulfil all their needs: that is the connection required. In its extreme form, this is madness (as is realised in popular folklore – the madness of love) or psychosis, to be more technical. Mostly, as therapists, transference theory helps us to rationalise our feelings, step back from the borderline and continue with the task of analysing the situation. Eros in its broader sense of love as well as desire, steps in to rescue the task. Usually, the patient does not want the madness confirmed anyway, and feels abused when the professional abandons the rules.

A patient, Shannon, referred to me because her first therapist was not Jungian and therefore could not conduct a training analysis, was angry and resentful comparing me contemptuously to her ex-therapist, B, a man with whom she had felt complete rapport. We worked on the various permutations suggested by this. Some time later, B wrote to Shannon suggesting a meeting to talk over what had happened. She followed this up and, she said, found herself engaging in passionate sex on his consulting-room carpet. He took the view that as their therapy relationship was over, there was no longer any reason not to act on their erotic attraction for each other. She was confused and drawn to have an affair with him. Why not? After all, she had known at the time that much of what she felt was 'transference', but not now, she thought, even if her fate with most men was to fall into sexual affairs because her attractiveness and low self-esteem both appealed to men and made her vulnerable to being seduced. Now she wondered if she should make up to B for having left him. As he was married, she was in a familiar place to her, of being part of a triangle. Usually, she had given no thought to the wife in the situation, except possibly to criticise her. In the analysis, we saw that there was now another triangle, the two analysts and the patient. I was in the position of the wife/mother and feared being jealous and possessive of my patient/child. Daringly, she had, like Persephone, responding to the Eros within her, sought a lover. My role, like Demeter, could be to lay waste and try to win her back, unless my inner Eros could continue to see the overall picture. By acting on her feelings for B, we now had the material to examine the complexities of her needs for love. After a while, she let go of the affair with B because her desire faded as she realised that the physical sexuality was in the context of her emotional development in the process of analysis. The actual sex enabled us to get a clearer insight into the part sex played in her life, but also how much resentful envy towards a powerful mother had motivated her. While she and I had work to do on the homosexual element of the transference, it began to be realised that her relations with men had been more to do with attacking 'the mother' and, thus, herself as a woman, than to do with a need for sex. In this situation, Eros, as Cupid often a trickster, had helped the analysis along by bringing B and Shannon together. The 'acting out', while appearing to be against the analysis, was more an acting-through than an attack on the process of Shannon's therapy.

With another patient, Dee, also referred after ten years of avoiding therapy, the sexuality had not been so useful. She recounted how in her previous analysis following rejection by her lover, she had been engaged in fantasies that her analyst, C, was so like him that she must have sex with him. Suddenly, C took her up on this in the middle of a session, inviting her to go to bed with him. She remained in the room discussing the subject but then left and never went back. Subsequently, she had an acute psychotic breakdown and was hospitalised. Here, it seemed that the need for physical expression had suffused both of them and avoided the meaning of her fantasies in the wider context of the transference. Dee had been too near to psychosis to cope with the concrete offer. Unlike Shannon's therapist, it seems that C misjudged the feelings and his acting on them constituted an abuse of their relationship. Presumably, in this case, the psychotic element had over-whelmed the couple.

In Jung's early discussion of transference phenomena (e.g. Jung 1935), he regards the transference as dangerous, something to be got rid of, a diversion from the work. He says that the transference is definitely not love and while both patient and analyst may be caught up in mutual projections, the analyst must manage to get over his or her feelings and help the patient to do so also. He seems to mean by 'not love' that the mutuality in life outside the consult-ing room must be recognised as different from that within. His professional persona excluded 'love'. He always maintains that he works from his own sub-jective experiences (Jung 1963). In a surrealist play, *Sabina* (Wilson 1998), the author is able to give a valuable insight into the involvement Jung had with one of his patients, at the beginning of his psychotherapist life early in the century, and which must have influenced such ideas about transference. Later, Jung does recognise transference and countertransference as a tool to be used in analysis.

The play manages to convey the psychotic element when sexual desire is overwhelming and experienced as love. It is not surprising that Jung felt it was something to be overcome. Sabina Spielrein (Wilson 1998; Carotenuto 1984) is portrayed in this play as a young patient in the Bergholzi hospital, taken over by sexual fantasies and masturbating continually in a flamboyant exhibitionism. She has been referred by Freud as requiring to be hospitalised and becomes Jung's first psychotherapy patient. In his professional self, Jung is a serious young psychiatrist, ambitious and well regarded. The play succeeds in showing how psychosis can permeate institutional as well as individual systems. For example, there is uncertainty about who has thrown faeces at a picture of Freud, who, at that time, is revered by Jung. Dr Bleuler, also in the play, assumes it was a patient's work but it seems to have been Jung's 'spirit guide' Philemon (Jung 1963), the device the author brings in to demonstrate the collective unconscious and how Jung became erotically intoxicated and was seduced by Sabina, whom he begins to refer to as his *anima* (feminine aspect). Through Philemon and Sabina all sorts of trickster-ish things happen as Jung and she have a romantic, sexual affair. Her symptoms diminish and the intensity of feelings recedes until, eventually, Jung realises he must end the affair, referring her back to Freud in Vienna. She is taken there by her parents and subsequently trains as a psychoanalyst.

This seemed to me to demonstrate how the bond which makes psychotherapy possible holds – in all its negative and positive aspects – until the relationship has fulfilled its function, because as 'opposites' both madness and sanity are there in the composition of the personality. Sabina, as a girl of her time, had a symptom designed to be shocking and which had overcome her in an extreme of hysterical compulsive behaviour. The contagion of her desperate need seduced Jung and split him off from his everyday persona. He was able to continue to do his job as a doctor while taken over by fantasy. As usual with his inner experiences, he was later able to make use of the involvement in his writing about analytical psychology. In this sense, again, Eros the trickster acted in the cause of Eros the connecting principle which could achieve what was needed in integration for himself and his patient. As an imaginative fantasy, the play is itself in the cause of Eros. Through it, I thought I could see how Jung might have been shocked into deciding that transference feelings were a danger.

Nowadays we, as therapists, enter this danger area deliberately. The special space of the analysis or the psychotherapy – secluded, quiet room, structured place or couch and chair, reliance on talking and silences, the 'rule of abstinence', the regular meetings with as few breaks as possible – all these 'conditions' create a special awareness, in both therapist and patient, that something different from daily life is going on. The therapy is in the present, the here-and-now, or to take account of the archetypal level of experience, the eternal Now. The experience can be 'shared' and is not confined to the boundaries of the physical self. Dreams are important, as are the images and physical sensations that arise – from sexual arousal or even small stirrings of erotic interest to physiological impulses such as headaches, backache, stomach and gut tremors and rumblings and gaseous sensations. Attention is concentrated, attention wanders. Thoughts arise and are translated into dialogue.

We call all this transference, the meeting of two beings in a universe on which each has a small perceptual window. By the time he writes of this phenomenon in 'Problems of modern psychotherapy' (1929), Jung tells us that it is necessary for the analyst to have been analysed in order that she or he is not lost in what occurs with the patient. Even so, to suspend the ego enough to let Eros make the necessary connections is to become vulnerable to being at the mercy of the patient's projections or one's own projective identifications, including sexual desire.

There is a paradox built into our contemporary ideas of the transference in psychoanalytic work. At the same time as we may think of interpretation as a logical process arising from application of a theory about development and/or technique, we believe in 'not knowing' of going into the consulting room 'without memory and without desire', to enlist Wilfred Bion's often used saying. We believe that each moment with the patient is unique and should not be predicted. At the same time, the patient is assessed and diagnosed, bearing in mind psychiatric states, to see if she or he is 'suitable' for psychotherapy, not too 'psychotic', etc. Increasingly, transference and countertransference are the main tools of the psychotherapist, offering the patient the possibility of reliving and thus changing the import of early (malignant) experiences. The 'here-and-now' is refined to refer to the infantile projections brought out in the process. It could be said that lying on the couch encourages the sort of regression which enables a response to invitations to consider that the earliest experiences are where the solutions to difficulties will be found.

Sometimes there is a belief that this is a microscopic investigation, akin to the micro-investigations of orthodox scientific tradition. Yet, at the same time, psychotherapists have to be aware that what is revealed in the consulting room is not to be understood in parts without the continual recognition that the human being which is the self seeks something we call wholeness or integration. The feeling of integrity means a capacity to recognise symbol, paradox, the relations between opposites, ambivalence: in other words, to deal with Eros as the connecting principle. Yet as Eros also flits about making connections, so each inner system, as part of other systems, can only be packaged for a moment before it fluctuates and changes balance. In the Kleinian model, this continual shift has been described as reworking the depressive position via paranoid/schizoid states. 'Not knowing' can thus be conceptualised as a kind of fragmentation of the feeling of integrated understanding. Where the therapist has arrived at a relatively integrated stage in development (the depressive position) the letting go of certainty (as in suspension of the ego), although unsettling, will eventually be followed by the realignment of the inner kaleidoscope in some comprehensible form. Chaos can be tolerated because it will be followed by order. Trust in the assessment which has been done allows the therapist to 'suspend the ego' and allow such inner realignments to occur.

The transference, in itself, is part of the whole process and where it is neglected neither patients nor therapist can see the role the therapist is playing in the analytic scenario. A patient was brought to supervision because he was continually 'acting out' and the therapist felt the psychotherapy to be 'stuck'. The patient, Jackson, felt he had become addicted to going to Turkish baths since coming to Britain from Africa. The atmosphere stirred flickering images of exotic excitements which the therapist, D, and he saw as regressive behaviour. He described the saunas as having 'warmth, wetness, darkness and timelessness', which they had been interpreting as 'womb-like'. Mostly, he lay about in sensual pleasure watching others. For sexual encounters, he went to a park where he met men silently and transitorily in the dark of night feeling after that he had a well of water inside which could engulf him. He kept sexuality away from loving feelings and kept everyone 'at a distance' from him. In line with this, in the therapy sessions he endlessly recounted sexual experiences and his times as an observer of human life. In describing his early life he had said that his father disapproved of him as a 'cissy' because he couldn't bear 'killing things' (i.e. he disliked fishing and hunting). Although he and his mother confided in each other in a confessional sort of way, he resented that she expected him to tell her everything and judged what he told her according to her strict religious code. He felt 'seen' by neither parent. They watched him but mistook what they saw. D felt herself to be imprisoned in the role of unseeing parent, unable to make the connections which might impinge on his insistently recounted, but curiously disconnected, observations. From Kleinian point of view, his anxiety unconsciously attacked the linking necessary to arrive at a more thoughtful (depressive) position.

With my encouragement, D acknowledged that she, too, had lived in Africa (although in a different country) and this began to loosen the split as she allowed her own inner identifications to surface in her thoughts. The Eros *coniunctio* could be realised in a more illuminating form through the feeling both experienced that at last she and Jackson could acknowledge something in common. She felt that she could begin to avoid her role as cleansing mother or critical father. When she wondered whether his family had had any black friends or servants, a whole new population entered therapy from his inner world. As is common with children brought up in a country where they learn to feel they do not really belong, Jackson had repressed his memories of his black nurse and her children, his first playmates. As he grew up, these relationships became forbidden and not spoken about. Jackson's mother thought his father particularly should not hear of any interest in his nurse or her family, lest he would be even more despicably 'soft' than he already appeared. In his adolescence, secrecy and sexuality became intertwined and love was feared as bringing catastrophe.

As with Sabina's masturbation, Jackson had found the thing which would most shock his father but at the same time that he needed in order to develop. His warmest relationships had been with his childhood friends but this was now a matter for shame. Sex became a secret sensual activity which gave a fleeting sense of Eros as an integrative wholeness. Because he could only have transient encounters in the dark, as when Eros visits Psyche in the darkness of night, he could not achieve internal acknowledgement.

When Psyche tries to see what her life and love really consists of Eros immediately flies away. Psyche has to face the wrath of the mother who wants to keep him from marrying a mortal. This archetypal triangle seemed to exist in D's consulting room. Jackson feared the wrath of the parent but began to find that D was interested in, rather than envious of, his individuality and did not subscribe to the view that it must be a secret or confessed as a sin. Her Eros, by taking an overview, let in the light.

D thought of the inner well of water as a need for rebirth as an adult man. The fear was of a cataclysmic change as the split-off sexuality was reintegrated with the whole Eros. As Psyche, in the myth, had been cast out to go through tribulations in the cause of developing consciousness, so Jackson feared what would happen if the water burst through. His addictive behaviour, going to the Turkish baths, was intended to alleviate the tension of the fear of destructive madness, but as is the case with any addiction, more and more of the 'drug' had been required. Jackson told how, before going on an important business trip, he had had to spend all night at his favourite baths. He avoided anxiety but was exhausted. In this sense, the steamy atmosphere is of Hades, where Eros and Psyche cannot meet and Logos, the capacity to have conscious thought, is lost until they can return to 'the light'. Can D's capacity for connections continue to enlighten her patient? Incidentally, it can be seen here that the black family had brought the possibility of a more integrated Eros to a white child born into a family rigidly imprisoned in their cultural bonds and into fears of sin and damnation, setting him on the path to eventual enlightenment. His sister remaining near her parents and, presumably, not having been able to find a way out, is constantly depressed and suicidal. Another sibling travels constantly from place to place, apparently also fleeing Eros.

SUMMARY

In this paper, I have tried to demonstrate that there is a connecting principle, Eros, in Jungian psychology, which is an instinctual underpinning for human development. Psychotherapy or analysis with the aim of integration of the personality, that is the body/mind/emotional system, is helped by this Eros to find ways of understanding the problems which arise in the course of development. In order to comprehend 'Eros', it is necessary to return to early Greek mythology, where Eros is the original 'connecting principle' bringing the environment into being as a psycho-physical system.

I finish with a quotation from Jung (1946: 27):

> Eros . . . belongs on one side to man's primordial animal nature
> which will endure as long as man has animal body. On the other

side, he is related to the highest forms of the spirit. But he thrives when spirit and instinct are in the right harmony. If one or other aspect is lacking to him, the result is injury or at least a lopsidedness that may easily veer toward the pathological. Too much of the animal distorts the civilised man, too much civilisation makes sick animals. This dilemma reveals the vast uncertainty that Eros holds for man. For, at bottom, Eros is a superhuman power which, like nature herself, allows itself to be overpowered and exploited as though it were impotent. But triumph over nature is dearly paid for.

REFERENCES

Bion, W.R. (1965) *Experiences in Groups*, London: Tavistock Publications.

Bohm, D. (1980) *Wholeness and the Implicate Order*, London: Routledge & Kegan Paul.

Carotenuto, A. (1984) *A Secret Symmetry: Sabina Spielrein Between Jung and Freud*, London: Routledge & Kegan Paul.

Grotstein, J. (1997) 'Klein's archaic Oedipus and its possible relationship to the myth of the Labyrinth', *Journal of Analytical Psychology* 42(4).

Hesiod, X. (1988) *Theogeny* (ed. M. West) World Classics edn, Oxford and New York: Oxford University Press.

Hopcke, R. (ed.) (1993) *Same Sex Love and the Path of Wholeness*, Boston, MA: Shamballa.

Jung, C.G. (1929) 'Problems of modern psychotherapy', *Collected Works* 16, London: Routledge & Kegan Paul.

—— (1935) 'Tavistock lecture 5', *Collected Works* 18, London: Routledge & Kegan Paul.

—— (1946) 'The psychology of the transference', *Collected Works* 16, London: Routledge & Kegan Paul.

—— (1955) 'Mysterium coniunctionis', *Collected Works* 14, London: Routledge & Kegan Paul.

—— (1963) *Memories, Dreams, Reflections*, London: Routledge & Kegan Paul.

—— (1972) *Synchronicity: An Acausal Connecting Principle*, London: Routledge & Kegan Paul.

Laing, R.D. (1965) *The Divided Self*, Harmondsworth: Penguin.

Neumann, E. (1973) *Amor and Psyche: The Psychic Development of the Feminine*, Bollingen Series L14, New York: Princeton University Press.

Redfearn, J.W.T. (1992) *The Exploding Self: The Creative and Destructive Nucleus of the Personality*, Wilmett, USA: Chiron.

Wilson, S. (1998) *Sabina: A Play*, London: private printing.

Zinkin, L. (1987) 'The hologram as a model for analytical psychology', in L. Zinkin and S. Gordon (eds), *Dialogues in the Analytic Setting: Collected Papers of Louis Zinkin*, London: Bloggs & Son.

Zohar, D. (1990) *The Quantum Self*, London: Flamingo.

Part II

Progressive and regressive aspects of the erotic transference and countertransference

4 Oedipus and the unconscious erotic countertransference

David Mann

INTRODUCION

In this chapter I will explore the universality of the erotic unconscious as it is linked to the presence of incestuous desire. The erotic is psychically binding and brings individuals into a deep relationship with each other. I will propose that both the patient and the therapist share unconscious erotic desires. The therapist aims to mediate these desires into what might be thought of as 'good enough' incestuous desires. Two clinical examples are given to show how erotic fantasy in the analytic relationship transformed the patient's repetition compulsions into a transformational couple.

Freud (1900: 262) had this to say about Sophocles' great tragic drama *Oedipus Rex*:

> If *Oedipus Rex* moves a modern audience no less than it did a contemporary Greek one, the explanation can only be. . . . There must be something which makes a voice within us ready to recognize the compelling force of destiny in the *Oedipus*. . . . [Oedipus'] destiny moves us only because it might have been ours – because the oracle laid the same curse upon us before our birth as upon him. It is the fate of all of us, perhaps, to direct our first sexual impulse towards our mother and our first hatred and our first murderous wish against our father. Our dreams convince us that this is so.

The enormity of these comments have still yet to take full effect on the practice of psychoanalysis. Freud was indicating the presence of incestuous and patricidal (I would add matricidal and homoerotic (negative Oedipal)) wishes into the fate of us all. From a psychotherapeutic point of view, we see this readily enough in patients and the transference. Psychoanalysis, especially in Britain, has not had a great deal of difficulty in coming to terms with the hatred and murderous wishes in the therapist's countertransference. However, the same cannot be said about incestuous desire in the therapist. The erotic countertransference still remains one of the least discussed and the most problematic part of any psychoanalysis. In this chapter

I wish to focus on the everyday nature of the Oedipal scenario and how we might think in terms of *a good enough erotic countertransference.*

OEDIPUS AND INCESTUOUS DESIRE

In the myth of Oedipus we find a variety of possible reactions to the incest taboo. The Oedipus tragedy starts when Laius rapes a young boy. The boy's father then curses Laius that he will be killed by his own son who will marry his mother. To foreclose this possibility Laius becomes celibate. Given his mistreatment of the young boy he has raped, we may assume that Laius was probably more concerned about losing his own life than he was about mother–son incest. However, his wife, Jocasta, gets him drunk and seduces him, even though she knows the prophesy. Presumably Jocasta is not worried much about the prospect of either incest or the death of her husband. Indeed, in the Sophocles version of this myth Jocasta is able to justify to herself and her son that their incestuous relationship is nothing more than what everybody dreams of. Even so, when the child is born both parents leave him to die on a mountain side but he is rescued and, being given the name of Oedipus, is brought up by the king and queen of a neighbouring country. From the Delphic Oracle Oedipus hears that he will kill his father and marry his mother. Thinking this applies to his relationship to his adoptive parents, he flees. Oedipus is shocked by the idea of incest and patricide and deals with it by repudiation. Interestingly, though repulsed by the incestuous thoughts, his flight from such a possibility leads to considerable achievements: winning battles at a roadside, defeating a sphinx, marrying a queen and becoming a king. Jocasta seems to have known the truth from early on, excusing their incestuous romance with 'Many a man before you, in his dreams, has shared his mother's bed'. Only once the incest and patricide have been discovered and proved does Oedipus' world fall apart: Jocasta kills herself, not because she has committed incest but because it has become known to her son and the public. So he does not have to witness the consequence of his deeds, Oedipus blinds himself. Both in this instance have overreacted, or acted out something destructive, which is indicative of the psychic damage of actual incest as opposed to merely unconscious desires.

Part of the beauty of myths is that they freely give themselves to a variety of interpretations. At different times I have seen new layers of meaning in the Oedipus myth (Mann 1989, 1993, 1995); other writers have also enjoyed a plethora of readings (Pollock and Ross 1988). The reading that I wish to emphasize on this occasion is that the Oedipus myth gives two dominant impressions about incest: either it should be eschewed, disavowed and repressed as quickly as possible (as in Oedipus' flight from his adopted parents), or, alternatively, it will be acted upon. Such a duality is also characteristic of the classical and traditional psychoanalytic attitude regarding the erotic transference and even more so the erotic countertransference: it is a problem that should be repressed or it will be acted out.

Oedipus flees from his adoptive parents so terrified is he at the thought of incest and patricide. So what do therapists do in his place? Do we flee or find a different stance regarding our own incestuous and filicidal fantasies to patients?

EROTIC SUBJECTIVITY AND THE UNCONSCIOUS

If we bring the mythic family into today's world we can play with some odd ideas. If Oedipus were a psychoanalyst how would he deal with incestuous and patricidal issues in clinical practice? If Jocasta, his mother, also practised as a psychoanalytic psychotherapist how would she work with incestuous desire? Likewise considering Laius, his father, what would he make of infanticidal or patricidal murderous wishes? I intend these propositions to be more than fanciful: the issues for Oedipus, Jocasta and Laius are the everyday material for the patient in clinical psychoanalytic practice. In various guises we see the patient dealing with Oedipal material in terms of his or her murderous and incestuous wishes; we also see how the adult patient has internalized and identified with both his parents. He or she will treat the child within him or herself as the parent did. We are also familiar with how the transference will lead the patient to experience the therapist as either the father, mother or child part of the self.

Now, in my view this cuts both ways. The therapist is caught up in the same cauldron of passions as the patient. The therapist, too, may experience the patient as child, mother or father; the therapist may also experience him or herself as the child, father or mother. We might then wonder what the therapist experiences in the various characters of the Oedipal drama. (I have explored in more depth elsewhere (Mann 1995) how the therapist may be identified with either Oedipus, Jocasta or Laius.) In my view, the therapist will unconsciously find him or herself drawn into the patient's Oedipal triangle transference. This will happen for several reasons. First, the patient will make sure that the therapist participates at an unconscious level: ego psychologists refer to this process as 'enactments' (Chused 1991); Sandler (1976) calls this 'role responsiveness'; Kleinians like Joseph (1989) describe how the patient will 'nudge' the therapist. Whatever the term used, the common ground in these descriptions is that in clinical practice therapists unconsciously find themselves playing parts in the patient's script; the therapist unconsciously repeats in the transference aspects of the patient's internal world.

I would also emphasize a second point, namely that everything a therapist does in the analytic situation is based upon his or her personal psychology. This subjectivity cannot be done away with. As Dunn (1995: 723) describes the process: 'Intersubjectivity in psychoanalysis refers to the dynamic inter-play between the analyst's and the patient's subjective experiences in the clinical situation'. In the context of this paper, I note the therapist's erotic subjectivity. The psychotherapist is not just a sexual object but also a sexual subject with passion of his or her own. This subjectivity is what the therapist brings to the analytic encounter: his or her own erotic unconscious. *The therapist's unconscious will unconsciously be in a relationship with the patient's unconscious.* The products of this union, the analysis of the transference and countertransference, is the attempt to bring this unconscious relationship into consciousness. In as far as the unconscious has the erotic at its core, the relationship between the therapist's and the patient's unconscious will also have the erotic at its core.

The American analyst Owen Renik (1993: 565) has written an interesting article on the analyst's irreducible subjectivity. He offers a variety of meta-phors to understand the analytic process which have a bearing on what I am attempting to describe. He writes:

> Instead of the analyst as surgeon or reflecting mirror, our guiding metaphor might be the analyst as skier or surfer – someone who allows himself or herself to be acted upon by powerful forces, know-ing that they are to be managed and harnessed, rather than com-pletely controlled. Of course, the forces with which an analyst contends in his or her work are internal ones. In this sense, perhaps we should think of effective clinical psychoanalytical practice as not unlike good sex, in that it is impossible to arrive at the desired out-come without, in some measure, relinquishing self-control as a goal. In making this analogy, of course, I am suggesting that interferences in both arenas may arise from the same causes.

Renik is alluding to subjectivity in general and not specifically to the erotic unconscious, though his imagery is closely connected to the point I am making here.

The incestuous and erotic issues are apparent in the psychotherapy patient and if they are not it is usually useful to ask why not. But how much are they present for the therapist? Can we imagine a therapist without erotic pre-Oedipal or Oedipal issues of their own? That is to say, is it conceivable that a therapist will not have an erotic unconscious? It becomes a problematic question when put as starkly as this. Given that, since Freud, therapists have acknowledged the universality of the erotic in psychic life, why is it perceived as so anomalous in analytic practice? Why is it perceived just as a rare occurrence in the transference and countertransference and, when present, is indicative of resistance to therapeutic procedures?

In the model I am presenting the therapist will participate with the patient in a deeply unconscious manner at the most erotic levels. This will occur for the dual reasons of being caught by the 'role responsiveness' or enactments brought about by the patient's unconscious obliging the therapist to participate in the patient's incestuous and murderous world. In addition, the therapist's own unconscious erotic subjectivity will be activated by the patient to bring the patient into the therapist's world. *We could say that the psychoanalytic encounter at this deeply unconscious level is where the unconscious incestuous and murderous desires of one individual meet the unconscious incestuous and murderous desires of another.* Just as every patient has Jocasta and Laius as well as Oedipus lurking inside, so indeed does every therapist. In my view, that is when psychoanalytic work takes off and can become highly transformational. It seems that if one is able to work intensely in a field and do fine creative work, it is most natural that the deepest desires will be functioning. In the intersubjective model of psychoanalysis the effective or ineffective nature of the work is crucially hinged upon the particular therapist's narcissistically based capacities authentically to involve him or herself with another human being.

Let me say by way of parentheses that I am not underestimating the importance of pre-Oedipal eroticism. Erotic experience and fantasy begin in infancy with one of the most erotic of all relationships, the mother and baby couple. This sensuous stage of contact is enveloped with all the prototypical features of sexuality characteristic of adult lovers: for instance, preoccupation with one person, prolonged eye contact, synchronized movements, continuous physical contact, faces very close, and so on (Stern 1993). The origin of erotic fantasy resides in the pre-Oedipal mother–infant relationship but culminates in the Oedipal stage of development. At this point unconscious fantasy has more opportunity to be mediated by reality when confronted with triangular relationships and the importance of the primal scene.

GOOD ENOUGH EROTIC SUBJECTIVITY

Having established the link between the analytic couple interchangeably embodying the psychology of Laius, Jocasta and Oedipus, I would now like to change that focus. In writing *Oedipus Rex* Sophocles was presenting us with tragedy in the form of gross acting out by all the characters: the Oedipus complex for Oedipus, whereby Laius and Jocasta were destructively constellated. Clearly we do not seek such a model for therapeutic practice so we need to think in terms of *the good enough Oedipal scenario.* Joyce McDougall (1995) uses terms like 'cannibal love and sadistic strivings' to describe the infant's search for love and satisfaction. I prefer to be a little more explicit when describing how these manifest themselves in the therapist: I would suggest that *what the therapist brings to the analytic encounter is an erotic unconscious, an erotic subjectivity that may be characterized as good enough incestuous and murderous desires.* Hopefully the ego of the therapist is more integrated than that of the patient. Just as the good enough parent is more likely to facilitate a good enough child, so the good enough erotic subjectivity of the therapist will mediate the patient's unconscious allowing a working through of the patient's erotic subjectivity. In that sense one of the therapeutic goals is to allow the patient to develop good enough incestuous and murderous desires.

There are myths that point in the direction of how this may be considered. In Hindu mythology there is a story very similar to the Greek Oedipus tale. Siva and Pavarti give birth to a son, Andhaka. He is then adopted. When grown, he spies a woman, his mother, on a mountain. Overcome with lust he tries to ravish her. Siva prevents this and at spear-point holds the boy away until all his sins are burnt away. Siva then acknowledges his son and makes him a commander of his army. In this tradition there is none of the excess of violence and incest of the Greek myth: there is a containment of passion that is worked through rather than being acted upon. (See Mann 1995 for a more detailed discussion of this story.)

It is also worth noting the mythic family described in Homer's *Odyssey*. In this myth, Odysseus has been away from home for nineteen years. Even so, his son, Telemachus, and wife, Penelope, remain loyal to him and each other. There is no Oedipal triumph or attempts to destroy the marriage. The turning point in the family's fortunes comes in what is called the Great Bow Scene. Penelope has set a test for her Suitors. She will marry the man who can string the great bow that belonged to Odysseus and then fire an arrow through a row of targets. The first person to try is Telemachus. He nearly succeeds but at the last moment a look from his father's eyes stops him. Each Suitor in turn tries and fails to string the bow. Eventually the bow comes to Odysseus: he strings it, hits the targets and then with his son's help begins the blood bath of killing all the Suitors. After his victory he re-establishes his relationship with Penelope.

I have had to be rather schematic in outlining this myth which leaves out a lot of detail. (A more thorough discussion is found in Mann 1996.) However, I would suggest that Odysseus and Penelope come close to being good enough parents: they allow their son appropriate space in their minds, they maintain strong boundaries and loyalties. Unusually for mythic heroes, they also love one another. Neither breach any boundaries and both have a positive sense of themselves as an erotic couple. Telemachus for his part shows no confusion about parentage. We might see his attempt to string the bow as his rivalry with his father for his mother but he voluntarily renounces his attempt, unlike Andhaka. As a family, they illustrate the good enough working through of the Oedipal triangle.

Taking the three traditions together we could say that, in a manner of speaking, Laius and Jocasta have a poorly integrated Oedipus complex. Oedipus' Oedipus complex was more advanced in as far as he had a recognition of the incest taboo, causing him to flee his adoptive parents and punish himself once he knew he had transgressed. Yet I do not believe he had integrated the incest taboo, since the incestuous thought was too shocking. Siva and Parvarti are at a more advanced level of development, though still the Oedipal issues for the family members come close to a detrimental acting out. In the relationship between Odysseus, Penelope and Telemachus, however, we see something closer to the healthy family. I would suggest each demonstrates a maturational stage of development of a good enough Oedipal scenario.

THE POSITIVE EROTIC TRANSFERENCE AND COUNTERTRANSFERENCE

Mythology points to constellations of psychic structures – how unconscious conflicts and desires may find a resolution in the mind. I would like to link this material with some thoughts in psychoanalysis.

If we begin thinking about a positive understanding of the erotic transference and countertransference we might well ask: what are the qualities of a good enough erotic fantasy or experience? Lichenstein (1970) has demonstrated that there is not a link between emotional maturity and the ability to sustain satisfying genital relationships. He proposes that sexuality is the earliest and most basic way available for the growing infant to experience an affirmation of the reality of his or her existence. May (1969) emphasizes the capacity for tenderness and concern expressed as 'genital identification': a full identification with the other without losing one's own identity in a love relation. Kernberg (1995) also subscribes to this view, adding that the most important boundaries crossed by sexual passion are those of the self.

Kernberg notes that identifications with the sexual partner lead to experiences of transcendence of the self and the fantasized union of the Oedipal parents as well as a transcendence from the repetition of Oedipal relations which can then be abandoned to a new object relation that reconfirms one's separate identity and autonomy. Merger with an object also replicates forceful penetration to the dangerous interior of the other's body (in fantasy the mother's body). Braving the dangers of merger implies the dominance of trust over mistrust and fear, a basic hope about one's own goodness in contrast to guilt about one's aggression. Kernberg (1995: 45) goes on to write:

> Sexual passion reactivates and contains the entire sequence of emotional states that assure the individual of his own, his parents', the entire world of objects 'goodness' and the hope of the fulfilment of love despite frustration, hostility, and ambivalence. Sexual passion assumes the capacity for continued empathy with – but not merger into – a primitive state of symbiotic fusion [Freud's (1930) 'oceanic feeling'], the excited reunion of closeness with mother at a stage of self-object differentiation, and the gratification of Oedipal longings in the context of overcoming feelings of inferiority, fear, and guilt regarding sexual functioning. . . . It is an important source of empathy with the loved person. Hence, the crossing of

boundaries and the reconfirmation of a basic sense of goodness in spite of many risks link biology, the emotional world, and the world of values in one immediate system.

Now, Kernberg is describing mature sexual passion. But it seems that his description applies just as well to a mature psychoanalytical relationship. To paraphrase Kernberg, we might say a good enough analytic experience necessitates an entire sequence of emotional states that assure the analyst and analysand of their goodness despite frustrations. It assumes empathy with the exciting relationship with the mother and Oedipal longings. It touches the core of the sense of oneness in the face of limitations of the procedures of abstinence and crosses boundaries between the analytic couple's unconscious; like a couple during sex, the analytic couple are symbolically inside each other. What Kernberg calls transcendence I have previously described as a search for a new transformational object whereby the self seeks to develop, progress and advance to broader and deeper stages of maturation (the progressive as opposed to the repetitive regressive transference) via an intimate relationship with another person (Mann 1997). In psychic life it is often the erotic that offers the most transformational opportunities in the life of an individual. The erotic in therapy may be thought of as incorporating regressive transference elements alongside the search for a new transformational object that will lead the individual into a new kind of relationship.

CLINICAL MATERIAL

Ms N was in her late 20s. She had had a number of long-term relationships that ended when her partners left her. The last of these relationships had recently finished after she became pregnant. Her boyfriend rejected her and wanted the pregnancy terminated.

Her family history was that she was closest to her father, recalling that he would take her and her sister, but not her brothers, out for special treats at the weekend. She felt her mother to be critical and jealous of this and felt a rival for her father's affections. The closeness with her father had been tempered by his frequent absences from home due to work: she would hardly see him during the week, and often he was away for weeks at a time; at weekends, apart from the treats, he spent much of his time out with friends.

Her primal scene fantasy was that her mother would have been frustrated by her father. She perceived her mother as a romantic and that her father lived in his own world. Ms N construed that her parents' sex life was a 'perfunctory duty' and believed this would bother her mother more than her father.

Ms N appeared to use her psychotherapy well. She associated freely, seemed to find my comments useful and made some important changes in her life. In that sense, we both appreciated the analytic hour and both looked forward to the next session. The only area that seemed to remain the same was her long-standing wish to have a family while remaining unable to begin, let alone sustain, a successful relationship.

It was at the point of thinking about this that I became aware of my erotic fantasies. I could imagine us in a long-term passionate relationship enjoying contraceptive-free sex but without the prospect of having babies as a consequence. That is to say, my sexual fantasies were entirely recreational and not procreational. I mention this because I began to notice the contrast with Ms N's fantasies. She would see happy couples and their children or just well-behaved children in a café, which would spark thoughts of desire – how wonderful these families were, and how they represented just what she wanted. There was never a thought about how difficult parents and children find it to get along with each other sometimes. There was no messiness in Ms N's fantasized family romances. I then asked her directly about her current situation with men. At first she said she did not feel ready for another relationship, but added that she must be giving a 'stand back' message to men because they were not taking an interest in her and besides she had no libido at present. She described a recent pattern that if a man asked her out she would agree but not turn up; if later he would ask for another date she would then say she had found somebody else. A dream from this period seemed to sum the situation up. She is going to meet a male and female friend. Ms N wears trousers and sees her friend is in a skirt. Her associations with this were that another friend had recently told her she had noticed that when Ms N was meeting friends, she would only wear a skirt if there were no men about. Ms N regarded skirts as more sexual than trousers, since they made her feel more attractive and showed her legs. This made her feel sexually vulnerable. In the dream Ms N was therefore locating sexual feelings and desires in others (her friend in the skirt) but not in herself who was now in non-sexual clothes (at least in her conscious fantasy).

I made some obvious comments that there would be no family without a partner to have sex with. What she seemed to want was an idealized end result without the intervening stages. Her fantasy image seemed like the Virgin Mary and Joseph, a miraculous conception and birth without intercourse. The contrast between Ms N's fantasies and mine could not have been more stark: I thought of sex without babies; she thought of babies without sex.

Now, I would like to draw out several trains of thought from this material. One possible reading of my countertransference was that I was identifying myself with her last boyfriend wanting sex and not a baby. She herself made a connection between her father and boyfriends, noting their similarities. In that respect, I might also have been identified in role with her father, having a special relationship with her but essentially lost in my own fantasy world. If we look at her fantasy we can see how she was drawn to unrealistically idealized and unavailable men, like her father, whereas the men she did have relationships with ultimately did not want to be with her. She would retreat from the mess and pain of relationships by cultivating what was essentially a virgin birth for her and a future family. Her desexualization was rather closely similar to how she imagined her father having sex with mother: father was 'perfunctory' and did his sexual 'duty', and she like him had also become uninterested. In that sense she was heavily identified with her father: sex was a troublesome intrusion from the external world that was an impingement on the preferred world of fantasy. We can also see her identification with mother in pursuing men who did not want to be with her and who were continuously unavailable. Later material brought to light her desire that I might rescue her, and also her annoyance that I had not yet done so. With this rescue fantasy we saw her identification with her romantic mother let down and frustrated by the uninvolved husband. We might say, then, that the transference and countertransference had become a symbolic re-enactment of her primal scene fantasy: we were two people going through the motions of psychotherapy, doing our 'perfunctory duty' but at a deep level nothing was happening, we were both locked in our private worlds.

After thinking about this material for a while, I asked Ms N what was the type of man she was looking for that was so hard to find. Her reply was somebody who would want to be with her and make sacrifices, who would listen and understand. I wondered if this was an idealized image of me (thinking to myself that my wife could put her straight about just how selfish and uncomprehending I can sometimes be!). Indeed this was the case but she knew it was not realistic.

At one level we could consider this material as confirmation of the classical psychoanalytic model that the erotic had been functioning primarily as a form of resistance to therapeutic change. Up to a point that might have been the case. However, I prefer a different understanding. What Ms N wanted was not more of the same experience be it with parents or sexual partners. She wanted a different end game to her usual scenario but did not know how to make things different. In my understanding of this process we symbolically re-enacted the unconscious erotic conflicts which manifested themselves in the transference and countertransference. But she was looking to me to break the mould. (This can be done only by having the mould there in the first place.) She was seeking a new transformational object. By subjecting this transference/countertransference material to analytic thought we could both be transformed – become what may be thought of as a 'transformational couple' – and create something new and renewing. I would stress that it was only a genuine depth of erotic feeling between us that enabled anything meaningful to emerge once consciously recognized. When she was at this point Ms N was able to perceive the nature of her relationship with me more realistically, no longer imagining me as the ideal rescuer who would give her babies with understanding and without sex. Because the depth of feeling and fantasy was genuine between us we had given her life scenario a different conclusion to the usual repetition of unsatisfactory relationships with men who did not want to be with her. Once she was able to achieve this with me and give up her idealization of me as the ideal but unobtainable man, only then was she able to establish a more meaningful relationship with a man outside the analytic setting.

Mr O presented a different picture. He was in his early thirties. He originally came to see me because of difficulties at work though it emerged that these centred around his female boss and this led us into discussion about his problematic relations with women, particularly his mother. He had experienced his mother as the person who wore the trousers in his house. He reported that she was vindictive and had remorselessly criticized his father. He thought she had been sexually inappropriate with him. He remembered at 15 his mother reading him excerpts from Philip Roth's *Portnoy's Complaint* referring to an adolescent boy masturbating, the book itself being about the effects upon the eponymous hero of a sexually humiliating mother. He remembered feeling totally embarrassed as she laughed at the story. His own relationships with women had been problematic. Women were largely to be avoided and he had limited sexual experience; he expressly stated his fear that a woman might destroy him. He was worried that a woman would be dependent on him but this anxiety thinly disguised his own fear of dependence on a woman.

Mr O presented himself as an uneasy mixture of strong intellectual and schizoid defences but with considerable insight and a willingness to be self-revelatory. His image for my interpretations was that they were 'like an oil drill straight into his unconscious and hitting the spot'. We worked with this metaphor for therapy, bringing out the valuable resources buried deep inside him. It was quite a while before I realized the parallel erotic nature of such an image: the penetrating drill, the receptive unconscious, the liberated lubricating oil – imagery also suggestive of the earliest sensuous/sexual transactions centred around bodily fluids in the mother–infant relationship.

Shortly after the massacre of school children at Dunblane Mr O reported that he was worried about being perceived as an 'odd ball loner' like Thomas Hamilton. I was surprised by this identification. I had a variety of thoughts about Mr O but had not connected him in my mind with an evil killer. This alerted me to the possibility that I had not grasped something in the material: not that Mr O was a latent paedophiliac child murderer but that less of his unconscious had been revealed than I had thought. At these points I often wonder about my own unconscious: what might I be resisting? I felt that, in some way, we had not got close enough or trusting enough to understand each other; something was inhibiting our intimacy. I was already thinking that perhaps there were homoerotic issues we had not grasped, but I did not say as much yet.

The following session Mr O reported that our last meeting made him very anxious. He was worried I was going to say he was a homosexual. He insisted he was not. He was attracted to women but could not have sex with them. The one time he tried he failed to get an erection and found himself thinking that if he put his penis inside a woman it might be 'chopped off'. After revealing his castration anxiety he then had a memory from his school life. His fellow pupils thought that a particular teacher abused children. Mr O recalled once being alone with this teacher and feeling terrified. Now in the session he was gripped with anxiety that I might put my arm around him. Until Mr O had said this I had no such thought, but once the idea was in my mind I realized that I had, indeed, felt very protective towards him and, in a manner of speaking, was trying to put my arm around him. At best, this was a wish to be protective but it alarmed me to think that it might have abusive undertones.

Thinking about these various associations, his spoken, mine silently thought, I interpreted that in the transference I was experienced as a combined male/female figure: penetrating and abusive but also potentially castrating. I would be the humiliating mother and the abusing teacher. I understood my own failure to grasp the meaning of his material in the following way: my detachment from the homoerotic imagery was parallel to his anxiety that if I 'drilled' into him I, too, might be 'chopped off'; also I was mirroring his need to stay uninvolved lest intimacy turned into intrusive dependence. In effect, the therapy, while interesting, had been manoeuvred to avoid discussion and feelings concerning homoeroticism.

This led us to looking at his relationship with his father. Mr O expressly asked if I could tell him what to do, though he was worried I would tell him to do something he did not want to do. In other words, he wanted a father to give sound paternal advice but was worried that I would let him down like he felt his father had done. I thought this material related more to the father transference as it revolved around questions about how he should be in the world. This brought us to his feelings about the father who had not been strong enough to protect him from his mother. In my view, castration anxiety is as frequently associated with the mother as it is with the father. Mr O's mother was experienced as castrating both his father and himself. His difficulty with homoerotic issues was, in part, a result of an unsuccessful homoerotic identification with his marginalized and ineffective father. My hesitation in recognizing the homoerotic material may also be considered as my 'enactment' or 'role response', identifying with his father, unable to give recognition to the erotic bond between father and son. Putting this into words seemed to leave Mr O feeling greatly relieved and considerably reduced his anxiety.

As with the case of Ms N, I considered that it was the erotic material that drew attention to the central underlying problem and indicated something of how a successful resolution might be found. Though we see in the transference much repetition and resistance, we also see the patient bringing the material and looking for a different conclusion, a new way of relating to his past as more than just a re-edition. In my terms, the patient was looking for a new transformational object but could only achieve this in the context of the relationship between two people, the transformational couple.

DISCUSSION

The erotic is at the heart of unconscious fantasy life. I am implying nothing special or exceptional about making such a statement. As I see it, normal erotic experience is inherent in the good enough maturational processes. The presence of the erotic, though subject to cultural variation and forms of expression, nevertheless seems to qualify as a ubiquitous universal experience. In adult life when the erotic is mixed with sensual or love components it becomes one of the experiences upon which humanity at large sets a high premium, even if there is as much anguish as pleasure involved. Not the least reason for this is that erotic involvement offers opportunities for fulfilment, maturation and transformation. Kavaler-Adler (1992: 536) describes it thus: 'In its full form, the erotic transference expresses the most passionate combination of genital cravings for the other, combined with deep longings for tenderness and for the reparative gift of love. A separate other is its prime target, and psychic fantasy charts the route to that target'.

From the point of view of clinical psychotherapy practice, how do we respond to the universal presence of the erotic? The history of psychoanalysis has not been encouraging in this regard. Many famous analysts have succumbed to erotic temptations with patients. More usually the erotic nature of the therapeutic transaction is ignored or not discussed at all. While proclaiming the universal nature of the erotic unconscious among patients and non-patients, astonishingly little regard has been paid to how this affects the transference and even less to how it affects the countertransference. Such scant literature that does exist has been treated with a monotonously singular view: if the patient falls in love with the therapist this is not real love: it is unauthentic, fabricated by the analytic encounter. Any expression of love or erotic feelings is considered an expression of resistance against the analytic process.

I will not review the literature about the erotic transference on this occasion (see the Introduction of this book and Mann (1997, Chapter 2) for an extensive literature discussion). I will, however, briefly note a few dissenting voices. Most notably in the 1950s was Harold Searles (1959) who saw the positive function of Oedipal love in the countertransference as demarcating a move from infantile to mature love. More recently, Wrye and Welles (1994) draw attention to the 'body love printing' between mother and baby. In their view, erotic experience has its origins in the contacts dealing with body fluids which create a sensual adhesion to the relationship with the baby. In their view the maternal erotic transference and countertransference recreate this sensual erotic contact between mother and infant.

Psychoanalytic therapists do not stand outside the experiences of the rest of humanity. The erotic unconscious which pervades every area of the patient's life will almost inevitably take its place in the transference. The same holds true for the therapist. Whether or not the therapist has an active sex life is irrelevant. All therapists have sexual experiences and a conscious and unconscious erotic fantasy life. I should say, though, that while I cannot imagine a therapist as not having an unconscious erotic fantasy life, I can well imagine all manner of defences against its recognition, everything from schizoid factors in the personality, repression, denial, disassociation and intellectualizaiton of psychoanalytic theories (e.g. the use of concepts like projective identification, when sometimes a therapist considers his or her own feelings as having been put there by the patient). Psychoanalytic theory makes use of the mother–baby couple to act as a model for understanding the relationship between two people. We should not forget, though, that *two* is also the number for sexual intercourse and procreation. The analytic encounter is equally infused with adult erotic undertones as is the mother and infant model. In my view, there is not necessarily a contradiction here: the mother and baby unit is highly eroticized for both.

I do not disregard the fact that working with erotic material in therapy can cause a good deal of anxiety in both participants. Kumin (1985) has aptly termed this 'erotic horror'; nor do I doubt that the erotic, like any other feature of the analytic process, can be used defensively to resist therapeutic change. Yet it seems to me that the erotic offers some of the most momentous opportunities for psychic change in an individual's life. Since this is often the case outside the analytic encounter then why should not it be the case in analytic work? In my opinion, to see the erotic as essentially fabricated and as a resistance is more often an indication of *resistance in the therapist* rather than in what is happening to the patient. Psychoanalysis has always had a fear of the erotic in therapy ever since Breuer's abortive attempts to work with Anna O. Later on Freud (1915a) likened the erotic or love transference to explosives: the anxiety for patient and therapist is that erotic or love feelings will get out of hand and who knows what the result will be.

Erotic fantasies will almost certainly be activated in both patient and therapist. Therapeutically it may be highly desirable that they should be. As the erotic is at the core of unconscious fantasy life it follows that any depth work, if deep psychological change is to occur, must surely come to terms with the erotic unconscious. If the erotic transference and countertransference are not developed and worked through it becomes difficult to envisage how this side of the patient's unconscious will be reconstructed.

CONCLUSION

In a now famous reference about the unconscious Freud (1915b: 198) wrote:

> It is a very remarkable thing that the Unconscious of one human being can react upon that of another, without passing through the Conscious. This deserves closer investigation, especially with a view to finding out whether preconscious activity can be excluded

as playing a part in it; but, descriptively speaking, the fact is incontestible.

In this passage Freud does not elaborate upon the significance of this process with regard to the relationship between analyst and patient, how the unconscious of each of them will react with one another. Other writers, however, have thrown light upon the implications for the therapeutic transaction. For example, Jung (1946) and Heimann (1950) consider the effect of the patient's unconscious on the therapist's unconscious while Searles (1958) explores further how the therapist's unconscious affects the patient's unconscious.

In my view, the patient and the therapist are continuously communicating at an unconscious level. The unconscious is best seen as porous and permeable, allowing experiences and affecting their passage between individuals. In the transference and countertransference the unconscious, with its creative and pathological constituents, will be passing between both participants in the analytic encounter. The therapeutic action can be described by seeing the transference and countertransference as a mutative process whereby both participants modify their unconscious fantasies about each other. The developing intimacy leads to a lessening of fantastical perceptions as both the therapist and the patient gradually come to see each other more realistically. The erotic is particularly significant in this respect: it is psychically binding, bringing each individual into a strong conscious and unconscious relationship with others. An erotic bond is forged at a deep emotional level that binds individuals into a relationship with each other at the deepest levels of fantasy. It seems that the transformational potential of the erotic goes right to the heart of the therapeutic transaction and the universality of unconscious erotic fantasy life is what connects and gives this process a good deal of its momentum. The patient and therapist unconsciously find themselves as a transformational couple working towards what may be considered good enough incestuous desires.

REFERENCES

Chused, J.F. (1991) 'The evocative power of enactments', *Journal of the American Psychoanalytic Association* 39: 615–39.

Dunn, J. (1995) 'Intersubjectivity in psychoanalysis: a critical review', *International Journal of Psychoanalysis* 76: 723–38.

Freud, S. (1900) 'The interpretation of dreams', *Standard Edition* 4, London: Hogarth Press.

—— (1915a) 'Observations of tranference love', *Standard Edition* 12, London: Hogarth Press.

—— (1915b) 'The unconscious', *Standard Edition* 14, London: Hogarth Press.

—— (1930) 'Civilization and its discontents', *Standard Edition* 21, London: Hogarth Press.

Heimann, P. (1950) 'On countertransference', *International Journal of Psychoanalysis* 31: 81–4.

Joseph, B. (1989) *Psychic Equilibrium and Psychic Change*, London: Routledge.

Jung, C.G. (1946) 'The psychology of the transference', *Collected Works* 16, London: Routledge & Kegan Paul.

Kavaler-Adler, S. (1992) 'Mourning and erotic transference', *International Journal of Psychoanalysis* 73: 527–39.

Kernberg, O. (1995) *Love Relations: Normality and Pathology*, New Haven, CT: Yale University Press.

Kumin, I. (1985) 'Erotic horror: desire and resistance in the psychoanalytic setting', *International Journal of Psychoanalytic Psychotherapy* 11: 3–20.

Lichenstein, H. (1970) 'Changing implications of the concept of psychosexual development: an inquiry concerning the validity of classical psychoanalytic assumptions concerning sexuality', *Journal of the American Psychoanalytic Association* 18: 300–18.

Mann, D. (1989) 'Incest: the father and the male therapist', *British Journal of Psychotherapy* 6: 143–53.

—— (1993) 'The shadow over Oedipus: the father's rivalry with his son', *Free Associations* 4: 44–66.

—— (1995) 'Transference and countertransference issues with sexually abused patients', *Psychodynamic Counselling* 1: 542–59.

—— (1996) 'The Odyssey of the Good Enough Father: the Relationship Between Odysseus and Telemachus', London: unpublished paper.

—— (1997) *Psychotherapy: An Erotic Relationship – Transference and Countertransference Passions*, London: Routledge.

May, R. (1969) *Love and Will*, New York: Norton.

McDougall, J. (1995) *The Many Faces of Eros: A Psychoanalytic Exploration of Human Sexuality*, London: Free Association Press.

Pollock, H. and Ross, J.M. (eds) (1988) *The Oedipus Papers*, New York: International Universities Press.

Renik, O. (1993) 'Analytic interaction: conceptualizing technique in light of the analyst's irreducible subjectivity', *Psychoanalytic Quarterly* 62: 553–71.

Sandler, J. (1976) 'Countertransference and role responsiveness', *International Review of Psychoanalysis* 3: 43–7.

Searles, H. (1958) 'The schizophrenic's vulnerability to the analyst's unconscious processes', in H. Searles (ed.), *Collected Papers on Schizophrenia and Related Subjects* (1965), London: Hogarth Press.

—— (1959) 'Oedipal love in the countertransference', in H. Searles (ed.), *Collected Papers on Schizophrenia an Related Subjects* (1965), London: Hogarth Press.

Stern, D. (1993) 'Acting versus remembering in transference love and infantile love', in E.S. Person (ed.), *On Freud's 'Observations on Transference Love'*, New Haven, CT: Yale University Press.

Wrye, H.K. and Welles, J.K. (1994) *The Narration of Desire: Erotic Transferences and Countertransferences*, Hillsdale, NJ: Analytic Press.

Understanding the erotic and
eroticised transference and
countertransference

Ronald Doctor

The major problem Freud posed in 1912 is why transference, basically an erotic phenomenon, is so well suited as a means of resistance in analysis. Freud (1915) recognised the universality of erotic strivings occurring within the transference which he regarded as induced by the analytic situation. The conceptualisation of erotic transference as a manifestation of both a strong resistance against treatment and an actualisation of past experience has been clearly expressed by Freud (1915). He convincingly shows that one of the motives for such passionate expressions of love for the therapist is the wish to interrupt the work of the analysis, and to attack the therapist's role by turning him into the patient's lover.

Joseph (1993) states that Freud emphasises how the patient's demand for love, their eroticisation of the transference, can be seen as a resistance, as a force that interferes with the continuation of the treatment; certainly understanding or being understood plays no part in the patient's wishes at such times. We can see how patients who eroticise the transference are bent on nullifying or actually defeating the treatment, of destroying the therapist's separateness as a human being, his capacity to help them, the very stuff of progress and life.

However, in every analysis there has to exist moments of love, of falling in love, because the cure reproduces the object relation of the Oedipal triad, and it is therefore inevitable (and healthy) for this to occur. The transference love that most concerned Freud in his essay of 1915, because of its irreducible tenacity, the sudden manner of its appearance, its destructive intention and the intolerance of frustration that accompanied it, seems more linked to psychotic than neurotic type of transference.

There are, then, various forms of transference love, which occur as a continuum and go from the healthy, to the neurotic pole of the conflict, to the psychotic one. To distinguish between the neurotic and psychotic pole, one speaks sometimes of erotic and eroticised transference. This differentiation originates with Lionel Blitzen and was taken up by Gitelson (1952) and Rappaport (1959).

In the psychotic transference love, or eroticised transference, it is evident that we can distinguish various forms; the most typical is, as Freud describes, 'tenacious, extreme and irreducible ego syntonic and refusing any substitution'. Racker (1968) described transference nymphomania in which the patient wants to seduce the analyst sexually. Nymphomania may be part of an erotic delusion, a persecutory delusion or an expression of a manic syndrome, and finally, if the disturbance is more visible at the level of sexual conduct than in the sphere of thought, nymphomania presents itself as a perversion with respect to the sexual object. Marco Chiesa (1994) conceptualises the erotic transference as a delusional manifestation originating from an intrapsychic pathological organisation which is established to protect the subject from the pains of the depressive position and the fragmentation of the paranoid position.

Nevertheless, Fidelio Cesio (1993) suggests that the direct emergence of the patient's transference love in a reasonably well-conducted analysis is exceptional. He makes the point that in the case of Anna O, transference mushroomed because the physician, Breuer, was unable to analyse it. Cesio investigates how the therapist's unconscious may lead him to collude with the patient and thus invoke a full-blown erotic transference. As Cesio (1993: 132) put it:

> The spirit of the dead that psychoanalysts invoke becomes manifested in the Oedipal, incestuous, tragic, transference love, and which, not adequately heard and interpreted, ends up destroying the treatment. When the analyst fails to address and analyse the incipient transference, he does, to a large extent, because of his own passion, – a primary drive-like affect, aroused by the situation.

However, Mann (1994) states that unless we take the view that all erotic desire and fantasy is a perversion or neurotic, and psychoanalytic theory tells us this is clearly not the case, then the therapist may experience healthy erotic feelings and these may be useful in the analysis if the therapist deals with the desire appropriately; if the therapist remains unconscious of the desire and does not analyse it effectively, then the erotic feelings are more likely to bring an unhealthy distortion into the work.

Joseph (1985) described the analyst's own experience as very important in sensing how patients draw the analyst in, how they act on us for many varied reasons; how they endeavour to draw us into their defensive systems; how they unconsciously act out with us in the transference, trying to get us to act out with them; how they convey aspects of their inner world built up from infancy, elaborated in adulthood and childhood, experiences often beyond the use of words which can only be captured through the feelings aroused in us, through our countertransference.

Blitzen's thesis is that if the analyst appears in person in the first dream during the therapeutic period, the analysand will eroticise the transferential link violently and the analysis will be difficult if not impossible. That presence in the first dream indicates that the analysand is not capable of discriminating between the analyst and a significant figure from the past. He or she understands by eroticisation a surcharge of the erotic components of the transference, which certainly does not signify a great capacity for love, but rather a libidinal deficiency, accompanied by a great necessity to be loved. In the transference, the analyst is seen as if he or she were the parent, while in the eroticisation of the transference he is the parent.

According to Gitelson (1952) if the analyst appears in person in the analysand's first dream, one must presume there is a grave disturbance, and following Blitzen, he maintains that the disturbance can originate from the patient having a poor capacity for symbolisation, or from the analyst having made an 'error of judgment'. Etchegoyan (1991) states that in an analysis that evolves normally, the erotic transference waxes and wanes gradually and tends to reach its climax in the final stages as opposed to the eroticised transference which appears at the outset. He also states that the analyst's appearance in the patient's dreams at any time in the analysis – and not only at the beginning – signifies that a real event or fact is in play, be this a countertransferential acting out, great or small, or simply a real and rational action; such as the giving of information on formal aspects of the relationship (change of timetable or fees, etc.). These dreams imply that the patient has a problem with the real analyst, not with the symbolic figure of the transference. This type of dream, then, where the patient alludes to the analyst personally, should always be taken as a warning concerning some real participation of the therapist, and may arguably represent an 'error of judgment'. However, this may also represent a real event or a fact of life.

A clinical example of an 'error of judgment' or real event, where there is a change in timetable and its precipitating of an erotic response, comes in the form of the following account. A patient, Mr A, who had recently broken up with his girlfriend, reported a dream on a Thursday after a Bank Holiday weekend: 'I was in bed with a boy pushing up against me. I was worried about it, it's edgy'. He then associated to the dream the following: 'On the bus, someone came to sit in front of me and I felt a bit uncomfortable. He was similar to the man in the dream; a scrawny, working-class person. I think it is a paranoia of my homosexual feelings and reminds me of a more difficult dream when for some reason you were touching me, stroking my lower back. I felt disgusted, but it was quite enjoyable'. He added, 'This dream occurred four days ago, at the end of the week. We were getting on well so I didn't want to tell you as it would spoil it. If we were getting on then it couldn't be anything else. The most worrying thing was that I didn't want to damage your friendly advances towards me'.

I responded that he wants me to feel the shame for having these feelings towards him, that I am the needy emaciated boy, resentful that he has a rich life, in which I am not included. He went on to say that he had only just realised what an amazing thing the analysis was and how lucky he was to be in analysis. At the end of the day, he said, I had my own life, but the extent of my involvement in his life was amazing: five times a week was a lot of my time. I said that though he wanted to caress and stroke me by telling me how amazing I was, it might be more difficult to face his needs and loneliness over the long weekend.

A couple of days later, Mr A reported two connected dreams about which he commented: 'I was in bed with my sister, kissing her and wanting to have sex with her. She said we should not and I said "Why not?" I get an erection and she feels scared. Then there is another dream where I am on the heath and standing in a hollow with trees around. Someone is trying to investigate what happened; a tragedy, in that a lot of people are shot trying to get out of the hollow'. He further reflected: 'My sister is you; it had an incestuous feel. I think it followed you saying you would know what it's like, that you had been through the same thing'. In the previous session, he had complained that I failed to understand him, to which I had responded that he cannot envisage the possibility that I might also have been through the same difficulties as himself and, therefore, there might be some understanding, contrary to what he assumed. He said that this made an impact on him. He went on to say, 'I feel some sympathy for you and some pride that I am the same as you but also afraid why you told me that. Was it a last-ditch ploy to make me relax? I was also worried about why you had said it; perhaps a homosexual or incestuous fear about it'. I concluded that he and I had joined up as a couple. Following my comment that I would know how he felt, he felt triumphant but it is a hollow victory, nothing would be achieved in this way.

My response to my patient's feeling that I would not be able to understand him unless I had been in the same predicament may have been an error of judgment on my part which produced his homosexual anxieties. On the other hand, the patient may have drawn me into enacting something with him in order to force me to experience his dilemma and for me to be in touch with his homosexual anxieties.

Although the eroticisation of the relationship fulfilled defensive functions, particularly against persecutory anxieties, it was also very closely linked with perverse areas of psychopathology in which the patient sought an exciting triumph over the togetherness of the parental couple, and in the transference over the therapist.

I shall discuss another patient, Ms B, in greater detail to illustrate the erotic transference and countertransference and what Wrye and Welles (1994) call the 'maternal erotic transference and countertransference', which represents the patient's intense longing for intimate physical contact with the analyst. Such transference illuminates unconscious beliefs about the condition for loving that these patients bring to treatment; as such, they frequently lead to a sense of deadlock and psychic paralysis for lengthy intervals of treatment.

Ms B is a 24-year-old single woman presenting with depression and problems of individuation and separation. She has been in analysis five times a week for four years. She initially organised the analytic sessions in such a way so as not to feel separate but to cling to me in a hateful and passive way, resulting in the paralysis and psychic deadlock, as Wrye and Welles describe. In fact, the only way to have me, to keep me attached to her, is to neutralise me, where we become versions of each other, so that we both experience the same feelings of tiredness, where any life, vitality or real interaction or intercourse is stifled and we are therefore unable to string two thoughts together or to think clearly. The net result is that there can be no sense of us being separate individuals.

Britton (1984) argues that the development of an eroticised delusional transference creates a reality which replaces any awareness of a dependent relationship on a separate person and the psychic reality of the early Oedipal configuration. He emphasises hatred for the real object world, which is at the root of the subject's idealisation of an alternative fantasy reality which is held to be greater and superior.

To allow her thinking to be used incisively was to allow a real interaction which was experienced as a hazardous kind of intercourse. The capacity to observe, to make judgments, to retain contact with reality seemed, in my patient, to lead her to recognise the state of her objects and to recognise her own impulses, and this appeared to make her afraid of what she would feel and what she would do. She could protect herself by splitting off and projecting these capacities but in the process was seriously disabled. She achieved this either by feeling tired; becoming an impenetrable blank wall where she takes an inert role and gets me to take the initiative, so that any curiosity about herself is lost, and any enterprise of analysis is defeated: or she obstructs the analytical process by controlling the session, where I do what she wants me to do by becoming docile and neutral, thus keeping the analysis barely alive.

She is fed up and angry, but cannot leave; she deals with feelings of hating and clinging by rushing about impetuously and dangerously. She hates the clinging but cannot leave me. If she leaves me, she has nothing and feels empty and desolate. In the last week before a summer break she has a dream: she is walking along a road in the dark and sees homeless people who are very frightening, so she crosses over to the other side, but these same people come after her. She feels very scared, so walks in the middle of the road. I interpreted that with the impending summer break she has rid herself of all her needs, her dependence, but in her ostensible independent frame of mind she feels uneasy, hounded by 'homeless' destructive cannibals. She has cut herself from needing a home and all the hungry needs are in me, and I become the threatening 'homeless monster'.

She feels stuck in a relationship with me and with her boyfriend C, which is unsatisfactory. She feels she wants something from me; an explanation or understanding, something that will make her love C. She cannot understand how she does not love someone who treats her well; what she loves is her bully of a father. She feels contempt for anyone who loves her, she thinks they are weak and submissive like her mother, and she despises them. She tends to feel that I am contemptuous of her and despise her if she is dependent on me: I am the impatient, intimidating tyrant, criticising and judging her, and she is the ineffectual and useless child; sometimes, conversely, her boyfriend C and I, are both inadequate in that we have remained loyal to her despite her attempts to be unlovable and unloving, and she has to ration the contact she has with us.

She did feel quite excited about the prospect of a new relationship outside of the analysis at one point and at the same time felt more lively in the analysis, but soon returned to the same tired and familiar way of being where nothing happens. I said that she was coming back to a miserable, tired and dead me, to which she replied, with loud sobbing, that there is this 'fundamental thing' which she cannot talk about: that is, she feels like dying, that I will get someone to take her away, and is angry that her mother did not know how ill she was. I interpreted to her that she would rejoice if Mum and I were to agree with her that there is a handicapped child in her, but we refuse to see it.

With her announcement that she was going away for five days, she had a very telling dream about being stuck with an evil woman, carrying a poisonous plant, in a garden littered with dead animals with daggers in each one, and, at the same time, she is trying to run away. She said that the terrifying thing is that she will go away and find out that she has no feeling for C, the same numb feeling of paralysis that a child would have on realising that its mother had left it, the moment before it starts screaming. I interpreted to her that she wanted to scream at me, that didn't I realise what it means to leave her, how difficult it is for her to go away, but the evil woman is her internal figure that kills all feeling; telling her it doesn't matter, it's not important.

Subsequently, after a long Bank Holiday weekend, she came back to say that she had felt disorientated on Bank Holiday Monday and had had a dream about me that made her feel better. However, instead of relating the dream to me she said the following: 'Last night, I went to see my friend and had a drink and a chat with him – his wife was away, it was just him. They are both successful and slightly intimidating. It's funny, I drank quite a lot and I woke up during the night, it was raining, I worried about it flooding, but it was fine'. There was a pause, whereupon I said: 'It seems that though the dream made you feel better, made you feel more loving to me, you are afraid that if you bring it into the open, your erotic desires for me are going to swell and flood and are not going to stop'. She continued by reporting the dream which had occurred on the Friday evening of the long weekend:

It was disturbing really, but then it wasn't. Well, the dream was about two kisses and a gap between them. I was kissing you, and it made me think of the kiss of life. I was able to go off and do something in between. On Sunday, I had another dream. I got a beetle stuck between my teeth, but went off to do something and forgot about it. Later I was surprised to find it alive and still stuck between my teeth. It would not come out in one piece, but came out in a few pieces.

She associated the first dream to being able to remember me over the week-end and not be too worried about not being able to come back directly after the weekend (i.e. a reference to the Bank Holiday Monday). She said that the second dream conformed to the same pattern: going away and coming back and remembering something: 'You always do forget it a bit'.

I interpreted that she appears to have a passionate longing, an erotic yearning for me. It seems to suffice initially, to give her life, but by Saturday the flood has turned into a deluge and it has to be killed off; she has to give it the kiss of death, pick it out bit by bit, and she feels she has become stuck to me in her usual cut-off, hardened way. She feels disorientated and falls apart. She responded by saying that 'little changes to the routine make you feel odd'.

A few days later she related a story about her cat who had developed an abscess that needed draining. The vet's advice was not to let a scab develop, and should it form, to pull the scab off and allow the pus to drain. I commented that the doctor-analyst's advice was not to hide behind her hard shell but to allow the past to emerge. She responded that the shell and the scab reminded her of a 'scarab beetle', which she had bought on a visit to Egypt.

The next day the patient had another dream:

I was in a dark little shop with a man cutting up a body like a butcher with a cutting machine. There were all these bits and it dawned on me that it was a person. There was this idea that the bits of meat would be sold and people would not know what they were eating; a good way to cover up a crime. It was scary. Then I was going on a boat past a row of houses and I could see through the window of a young man's house; his grandmother was about to die. I then went into the house and I was aware that there was a body and the murderer was in the house.

Ms B, in a rather hesitating way, associated to the dream: 'It sounds sort of better, in that if I can dream about it and face it, it seems a bit better'. I responded that if she took back from me her capacity to observe, 'to look through the window', to discover her archaic memories, her 'scarab beetle', she would be more incisive and make decisions, but would come up against death and my or her own murderousness. However, she could begin to think about it and have a more creative intercourse with me. She replied:

I had a thought about being able to leave, thinking it might be possible to leave without losing the whole thing; I was able to think clearly about being separate. It's about having a very unfamiliar feeling, indeed, I never thought it possible; leaving before, missing something, loneliness, requires a bit more of a contained person, a bit of a more separate person.

I think she was saying that she could feel more an experience of loss rather than fear and a denial of the loss. To take back her own impulses and fears was equivalent to letting me go which she had always felt was not possible in that she would not survive. She was able to bear the pain of separation and feel more her own self. Though the erotic transference was a resistance it also paved the way for relinquishing her deadness, her refuge, her scarab beetle. Ms B's eroticisation seemed more like a dream state, in which she lived in her idyllic world as an escape from unbearable inner realities. Her erotic transference was the expression of her unconscious effort to remain in contact with an external object, in order to keep at bay a potential breakdown of her mental capacities.

Joseph (1993) suggests that Freud's ideas on transference love cannot be understood in terms of libido only; we must also take account of the destructive drive, for when Freud wrote about transference love he was still five years away from formalising his understanding of aggression and destructiveness. She also states that what is transferred is not just figures from the past, from the patient's actual history, but complex internal fantasy figures that have been built up from earliest infancy, constructed from the interaction between real experiences and the infant's fantasies and impulses towards them.

CONCLUSION

Chiesa (1994) states that the erotic transference serves manifold functions which are operative in patients in different degrees and which change as therapy develops. These functions are shaped by the nature of the patient's early experiences, which may account for the different presentations, intensity and development in each particular case.

Mr A demonstrates the paranoid-schizoid position, in which gratification brings not only gratitude but also envy. It is in the balance of envy versus gratitude that the security of the infant lies, since envy destroys love and gratitude. Mr A deals with this by splitting off an 'ideal' gratifying object, towards whom gratitude is felt, from an envied and hated persecutor. However, this splitting brings a form of insecurity in itself, since any degree of frustration results in an abrupt switch in the impulses to hatred, and in the object, which suddenly becomes a persecuting one.

On the other hand, Ms B reveals aspects of the depressive position and conveys the qualities of a particular, poignant kind of love; a pining. Love in the depressive position is for the non-ideal object, and as this becomes established, the love, in spite of the flaws, tends not to switch so violently to hatred and a degree of emotional stability begins to develop. There is here the capacity for tolerance and forgiveness. However, the flawed whole object gives rise to the experience that the good object was perfect and has been injured and damaged with the arousing of an anguished concern. In turn this concern gives rise to the wish to restore and repair.

In these patients' eroticisation of the transference, although it can be seen as resistance to the analysis, the resistance is only a part of their way of loving, hating, controlling and preventing any shift in the structure they have established of omnipotent superiority and therefore, avoidance of a more realistic relationship. However, as we have seen, the picture is far from pessimistic, for though the erotic transference may emerge as a resistance to progress in the analysis, the upshot of its appearance can be a way of exhuming ancient psychic relics of the patient, which, of course, augurs well for the analysis in the long run.

We can take for granted, not just as Freud describes, that the patient's falling in love with the analyst is inescapable, but that the characteristic nature of the patient's loving will inevitably be enacted in the relationship with the analyst. It may be acted out noisily, with protestations, demands or threats, as in the cases described by Freud (1915). Or it may not appear as falling in love at all, but the patient's way of loving or not loving, will inevitably emerge in the transference. The patient may be rejecting, silent, withdrawn and independent or subtle and perverse as in the two case studies related here.

The analytic situation evokes the patient's love, which is the unavoidable consequence of the treatment; and therefore the sole responsibility for handling the situation must lie with the analyst. It is after all the patient's prerogative to try to misuse the situation, according to his or her personality and pathology, but once we understand and elucidate the transference, it becomes an opportunity to explore what is going on rather than a burden.

REFERENCES

Britton, R. (1984) Personal communication to Marco Chiesa.

Cesio, F. (1993) 'The Oedipal tragedy in the psychoanalytic process; transference love', in E. Spector-Person (ed.), *On Freud's Observations on Transference Love*, New Haven, CT/London: Yale University Press.

Chiesa, M. (1994) 'Some thoughts on erotic transference', *Psychoanalytic Psychotherapy* 8(1): 37–48.

Etchegoyan, R. (1991) *The Fundamentals of Psychoanalytic Technique*, London: Karnac.

Freud, S. (1912) 'The dynamics of transference', *Standard Edition* 12, London: Hogarth Press.

—— (1915) 'Observations on transference love', *Standard Edition* 12, London: Hogarth Press.

Gitelson, M. (1952) 'The emotional position of the analyst in the psychoanalytic situation', *International Journal of Psychoanalysis* 33: 1–10.

Joseph, B. (1985) 'Transference: the total situation', *International Journal of Psychoanalysis* 66: 447–57.

—— (1993) 'On transference love: some current observations', in E. Spector-Person (ed.), *On Freud's Observations on Transference Love*, New Haven, CT/London: Yale University Press.

Mann, D. (1994) 'The psychotherapist's erotic subjectivity', *British Journal of Psychotherapy* 10(3): 344–54.

Racker, H. (1968) 'Considerations on the theory of transference', in *Transference and Countertransference*, London: Maresfield Library.

Rappaport, E. (1959) 'The first dream in an erotized transference', *International Journal of Psychiatry* 40(4): 240–5.

Wrye, H. and Welles, J. (1994) *The Narration of Desire*, London: Analytic Press.

6   'O tell me the truth about love'[1]

Nathan Field

Love is of particular significance in psychoanalysis because it sabotaged the very first analytic treatment, that of Breuer and his patient Anna O. Breuer became so fascinated by his attractive young patient that he talked of little else. Breuer's wife, recognising her husband's infatuation long before he did, became morose with jealousy. When Breuer eventually realised the cause of his wife's depression he abruptly terminated the treatment. Anna O, who until then had never made a single allusion to sexual feelings for her therapist, reacted hysterically by developing a phantom pregnancy. Breuer calmed her down with hypnosis, and left 'in a cold sweat' the very next day with his wife for a trip to Venice (Jones 1964).

The Anna O case made a profound impression on Freud. He discussed it with Breuer again and again. Freud realised that Breuer and his patient had stumbled on to something remarkable, namely psychoanalysis; but he also recognised that the patient–therapist erotic involvement could pose a very considerable challenge. Freud encountered the problem of erotic attraction again, not only with his own female patients, but notably in two of his most gifted disciples: Ferenczi and Jung. Ferenczi fell in love with, and eventually married, one of his patients – who just happened to be the daughter of his mistress (Stanton 1990); and Jung had an intense love relationship with his young patient Sabina Speilrein, who thereafter consulted Freud (Carotenuto 1984).

It is in this context we must read Freud's paper 'Observations on transference love' (Freud 1915). Here he sets out the correct attitude the analyst (male) must adopt when the patient (female) 'falls in love' with him. Freud rejects, at the outset, three possible outcomes: the abandonment of the treatment (like Breuer), marriage (like Ferenczi) or an illicit sexual relationship (like Jung). He regards the latter alternative as impossible simply on the grounds of 'conventional morality and professional dignity'.

This last point about 'conventional morality and professional dignity' is hardly worthy of a pioneer like Freud, whose sexual theories anyway offended the medical establishment. But the last thing he wanted was to see his fledgling psychoanalytic movement brought into disrepute. His argument becomes more impressive when he describes transference love as resistance to the treatment. 'The outbreak of passionate demands for love', he observes, invariably occurred just as the patient was on 'the point of confessing or remembering one of the particularly painful or heavily repressed vicissitudes in her life-history'. Freud further declares that given the fact that none of us is totally immune from temptation, 'it is not permissible to disavow the indifference one has developed by keeping the countertransference in check'. We might note here the double negatives that render this statement so laborious, as if Freud himself was not wholly convinced. Indeed he concedes he would not 'insist that the analyst must never in any circumstances accept or return the tender passion proferred to him'. This is a puzzling qualification. Is Freud suggesting that the analyst *may*, in certain circumstances, actually 'return the tender passion'? Clearly he thinks better of it, because he then lays down very firmly the basic principle that analysis must be *'carried through in a state of abstinence'* and this rule remained thereafter central to orthodox psychoanalytic method.

A TREATMENT THAT FAILED

Freud's caution would appear to be amply justified by the first case I shall present. When Mrs K started therapy with me she had previously been in treatment for several years with an analyst about the same age as her father. But over time things had gone badly wrong. In the latter phase of the therapy a ritual had developed where therapist and patient would lie together on the couch, with their arms round each other. From what I could make out, this was apparently the limit of their intimacy. Mrs K had originally regarded her former analyst as a caring and experienced practitioner, but bit by bit the boundaries crumbled, and over time she became increasingly convinced either that he was exploiting her or that he was in love with her. Either way, the therapy had become a sterile enterprise, and eventually she left him.

This was her main topic in the early months of therapy. I found it uncomfortable to listen to, as if she was sending me a message I did not want to hear. At this stage I deliberately avoided any exploration of what part she might have played in such an interaction. I also expressly asked her not to tell me her therapist's name. I think my discomfort arose from a sense that she was warning *me* not to fall in love with her. For good or ill, it did not help.

As well as criticising her former analyst, she also repeatedly criticised herself for 'paying for the privilege' of talking about herself, and she constantly discussed stopping. With hindsight, I think it was not guilt that bothered her so much as fear: fear not only of her hunger to be loved but of the power of her seductiveness. I did not see this at the time and reacted rather naively by challenging her punishing superego: in effect, urging her to continue. The truth was I liked her, I felt she had real potential, and I did not want to lose her. She let herself be persuaded; she said she ought to leave but could not, and slowly I began to realise that she was telling me that she had become deeply bonded to me, and had in fact 'fallen in love' with me.

Although I told myself this was purely transferential, the effect was to put me under some kind of spell. I found myself increasingly captivated by the way she looked, the way she thought, and especially the way she spoke. I sometimes had the distinct fantasy that her words palpably enveloped me in a shower of kisses. She habitually dressed in plain, clean, second-hand clothes, but I had the fantasy that she was a princess in disguise. This was reinforced by the fact that she was in fact the daughter of an aristocratic family, but had spent her life in revolt against them. She had been married to a well-known sculptor but now lived alone, struggling to bring up her two young daughters.

I found myself entertaining other fantasies towards her, including our being happily married. My fantasies were deeply tender, romantic and protective rather than lustful. This puzzled me: I was no stranger to sexual fantasies towards women patients I had found much less attractive. It is possible that much of this idealised and innocent tenderness was introjected from my patient's unconscious. I could well understand how her former analyst had fallen in love with her. But, unlike him, it was no struggle to resist breaking any professional boundaries. I did not need to: I had all the gratification I wanted just being in her company. The work of analysis seems to move by its own momentum: I would barely begin an interpretation when she had already understood it. If ever I challenged her, she felt so profoundly accepted by me that nothing, however confronting, ever hurt her. The therapy itself felt like a joyful lovemaking. Given the rapport between us, Mrs K herself had by now reached a state of well-being such as she had never known before. Her habitual depression and sense of deep inadequacy had vanished; instead she appeared radiantly alive, confident, purposeful and looked increasingly beautiful. Her happiness seemed to go on and on, month after month. As her therapist, I rejoiced in this blessed condition. At times I even envied it: I could not recall ever having myself enjoyed a state of such prolonged well-being.

And yet, at the same time, I felt it was too good to be true. As her attachment grew so did my anxiety. I began to fear that she harboured the hope that we would actually live out the happy existence we already enjoyed in the consulting room. All my training told me that her transformation, like that of Breuer's 'Anna O', was merely a 'transference cure'; that she was floating above everyday life in a hot air balloon and the crash, when it came, would be catastrophic. I decided it was my duty, as her analyst, to bring her safely back to earth. Much as I hated doing it, I now proceeded to interpret her feelings as simply transference. I told her that being 'in love' with me was really a form of resistance against insight.

Within weeks the spell was broken. She became manifestly depressed, mortified at having fallen victim to the illusion that I had ever really cared about her. Our relationship rapidly began to deteriorate. Previously even my half-finished sentences were intuitively understood, now the most carefully worded interpretations became hopelessly misconstrued. Her old, persecuting superego re-established its dominance, she talked increasingly that therapy was mere self-indulgence, and saw no point in continuing. I struggled on with my interpretations, but in vain.

The end came about in an unexpected way: I returned from the Easter break to be told that she was getting married. I was astonished: it had all happened in the two weeks I was away. My response was mixed: professional satisfaction that the therapy seemed to have worked after all, since her life was now entering a more settled phase; and personal sorrow that I had 'lost her' to another man.

I was wrong on both counts. Within just a few weeks of her wedding I began to realise she was far from happy. The man she married was a friend of her family, by all acounts an able and generous-spirited person, who had been in love with her for years. But she now told me that, while she admired his achievements, she had never found him personally attractive. Next I heard that she had moved to a separate bedroom. The marriage was deteriorating fast, and I became filled with concern for her, indeed for both of them. When she let drop that she found her husband physically repulsive, because his chronic alchoholism had rotted his teeth, I blurted out: 'Then why did you marry him?' She countered: 'Why did you go away?'

Her retort stunned me: I now realised that my decision to deflate the transference had been construed as a totally unacceptable withdrawal of love, and my holiday had killed off the last of her illusions. It was, for her, a repetition of what had happened with her father: throughout her childhood they had adored each other, but when she had reached a certain age, he had unaccountably withdrawn, perhaps through his own Oedipal anxieties, but she had seen it as an intolerable rejection. Her impulsive marriage was a kind of vengeful suicide, as if to say: 'Look what you drove me to'. At the same time she revenged herself on her family by marrying a man they approved of, going through the fashionable wedding they had arranged for her, then sabotaging the whole arrangment. The sheer destructiveness of it left me feeling like an accessory to murder.

All attempts to analyse this new turn of events were met with personal criticism. Previously she reproached me that I had misled her into thinking I had cared for her. She now reproached me that if, in fact, I really *had* cared for her then, like my predecessor, I had seriously failed as a therapist. With punishing clarity she put it to me that no matter what *she* had felt towards me, it was my task to have resisted all temptation. I could have replied that, unlike my predecesor, I had done just that, but thought it better not to defend myself. Instead I tried to analyse the chain of events, but she was in no mood to debate anything and terminated.

SHOULD THERAPISTS LOVE THEIR PATIENTS?

The failure of my treatment of Mrs K left me deeply troubled. I felt that I should, from the outset, have followed Freud's recommendations: that is, interpreted that her attachment to me was simply a resistance to the analytic process, kept a strict guard on my feelings, and explored her role in her former analyst's deviant behaviour. But with the passing of time, and further reflection, I have become less convinced of Freud's prescription. By what right could I have decided that her love was a transference illusion evoked by the analytic situation? To have consigned it to the realm of unreality might have helped to protect me from the involvement that followed, but only by invalidating her experience; and that felt to me to be decidedly non-therapeutic. Nor does it seem realistic that therapists can, as Freud recommends, develop an 'indifference' by 'keeping the counter-transference in check'. Jung (1954: 176) takes a different view:

> The patient, by bringing an activated unconscious to bear upon the doctor, constellates the corresponding unconscious material in him, owing to an inductive effect which always emanates from projections to a greater or lesser degree. Doctor and patient thus find themselves in a relationship founded on mutual unconsciousness.

I suspect it is a piece of self-delusion for therapists to imagine that they can hide their feelings from their patients. I know from my own analysis that patients watch and listen for every clue that betrays the therapist's true feelings, as distinct from their professional responses. Even when the analyst is out of sight behind the couch, a pause or a sigh tells the patient just as much as a carefully worded interpretation.

Freud's paper reflects a deeply sceptical attitude towards transference and countertransference love; in his view analytic interpretation was the sole instrument of therapeutic change. And this determined the classical psychoanalytic attitude for at least the next half-century. It was well into the 1950s before Freud's original drive theory was to become superseded by object relations theory, which took into account the healing effect of the patient–therapist relationship.

The decisive influence of pre-verbal, mutually attuned, relationships between mother and baby is now beyond question. Current research in neuroscience has demonstrated that the failure of responsive mothering in early infancy physiologically impairs the post-natal development of the prefrontal cortex, which is largely responsible for emotional self-regulation. Thus the enduring susceptibility to psychiatric disorder can be laid down in this very early phase of life (Schore 1996). But matters are not irrevocably determined in infancy: the human brain is of such an unimaginably complex and fluid nature that early damage can, in some degree, be repaired. The evidence suggests that any significant experience that reaches a certain level of intensity redistributes synapses and reinforces neural pathways, so that even talking or imagining alone actually produces physiological changes. It follows that after therapeutic treatment the very brain of the patient is different (Tresan 1996).

Patients, like infants, thrive on love, since it promotes authentic self-regard. In this respect my loving feelings for Mrs K were soundly based. If helpful insights and sensitive interpretation serve to confirm this internalised self-regard then they act therapeutically. Love in all its forms, which encompasses understanding, confrontation and the maintenance of safe boundaries, is the basic healing factor. This includes both the therapist's love for the patient, and the therapist's readiness to be loved by the patient, and not to be afraid of it.

Of course love has its dangers, but far more dangerous, in my experience, have been those cases where, try as I might, I have been *unable* to love my patient. The American psychoanalyst, Thomas Malone (1976: 401), says this on the subject:

> I came then to the most significant discovery I have come to in thirty years of psychotherapy. Before you can help anyone be different, you have to accept them as they are. . . . Unless this occurs, nothing eventuates in the therapy. This means loving – enjoying – being with them as they are, without any insistence they have to be different for you to love them. . . . Some I cannot accept even after months. And I cannot help them. Others I can accept – it may take weeks or months – and I can help. But it is my first order of business in therapy.

Furthermore, Harold Searles (1965: 284–303) said: 'Since I began doing psychoanalysis and intensive psychotherapy, I have found, time after time, that in the course of the work with every one of my patients who has progressed to, or very far towards, a thoroughgoing analytic cure, I have experienced romantic and erotic desires to marry, and fantasies of being married to, the patient'. What Searles seems to be saying is that as the patient grows to feel more whole, the analyst finds them more attractive. The implications are simple but stunning: the more I feel myself to be lovable, the more people will love me. This may be, in part, the result of projective identification, but because we are so familiar with it, that does not make the phenomenon any less remarkable – or less therapeutic.

In Chapter 1 of this book Jackie Gerrard concedes that 'until and unless there can be felt moments of love for the patient by the therapist, the patient is not able to develop fully. I think it is only when a patient can arouse our deepest loving feelings (not empathy) that we can truly hope for a positive outcome from our work'. Andrew Samuels (1989: 82) says the same thing in another way: 'Numerous problems met with clinically stem from an *insufficiency* of kinship libido or incest fantasy, not an excess of it. The father who cannot attain to an optimally erotic relation with his daughter is damaging her in a way that deserves therapeutic attention'.

I brooded over my encounter with Mrs K for years. I now think my mistake was that, by following the analytic precept of abstinence, I sent her the message that I had stopped loving her, or had never really loved her. I did what her father did, and for much the same reasons. In retrospect my failure consisted, not in responding emotionally to her transference love but that, lacking the confidence to let it live out its full development within the boundaries of a professional relationship, I took it on myself to abort it prematurely.

THE SPECTRUM OF LOVE

Now what do I mean by letting transference love 'live out its full development'? Gerrard differentiates three types of love: 'genetic' (part-object) love; 'narcissistic' love; and ultimately 'mature' (whole-object) love. These can best be understood as reflecting successive stages, or dimensions, of psychological functioning. I will indicate each dimension very briefly.

The way in which very small infants experience their existence is profoundly different from that of adults, and any attempt to delineate the 'genetic', or *one-dimensional*, level of mental functioning must involve a considerable measure of speculative reconstruction. It is a world where the mental and the physical are relatively undifferentiated; that is, mental distress may well be experienced by an infant as physical pain. There is minimal differentiation between self and other: thus what happens to the infant virtually happens to its mother and vice versa. Kohut (1977) hypothesises an initial state he calls 'self-object', which is intended to convey that subject and object, infant and primary caregiver, are merged in a single experience. Likewise there is no differentiation between appearance and reality: thus there is no concept of play, which even young animals soon develop, and therefore no sense of 'as if'. The person who never quite knows if someone is joking operates, in part, one dimensionally. The psychoanalyst Matte Blanco (1975) sees this phase as dominated by 'symmetrical thinking', a pre-logical type of thought where the part comprises the whole. Thus if there is pain, the entire world is composed only of pain. This type of thinking is readily revived in adults in times of strong emotion.

In the normal course of development the baby becomes a child and the one dimensional is encompassed in a larger framework we can call *two dimensional*. This is equivalent to Melanie Klein's 'paranoid-schizoid' position, Balint's 'area of basic fault' or Gerrard's 'narcissistic' level. The two dimensional is flat, like a map. We know that a map, thanks to geometrical projection, distorts the shape of the continents, compared to the way they are shown on a globe; in an analogous manner paranoia or idealisation distort how we see the people we become involved with. The two dimensional may also be compared to a coin, with one side heads and the other tails. This is to indicate that it is characterised by opposites; things are experienced as either black or white, good or bad, love or hate. My relationship with Mrs K would qualify as two dimensional: when she felt loved and loving she found it extremely difficult to see a blemish in me. But when the relationship began to deteriorate she became devastatingly critical, and the love that preceded it was proved a delusion. At the two-dimensional level whichever feeling is uppermost virtually defines reality and its opposite becomes inconceivable.

But I want to make it clear that although two-dimensional love is not 'true love', that does not mean it is false. In everyday life falling in love is commonly regarded as the preparation for something deeper. Optimally 'falling in love' grows into 'loving': the two dimensional grows into the *three dimensional*, by which I mean adult, reflective, resilient, capable of integrating love and hate, good and bad. You could represent the three dimensional geometrically by a sphere. Psychologically it means there is a space inside where thoughts can be held. Melanie Klein called this the depressive position – depressive because it involves the loss, among much else, of that fragile enchantment Mrs K and I had both basked in. And had I not, with the 'best intentions', prematurely terminated that enchantment we might have worked through to the birth of something more durable, something that could take knocks and not crack up; something perhaps less exciting but more deeply satisfying.

The achievement of the three dimensional, or mature, relationship cannot be overestimated. It requires the emergence of a flexible, well-functioning ego, which is what psychotherapy aims at. But by true love I actually mean something more, something *beyond* the three dimensional, beyond Klein's depressive position, beyond Freud's secondary process; something which incorporates, underlies and transcends the ego. I want to suggest the possibility of a four-dimensional relationship. I have in mind those moments – and they are usually very brief – where two people feel profoundly united with one another yet each retains a singularily enriched sense of themselves. Because it feels to be of quite a different order from everyday experience, we are inclined to call it an 'altered state'. But when we are *in* it we realise with a shock of joyful recognition that it is our *true state* and everyday experience is, by comparison, a shrunken form of consciousness.

Although it happens but rarely in the life of each individual, many people have actually experienced it, either in the company of a particular person, or it has come to them in solitude, as a moment of pure illumination, often termed a 'peak' experience. In the one-to-one therapeutic setting such moments are usually characterised by stillness and intense mutuality. This was the state that emerged after many years of work with my patient Mrs R, originally described in my book *Breakdown and Breakthrough* (Field 1996).

ANALYSIS INTERMINABLE?

For the first two years Mrs R came twice a week, lay on my couch, talked about her unhappy marriage, and seemed to find my carefully thought-out interpretations acceptable. Unlike the magical rapport with Mrs K my relationship with Mrs R was neither close nor distant but conformed to the correct analytic attitude of benevolent neutrality. I sometimes wondered if our working alliance resembled a passionless marriage, rather like the one she was already in. It was only later she was able to tell me that this seemingly unremarkable phase had been one long misery: she hated coming, hated my interpretations, had been deeply afraid of me, and soldiered on out of sheer determination. I realised that, even after two years of analytic work, I had not even begun to reach beyond her defences to where much more serious disturbances lay.

The second phase seems linked with the actual ending of her marriage and the beginning of a period where she lived alone. Our communication during this time was characterised by utter mutual incomprehension. The harder I tried to understand what she was telling me, no matter how simple, the more confused we both became. Repeatedly I would reach a stage where I felt myself becoming unbearably frustrated – whereupon something in me would just give up. But I began to notice that it was just at that point of giving up that something clicked and our minds synchronised. I would say: 'Then you simply mean . . . (whatever)?' and she would respond: 'Exactly!'

I noticed that when this happened she involuntarily pulled out the comb that held her bun in place and her hair would cascade down her shoulder, while she looked at me with a satisfied smile. This evoked in my mind the crude metaphor that I had been, as it were, enlisted in a heroic effort to give a frigid woman an orgasm – albeit a cognitive one. Even stranger was the fact that she could get one only at the moment when I admitted my impotence. This same agonised struggle was repeated at nearly every session over the next year, and slowly I realised that she needed me to experience this disoriented state, because that was how she felt most of the time.

The third phase began when she talked about ending the therapy. After all these years it seemed perfectly reasonable. But as we discussed it, she con- fessed to a fear that she was getting ever more involved with me. I recalled my metaphor of the orgasm, and began to explore if she harboured unacknow- ledged Oedipal feelings towards me. She looked blank and said she might well be denying such feelings but she had no conscious knowledge of them. I came back to the Oedipal situation on various occasions but got nowhere. Eventually she replied: 'When I say I have become more involved with you, it's something far deeper, far more exciting, than sex'.

Her reply put me in my place and I dropped the subject. Moreover she had met a man of her own age and was in love with him in a way she had never been with her husband. Yet I suspect the Oedipal connection between us had done its work, even though unacknowledged and unanalysed. In time she remarried and had a child. Once again we discussed ending, but she wanted to continue and a new phase emerged. It was signalled by each session beginning with a silence. At first it was just a few minutes but the silences gradually stretched to half an hour. For some reason I found them very difficult to bear. I never knew whether she needed my help to break them, or whether she wanted them to continue. In the previous phase I had felt crazy trying to grasp what she was telling me; now I felt even crazier trying to guess what she might be silently thinking. Then one day she said: 'This is the only place I can come and not have to talk'.

This released me from all anxiety, so again I gave up and went off into my own thoughts. The silences became even longer and now filled the entire hour. Within moments of sitting down, Mrs R's eyelids would begin to flicker, then close, as she slipped into a strange, almost trance-like condition. It induced a similar state in me, accompanied by a deep feeling of personal connection with her that was unbelievably peaceful. Having struggled for years to communicate, we seemed to have now reached a state of communion, but one in which I felt an enhanced sense of myself. The hour seemed to pass all too quickly and Mrs R would leave, saying nothing but a heartfelt: 'Thank you'.

After many weeks the silences shortened; she would 'wake' with a warm smile, as if to say: 'Oh hello – you're there . . .' and then begin: 'I've been thinking . . .'. What followed was an interchange as alive and clear as our previous exchanges had been fraught and mutually incomprehensible. We were no longer patient and analyst, but more like two instrumentalists freely improvising, each creatively elaborating on the other's responses.

Eventually I asked her to describe what happened in her silences. She thought for a long time, then replied: 'They vary. But at their best all my thoughts, all my confusion, settles and I begin to see. Just *see.* You, for example. The fact is, for years I never really saw you, only what you would call my projection of you: you looked positively ugly when I hated you, attractive when I was idealising you. Then, at a certain moment, my eyes really opened and I saw you'. She hesitated: 'Don't laugh please, but I think what I saw was your soul'. I did not feel at all like laughing but felt very exposed. She continued:

> 'I know you think I've been coming a very long time, but I'm sure it has had to take this long. When I first came I was locked into my private world; I was always tense but at the same time secure. I actually thought that, apart from my marriage, I was a happy person. It was you, with your interpretations, who made me unhappy and horribly insecure and I hated you for it. Inside me I fought everything you said, I had to, or I would really have had a breakdown. I don't think you really understood. In my eyes you knew all the answers, and if you didn't understand me, it was because I was too sick. I must be the one in the wrong. You broke into my safe

world. It's true you let the light in, but it was horribly blinding.
I could only take it in tiny bits. It meant I could never really look
at you. I don't think you realised that either. But I can look at you
now,' she said, smiling, 'and not be blinded'.

I found it painful to realise how little I had understood. But what I understood now was that she had made a long and difficult journey from a two-
dimensional level of polarised certainties to a three-dimensional level of
ambivalence and confusion and thence, by means of the silences that she
had imposed, and which I learned to accept, to intermittent glimpses of
the four-dimensional level of clear sight.

A four-dimensional relationship is not especially rare, but something that
happens to many people at particular moments of their lives. It is very much
part of human experience but not easily talked about. I think this is because it
can sound pretentious, or mystical, and thanks to its paradoxical nature,
cannot be mentally grasped: we have to let it grasp us. Bion (1970) said
the same thing of his concept 'O': you can't know it, you can only be it.
I see it as analogous to Einstein's four-dimensional union of space and
time, in that it involves the paradoxical *union and separation of self and other*.
We are not lost in one another – that would be one dimensional – but found.

The four dimensional is reached in many ways – in art, in nature, in prayer,
in mystical experience, sometimes in childbirth, and also in the therapeutic
encounter. In fact therapy, with its unique combination of intimacy and
boundary, is especially well suited to facilitating it. It can only happen
when each party unreservedly accepts the other and themselves as they are.
And just as the shift from the two dimensional to the three dimensional
requires the transcending of primary fusion in order to achieve separateness,
so the shift from the three dimensional to the four dimensional requires
the transcending of the ego in order to achieve this paradoxical state of
communion/separation.

When the moment of communion happens there is a sense that healing
takes place. I think this is because the experience provides a powerful feeling
of mutual trust, in the absence of which interpretation is merely a cerebral
exercise. Nor would I want to imply that a single 'dose' of the four dimensional is sufficient to bring about a lasting transformation. For long-term
change to establish itself these intense experiences need to be repeated, perhaps many times, in order to undo the massive mistrust so many patients
acquire in childhood.

Looking back on my work with Mrs R, it also became clear that we seemed
able to make the transition from one level to the next only when we both
reached the end of our tether and I was forced to give up. Giving up
seemed to leave a space where something new could enter. In practise I did
not give up but carried on; and I did not give up so much as give it *over* to
some healing process that we had managed to initiate. Each breakthrough
seemed to come only after I allowed something in me to break down.

To my profound regret I never gave Mrs K the chance to go through this process with me.

NOTE

1 This quotation is from a poem by W.H. Auden.

REFERENCES

Bion, W.R. (1970) *Attention and Interpretation*, London: Tavistock Publications.
Carotenuto A. (1984) *A Secret Symmetry*, London: Routledge & Kegan Paul.
Field, N. (1996) *Breakdown and Breakthrough*, London: Routledge.
Freud, S. (1915) 'Observations on transference love', *Standard Edition* 12, London: Hogarth Press.
Jones, E. (1964) *The Life and Work of Sigmund Freud*, London: Pelican.
Jung, C.G. (1954) 'The practise of psychotherapy', *Collected Works* 16, London: Routledge.
Kohut, H. (1977) *Restoration of the Self*, New York: International Universities Press.
Malone, T. (1976) 'The Christian sacred tradition and psychotherapy', in J. Needleman and D. Lewis (eds), *On the Way to Self Knowledge*, New York: A.J. Knops.
Matte Blanco, I. (1975) *The Unconscious as Infinite Sets*, London: Duckworth.
Samuels, A. (1989) *The Plural Psyche*, London: Routledge.
Schore, A.N. (1996) 'The experience-dependent maturation of a regulatory system in the orbital prefrontal cortex and the origin of developmental psychopathology', in *Development and Psychopathology*, Cambridge: Cambridge University Press.
Searles, H. (1965) 'Oedipal love in the countertransference', in *Collected Papers on Schizophrenia*, New York: International Universities Press.
Stanton, M. (1990) *Sandor Ferenczi*, London: Free Association Press.
Tresan, D. (1996) 'Jungian metapsychology and neurobiological theory', *Journal of Analytical Psychology* 41(2).

7 Primal absence and loss in erotic transference

Martin Stanton

'Transference' ranks high in the list of technical terms that Freud bequeathed both to the medical profession and to popular language. It is standardly listed in psychiatric textbooks as a major distinguishing feature between psycho-analysis and other psychotherapies (cf. Katona and Robertson 1995: 68), and is separately itemized as a psychoanalytic term in most English and foreign-language dictionaries. Despite this broad and general currency, surprisingly little attention is given either to its specific etymology, or to the particular manner of its operation in clinical work. Even in clinical case presentations, it is often assumed to be a simple projection of unconscious material relating to parental figures on to the analyst. As my reading of trans-ference differs significantly from this popular conception – particularly with respect to the residual unconscious nature of transference – I propose to preface this chapter with some discussion of my own conceptualization of erotic transference, and how this relates to the clinical case history I will present later.

Let us begin, then, with a brief exploration of the etymological origins of the term 'transference'. In Freud's German, the term 'transference' (*Uber-tragung*) conveys two main commonly used meanings: first of all, it denotes the carriage of something from one place to another, such as shifting a vase from one table to another; and secondly it denotes the transferral of something from one language to another, for example from German to English – a use which closely links the term 'transference' (*Ubertragung*) with 'translation' (*Ubersetzung*).

In clinical work, transference is traditionally used to convey the first of these meanings. When psychotherapists talk about patients 'transferring' psychic material, they usually mean that the patient carries over material from their own inner world to the psychotherapist. Similarly, countertransfer-ence usually involves the psychotherapist carrying over their own material to the patient.

In contrast, the second meaning of transference as translation from one language to another has been left relatively unexplored, with significant exceptions (e.g. Lagache 1993; Lacan 1991; Laplanche 1993; cf. Stanton 1997: 47–60). Freud centres his own discussion of this second sense of transference on two specific clinical issues: first, the issue of multiple levels of psychic inscription of unconscious material, and the evident 'transfer' of symptom-presentation in sessions from one level of narrative (such as speech) to another (such as the body) (Freud, 'Letter to Fliess' of 6 December 1896, in Freud 1985: 207–15). The second related clinical issue is the transfer (or 'translation') of visual to verbal material – an issue Freud argues is central to problems of representability and subsequent interpretation in dreams (Freud 1953–74, 5: 343–4). Here Freud stresses the structural limitations of the transference-translation process in dream narrative, and draws particular attention to the 'untranslatability' of some visual material into verbal form, and vice versa. A leading article in a newspaper, for example, cannot readily be rendered into pictorial form (p. 340). For Freud, the visual articulates earlier and deeper levels of psychic inscription of symptoms, and the verbal remains secondary and elaborative. For this reason, he draws a sharp distinction between the dream experience itself, which remains residually 'unconscious' and substantially unrepresentable and untranslatable, and the *account* of the dream, which forms the focus of interpretations (p. 506).

Let us now explore how both these clinical issues powerfully endorse arguments for the residual unconscious nature of the transference – that is, its ultimate non-translatability – and also serve to highlight the severe limitation placed on any potential interpretation of the transference. For Freud, the secondary elaborative and associative function of interpretation implies an ultimate failure to capture or decode residually unconscious material, so interpretation itself inevitably becomes symptomatic in its own right – symptomatic of its own failure effectively to represent an original transference structure. For this reason, following Freud, it is important to draw a clear distinction between interpretation *of* the transference (an impossibility) and interpreting *in* the transference (an option which takes full account of the complex and symptomatic nature of interpretation itself).

In this way, Freud's development of the translation-transference issue cogently illustrates the sacrifices and substitutions involved in the attempt to attribute meaning to any communicative expression. A translator from German into English, for example, may well transfer some 'sense' from one language to the other, but will inevitably lose both the primal sound or written shape of the original, as well as substitute new syntactic structures to enable the 'flow' of meaning in the translation. Similarly, the associative range of original words will be lost and replaced by a whole new set of associations built into the language of translation – as indeed our present discussion of the translation of the German term *Ubertragung* into English has aptly illustrated.

None the less, the crucial clinical issue posed by this level of inquiry is not the recognition of fundamental differences between languages (such as German and English, or even your use of the English language and mine), but the presence of formally distinct registers in which psychic material may be processed, or may, through repression, be distorted, or avoid process altogether (as in autism). Following Freud, two original categories of register therefore need to be identified in the communications that take place in psychotherapy sessions: a primary visual, auditory and sensorial register, and a secondary elaborative, interpretative, verbal register. Transference will intrude and make its presence felt precisely at points of non-translatability between the first and second registers – when either distortions will disrupt the 'flow' of meaning, as with parapraxes, or when unprocessed visual material will stall secondary elaboration, as with dislocated auditory or visual hallucinations. In clinical work, such distortions and stallings reveal both the inadequacy and incompleteness of either patient's and/or psychotherapist's symbolizations (which Lagache calls the 'Zeigarnik Effect'[1] (Lagache 1993)). Crucially, if these distortions and stallings are left uninterpreted – that is, the analyst desists from theorizing or interpreting them – such impasses may promote the emergence of primal complex structures of unprocessed unconscious psychic material. Freud conveniently identifies these sites as 'primal scenes', probably in part at least to emphasize his view of the primacy of the visual and dramatic power of stallings. Laplanche (1993) in particular has drawn attention to the *dissociative* function of such scenes in transference stallings: he argues, for example, that Freud's use of the word *Lösung* in relation to these aspects of transference indicates a 'loosening' or 'unbinding' of primal scene elements (as in *ablösen*, 'to unloose', *auflösen*, 'to untie or unravel' and *erlösen*, 'to release or redeem'), rather than a 'resolution' or 'dissolution' of transference (as is proposed in the Strachey translation of Freud's term).

Erotic transference assumes a further dimension of impossibility and unprocessability in such formulations. In 1954, Lacan proposed a preliminary focus of any discussion of erotic transference on Freud's use of the German term *Begierde*, which is standardly translated as 'desire', but more specifically means a consuming desire, such as the craving for food or covetous or incestuous desire (Lacan 1977: 301). For Lacan, we can never 'know' or 'master' such desire through knowledge (*connaissance*) because the desire itself originates in a primal misrecognition (*méconnaissance*) through which we all identify what we are with what we see reflected in the other: either we substitute the image in the mirror for our bodies (in the 'mirror stage' – the primal scene in which we enter language and symbolization); or, to follow Winnicott's reading of Lacan, we identify and secure our own sense of feelings by how we see them reflected in our mother's face (Winnicott 1985: 130). 'Desire' therefore always returns us to all that we have to repress in order to maintain this primary identification with the other. It returns us to the residual 'otherness' of other, the fact that others as objects of our desire do not conform to the dictates of our 'knowledge'. Hence our compulsion to 'consume' others in our desire (*Begierde*) and the endless desire to repeat the rituals through which we aim to merge with the other, notoriously and pleasurably through sexual intercourse, or through meditative *extasis*. Ultimately, then, *eros* is unknowable: it is *atopic* (ατοπία following Socrates in *The Banquet*) – it is unsituatable in our consciousness, and unclassifiable in knowledge ('L'atopie d'Eros: Agathon', in Lacan 1977: 117–34).

How might such an erotic transference operate within the clinical session? If we return to the 'translation' paradigm, two main options emerge. First of all, erotic transference might operate a stalling of the specific identification of desire with an object, so the desired object becomes 'other', alien or distant. This can transmute desire into a loss-of-object form of 'yearning' (*Sehnsucht* in Freud's terminology (cf. Laplanche 1989: 96–7)) – the yearning for some-thing lost, such as beautiful forests, or something to be lost, such as the yearn-ing to see the hour end, or something never ever attainable, as in the 'Wolf Man's' case, the yearning for sexual satisfaction from the father (Freud 1953–74, 17: 27–8).

Secondly, a dissociation may occur between the primary sensorial articula-tion of transference and the specific symbolizations of desire: the object of desire, for example, may fragment – in the case of a desired person, parts of his or her body may displace the whole, or fundamentally disrupt or even fore-close set erotic narrative and ritual. Unprocessed elements – bizarre and intru-sive images and sounds in hallucinatory or 'flash-back' episodes – may also significantly loosen and shift through various repetitions: a process I have described elsewhere as the 'bezoaric effect' (a concept analogically developed from the process of periodic regurgitation of undigested material in animals (Stanton 1997: 69–88)).

Let us now explore how these options might usefully inform clinical work in a specific case history.[2] I would like to discuss in this context my work with a woman who had a strong and sometimes overriding visual sense, which prompted her to draw, paint or sculpt scenes and images that she felt unable to represent fully in words. I should mention at the outset that there was neither any obligation for her to produce these works for therapy sessions, nor indeed to show me any of her creative efforts. In fact, she often talked about the technical difficulties encountered in rendering images without actually displaying them. She also made it clear that she regarded some images as potential works of 'art' which progressed through various creative stages, and others as raw material in a voyage of personal discovery.[3] During one period of the therapy, for example, she found it useful to take photographs of herself to attempt to gain some sense of how others may see her, and what emotions were expressed in her face. The few photos she found it important to show to me were significantly all of facial expressions with which she could not identify, so wished to destroy. Finally – and even more important for her – was the need to rework and relocate uneasy images into an artistic context in which she might discover some aesthetic potential. In this context, her attempts to process her own visual material in sessions also vitally engaged with other artists' work where she could identify her own raw response: Cindy Sherman, Jo Spence, Robert Mapplethorpe periodically enabled her own 'self-portraiture'.

My patient was an attractive woman of 35, who came into psychotherapy to resolve difficulties in forming long-term relationships with men. She was currently very much in love with a doctor she had known for two years, but had met originally when he successfully treated her for a serious back injury. They dated each other regularly and particularly enjoyed dining out together. They had twice gone away together on holiday to romantic locations. Despite this intimacy, their physical relationship had not progressed beyond hugging and kissing on meeting and departing. My patient had tried to let him know that she would like to have a full sexual relationship with him, but could not work out why he failed to get the message. They shared a room together while on holiday, and she went out to buy 'special' lingerie to highlight issues of sexual intimacy, but he remained resolutely inseparable from his underclothes. She became increasingly desperate, but felt totally unable to approach the matter directly with him. She eventually became convinced from a passing reference he made to an 'unsharable secret', that he was a sensitive tortured soul who might eventually open up his heart, mind and even his body, once he felt totally secure in a woman's love. She hoped that she could gain a better understanding of his soul and its secret through her own explorations in psychotherapy.

My questions about her previous relationships with men produced a chronicle of severe deception. In the summer after 'A' levels, she had a first affair with an 'older' man (who was 26 at the time) who taught in an art college in a nearby town. She travelled daily on the bus to see him, and they spent all day in bed together. She thought the sexual side of the relationship was wonderful, and he professed to be 'totally in love with her'. She found out, however, after he had unceremoniously 'dumped' her ten days later, that he was married. Later still, she also discovered that he had engaged in more or less regular sexual relations with several other women at the same time. She was devasted and confused, as she could not understand how he could walk out on their mutual sexual bliss.

Once over her distress, she determined to find out as much as possible about male sexual needs, and set out to seduce as many attractive men as possible. She had no difficulty at all in achieving her aim, and enjoyed a new found sense of power and control in walking out on brief sexual encounters. She recognized at the time that this had nothing at all to do with love, but, at the end of this brief intense epoch, she at least felt herself to be secure in the 'knowledge' that she would be one of the best sexual partners her future potential lovers would ever encounter.

Nevertheless, her deception in love seemed inexplicably and cruelly to persist. She fell deeply in love with a colleague at work. They shared similar interests, loved to visit art galleries together, and enjoyed long profound conversations into the early hours. They slept together regularly and became sexually intimate, though he never penetrated her. She wanted him to, but he refused on the grounds that he wished to remain faithful to his first love back home in Sri Lanka, and he intended to return to her one day. Two-and-a-half years later, he did indeed return home to her and left my patient heartbroken.

In the aftermath of this, she re-entered a more distant and cynical phase of relationship with men, and soon after started a two-night-a-week arrangement with someone eight years older (the same age as the art college lecturer). He claimed to be separated from his wife and small daughter. She described herself as fully aware of the limitations of this arrangement, but was appreciative of the sexual side of the relationship, which both satisfied her sexual needs and left her with a secure sense of her own attractiveness. Just over a year into this arrangement, she began to become suspicious of this man's 'other life' on the five days of the week when she lost all contact with him. She also became increasingly disenchanted and irritated with his 'voyeuristic' behaviour towards her, particularly his insistence that she always wear tight revealing clothes and his repeated request that she give him 'titillating' photographs of herself (a request she never answered). She had neither the energy nor the commitment at this time to find out more about his 'other life', but simply decided to end the arrangement and return to her home town. During our discussion of this relationship in therapy sessions, she became increasingly convinced of his abusive character. She recalled vague memories of dreams in which he was anally raping small oriental women, and she suddenly became very distressed and tearful over concern for the welfare of his young daughter.

My first set of concerns in our discussion of these and similar relationships, centred around establishing the degree of her own awareness of the 'sacrifice' involved. What sense did she have of her own welfare with these men? It was very striking indeed that the only and overpowering sense of awareness she could confess was her urgent and compelling need to enter into psychotherapy. Our initial work with this 'uniqueness' loosened up a profound sense of no one ever listening to her: either no one was there to listen, or they were not able to listen to what she needed to say. Immediately after the art college lecturer had ejected her from his flat, she had found herself in the street terrified by the fact that she could tell absolutely no one about her feelings.

Her account of this sense of 'no one to listen' led her in sessions to lengthy and painful descriptions of a primal erotic transference scene. This scene focused crucially on her memories of losing her father when she was 4 years old. He died after a long and extremely painful fight with cancer, and her recall of the last year with him mingled strong physical sensation of being lightly hugged by him in bed on Sunday mornings with horror at the sight of his body wasting away. She was deeply shocked when she was told he was dead, and was going to heaven rather than returning from the hospital. She did not attend the funeral, and for years harboured the secret thought that perhaps she had not been told the truth and he would just come home one day. The sense of the physical absence of her father was poignantly marked by the family's immediate loss of home (necessitated by impecunity). She moved with her mother and younger brother into a very small flat. In this flat, she was obliged to share the parental double bed and bedroom with her mother right up to the age of 18, when she left home. Her younger brother occupied the other bedroom, which left him as a remote figure in her childhood. The masculine seemed confined to a separate room.

Until it came up in sessions, the primal site next to her mother in the parental bed did not seem unusual or particularly important to my patient. Once mentioned, it led her to two major realizations: the first was that the place she lay her head every night literally marked her father's absence and his loss; the second was the conclusion that her mother had experienced no active sexual life after the death of her father because she had spent every night thereafter beside her. In fact, there was absolutely no expression of sexuality at all in her and her mother's bedroom. Her mother undressed in the bathroom, and always emerged in her nightgown, and my patient had to withdraw to the bathroom if she wished to masturbate. She assumed that her mother never masturbated, so her sexual drives must be extinct – a classic case of *aphanisis*, to follow Ernest Jones' terminology (Jones 1950). In this primal scene, then, the erotic was either formally absent or removed to the adjacent 'men's' room.

In the next session, she brought a clay sculpture she had just made of a woman in a bath (see Figure 1). She had made this to try and capture

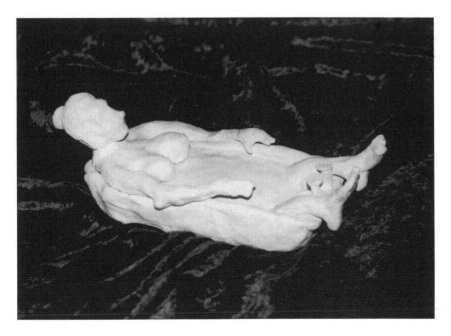

Figure 1

a sudden image that came to her in the early hours of the day following her previous session. She was exhausted, so unsure whether the image was 'half-awake' or had emerged from a dream. She was unsure also whether the figure in the bath was herself or her mother. The head and arms looked elderly, but the breasts were 'young, full and voluptuous'. I pointed out to her that the figure appeared far too large for the bath, and that the waist section of the woman seemed unusually deeply submerged.

In association, she informed me that the last session had provoked her to confront the doctor about the absence of sex in their relationship. She had invited him round to her house to dinner, ensured that he consumed a fair quantity of wine, and then asked questions she felt she had rehearsed in sessions: why did he share a bed with her on holiday if he did not wish to make love to her? What was his 'secret' and why could he not share it? To her utter surprise, he did not declare that he was unaware of her feelings, but told her that he could not make up his mind whether or not to 'take the plunge' and have sex with her. She was horrified, and severely berated him for sadistically allowing her to build up her expectations. He refused to tell her his 'secret' and left. Later, when on her own, she had drawn a detailed and 'loving' picture of her pudenda – the part of her he had not 'known' – which she said was inspired by Gustave Courbet's *Origin of the World* (1866), a painting she had seen in the Musée d'Orsay in Paris a few weeks earlier. It had struck her at the time that this painting had been donated to the Musée by the French psychoanalyst Jacques Lacan – a figure of some importance in my own professional life as a therapist (a fact she may or may not have known). Once finished, she had torn up her own drawing with some pleasure and feeling of breakthrough, and something of this 'flowed' into the bath sculpture. I pointed out that it was not just that the pudenda were *not* represented in the sculpture, but they also seemed to weigh the figure down. The title of Courbet's associated painting ('Origin of the World') also seemed to open the whole question of mother's body and where we come from. In my patient's sculpture, this site was radically submerged if not absent.

Her separation from the doctor had a major impact on our therapeutic relationship. She began to feel anxious and apprehensive before sessions, and very fraught during them. She felt that she was 'losing it', and wrote me a long impassioned letter demanding that 'you explain to me how my present feelings will help rather than hinder my progress'. A few days later she wrote again to tell me that she was powerfully sexually attracted to me and felt very much out of control in this area too. She had read in a book that this was not unusual in therapy, and was called 'transference', but she needed my assurance that I was not going to hurt her much worse than all the other men, and abuse my position.

In the next session, we discussed what indeed might be frightening and abusive in my position, particularly that I was now in a unique position. Effectively, for her, I was both the very first person to be there to listen attentively, and I was also a man. Like her father, I might disappear or just withdraw my 'gentle holding' (as she frequently described my presence). An important mutual recognition emerged that she also put me in the position of mother, particularly to look at and 'dress' her wounds. Her mother too was 'absent', sexually absent. My patient had some initial thoughts in this connection that her fraught compulsion to be immediately and dramatically sexually intimate with men might directly relate to her mother's *aphanisis* (extinction or annihilation of desire). In this context, she began to talk about her compulsion to fellate men on the first night. To some extent, she felt her compulsion was relative to the size of the particular penis: the smaller the penis, the more she felt compelled to show her desire to 'accept' it in this way, so he would not feel compelled to leave.

I asked her what determined her sense of size here – wondering why she addressed this well-publicized male concern in this way, particularly as men in particular often fantasy-elaborate such issues around their mother's vagina (cf. Horney 1967: 133ff.). Did she have some particular penis in mind? At this point, she disclosed to me that her grandfather had sexually abused her when she was 7 years old. She was unsure of the extent of the abuse: he used to sit her on his knee and push his erection up against her, and expose himself to various degrees (in particular he used to chase and threaten her in his long-johns). None the less, she was certain that he had never penetrated her – and declared herself grateful for this certainty, though fearful for other female members of her family whom she felt may have suffered a worse fate. As we worked through the details of her experience with her grandfather, she gradually came to the disorienting feeling that the abuse – horrendous, frightening and damaging as it was – remained in some important way secondary. The pain, horror and anxiety were built on something else. The primal elements for her all seemed to be engaged in the act of telling me – indeed she has frequently told me since that this was the 'hidden' purpose of her seeking therapy. In telling me, she saw how primal it was *not* ever to be able to tell her mother (her grandfather's daughter), or deeper still, her father, *who was not there*. Not surprisingly, she was terrified that her mother would deny her disclosure – precisely because she intuited that her mother's sense of the 'reality' of sexuality may have become extinct – or that her mother would tell her that it had become extinguished, or that the grandfather had abused her too. In fact, neither of these stark options occurred. She did tell her mother, who was deeply shocked, but never questioned for a minute the basic veracity of her daughter's testimony. Indeed, she set about discretely researching on her daughter's behalf issues of grandpaternal abuse with the previously identified vulnerable and exposed members of the family. Most important, my patient also told her brother about the abuse, and the emotional non-communication between them seemed to start to transform radically as a result.

The negative grandparental associations were clearly neither fundamental nor formative in the transference loosenings provoked by our work on her sense of abuse. Instead, primal pre-genital issues underlay the erotic compulsion, namely the absence of her father and the *aphanisis* of her mother. Furthermore, other primal and complex issues loosened up surrounding the images of phallic size and intrusion. She had an 'almost overwhelming' and vivid dream, which she described in her dream notes as follows:

> I am going into an art class. There are panelled walls and the tutor has her art displayed. It is very colourful and bold. I like it. The tutor is very aggressive about other people's taste. I feel very vulnerable and wish to make a good impression. We talk at the end of the class, discussing art. She shows me a sculpture – smooth surfaced – one foot high. The body parts are intermingled. There is a mouth between the breasts and pubis along the mid ascillary line on one side and an ear on the other side. I enjoy touching the sculpture. I feel the tutor's attraction for me and mine for her. She talks to me with her head close.

My patient immediately associated the tutor with me and the art class with the psychotherapy sessions, but was puzzled by the fact that I was a 'very feminine' yet 'caustic and aggressive' woman in the dream. Also she wondered why I am the one who produces the sculpture in her dream. Did the sculpture represent my own desire, and if so, what did it represent? Did she identify with my desire? This line of questioning so haunted her that she decided to make her own version of 'my' sculpture, which she brought to the next session (see Figure 2). The figure had identifiable phallic features – such as a glans and meum – but was also deeply riven in the middle with a vaginal 'mouth'. We discussed at some length the option that it might contain a representation (in the dream) of some complex structure of the tutor/therapist's desire – namely in its abstract and amalgam form, shaped androgynously with a solitary ear, a figure perhaps bent over in concentration, pain or even *aphanisis*. This figure was trying to bring out something that was unidentifiable and uninterpretable. My patient was obviously very taken with this thought, but was unable to reach any resolution. She described the image as intrusive and deeply disruptive of her daily thoughts. She told me she had been tempted to destroy it, but then realized that she may well treasure it for the rest of her life.

Ten days later she had another 'important' dream, this time of a cat fellating itself. The cat was quite serene, and the dream seemingly went on for ages. Again, she associated the cat with me, but was puzzled by the fact that this very feminine feline should also be prodigiously phallic. She tried to capture this image in another sculpture which she wished to give me as a present (see Figure 3). We spent some time looking at both sculptures, and noted the marked difference between the dissociated body parts in the first and the unified serenely stretched out body in the second. She was at first considerably amused by the thought that I might be able to satisfy myself in this way,

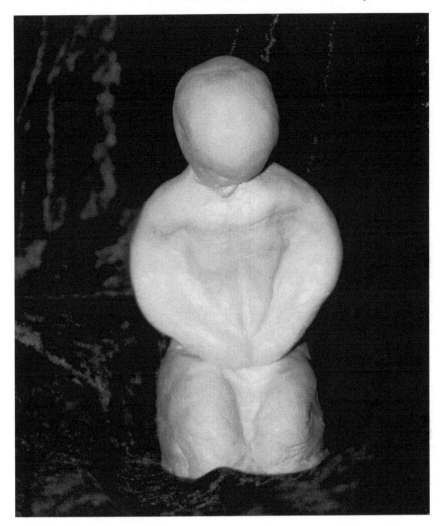

Figure 2

but then became profoundly troubled by the corollary need for *no one* else, as I could presumably fulfil my own desire. Again I suggested that this image might contain some representation of the therapist's desires, but this time with the maternal and paternal elements welded together in some unified and identifiable icon – a cat. In short, this image put her in the position of picturing my own desire independently of her own: she had no compulsive need to fellate me or do anything else except simply observe.

What basic features of erotic transference might this case indicate? First of all, the basic non-viability of any equation which directly projectively

Figure 3

identifies the therapist with single problematic figures in the patient's life: it is clear, for example, that my patient did not simply project her unprocessed feelings for her lovers, grandfather or even her mother and father on me. Instead, the stallings — the nowhere-forward/fear of abuse/out-of-controlness — that indicated the shifts of transference in the therapy, all contained primal elements of absence and loss. My patient felt both cornered by these elements and compelled to *do* something to escape them, and avoid imminent loss of intimacy. The experience of transference for her was therefore ultimately unworkable, unintelligible and intrusive: this experience underlay her basic rhetorical challenge to me to 'explain to me how my present feelings will help rather than hinder me'.

Similarly, the erotic impulses in these transference stallings were all intro-jective or literally incorporative: my patient wished to devour her primal anxieties of loss and absence, as is clearly marked in the *fellatio* rituals. These erotic impulses are also clearly not gender-specific. They are neither primally aimed at the father nor at the mother in some fantasy gratification, nor do they articulate some other restitutive fantasy (such as forms of narcissistic self-enhancement and gratification); rather they are complex, incorporating different erotic aims, and are fundamentally androgenous. This is nowhere more clearly illustrated than in her erotic dream and sculptural figurations of her relationship to me. Particularly striking here is the complex and shifting juxtaposition of different genital and gender images – and the intense concern about their size, change and fluctuation. Again, there are clear indications of primal loss and absence here which she herself comes to recognise as underlying the genital erotics of some of her dreams and fantasies. The sculptures assume a special role in the therapy in this respect. It seems easier for her to mould some images in clay than to attempt to describe them in words. This could well be because the dream and fantasy material itself cannot be readily translated/transferred into words. This is particularly the case with the tutor's 'abstract' sculpture in my patient's dream – whose enigma in some way encapsulates the residual and unprocessable elements of desire in our mutual transference.

Finally, this case also confirms the specific and unique nature of psycho-therapeutic transference – as opposed to any culturally generalizable form (such as 'falling in love'). In an important way, my patient's last two sculp-tures (Figures 2 and 3) do illustrate the actual 'impossibility' of those forms of psychotherapy that work in the transference. By abstinence or dis-inclination, the therapist is bound to figure at one point or another in the therapeutic process as either fundamentally absent or lost/losable in their own self-gratifying position of 'knowledge'. In short, their profession of no-desire ultimately provokes all the primal impossibilities of desire: in the end, any supposed therapeutic 'knowledge' transforms into something symp-tomatic – a symptom of an erotic enigma. This enigmatic power is high-lighted in this case by all that resists symbolization and interpretation in my patient's sculptures. It is this power which renders them permanently precious and enhances their potential as desired objects or, indeed, works of art.

NOTES

1 This evokes Zeigarnik's 1927 experimental discovery that unfinished tasks are much more often recalled than completed ones.
2 The psychoanalytic psychotherapy with this person terminated some time ago, and she has kindly given me permission to use the material and images reproduced here. I have made every effort to conceal both her identity, and the identity of others mentioned. The case history recounted here is therefore essentially fictional, and has been con-structed around the images provided to illustrate my own clinical concerns and views – some of which I am sure she may not share or endorse. We mutually hope that this 'fiction' may prove useful to others.
3 In this context, her conception of her own 'art' formed a peculiarly complex relation to issues of 'free drawing' (to follow Marion Milner's famous dichotomy), as her works of art always contained the potential to shift backwards and forwards through raw visual material (cf. Milner 1971: 71ff.).

REFERENCES

Freud, Sigmund (1953–74) *The Standard Edition of the Complete Psychological Works of Sigmund Freud*, 24 vols, London: Hogarth Press.

—— (1985) *The Complete Letters of Sigmund Freud to Wilhelm Fliess 1887–1904*, Cambridge, MA: Harvard-Belknap.

Horney, Karen (1967) 'The dread of woman. Observations on a specific difference in the dread felt by men and women respectively for the opposite sex', in *Feminine Psychology*, London: Routledge.

Jones, Ernest (1950) 'Early development of female sexuality [1927]', in *Papers on Psycho-Analysis*, London: Bailliere, Tindall & Cox.

Katona, Cornelius and Robertson, Mary (1995) *Psychiatry at a Glance*, Oxford: Blackwell Scientific.

Lacan, Jacques (1977) *Ecrits – A Selection*, London: Tavistock Publications.

—— (1991) *Le Seminaire Livre 8: Le transfert*, Paris: Seuil.

Lagache, Daniel (1993) 'Some aspects of transference', in *The Work of Daniel Lagache – Selected Writings*, London: Karnac.

Laplanche, Jean (1989) 'Terminologie Raisonnee', in *Traduire Freud*, Paris: Presses Universitaires de France.

—— (1993) 'Du transfert', in *La revolution copernicienne inachevée*, Paris: Aubier.

Milner, Marion (1971) *On Not Being Able to Paint*, London: Heinemann.

Stanton, Martin (1997) *Out of Order: Clinical Work and Unconscious Process*, London: Rebus.

Winnicott, Donald W. (1985) *Playing and Reality*, Harmondsworth: Pelican.

8 Erotic transference in clinical practice

Marco Chiesa

Freud's revolutionary and original formulations on the central role played by libidinal drives, which he believed operated from birth, formed the cornerstone of the emerging psychoanalytic theory. The notion of libido, the original sexual drive, which governs psychic development, inflicted a serious blow to the belief that sexuality was confined to genitality. His account of infantile sexuality represented a cultural shock for Western society at the turn of last century, but paved the way for building psychoanalysis as a theory of mind and as a treatment for neurotic conditions. Freud's convincing illustration of the ubiquity of erotic feelings was not matched by awareness of their expression in the analytic encounter, and it was not until 1915 that he wrote about the subject (Freud 1915). Since that seminal publication contributions on transference love had been few and far between until the last ten years, probably due to inherent difficulties in writing publicly on the subject – Freud used the fire metaphor to refer to the impact transference love has on the analytic situation. In contrast, the last decade has seen a significant increase in the number of publications on erotic transference: twenty-two articles in the main analytic journals between 1993 and 1997 as opposed to only thirteen in the previous nineteen years (1974–92) in the same journals.[1] This signals greater scientific interest on the manifold aspects and clinical manifestations of erotic transference. Freedom to communicate about the subject and awareness of a possible increase, and a better recognition, of the incidence of erotised manifestations within the transference may also account for such a sharp growth of published material.

In addition the technical implications with regard to the analyst's counter-transference and to the optimal management of the analytic situation have been the object of discussion and in-depth inquiries. The recent discovery of the relatively high incidence of sexual boundary violations within the analytic setting, some of which following the onset of erotic transferences, has led analysts to present more openly clinical material as a way to deepen our knowledge on the nature of erotised forms of transference. The finding that acting out of erotic feelings between therapist and patient has occurred more frequently than it was believed in the past (Gabbard 1995; Gabbard and Lester 1995) is a testimony to the power which eroticism plays in the consulting room. A better understanding of erotic feelings evoked in patients and analysts, and of the interplay between transference and countertransference phenomena, is required.

The literature shows that there is no universally agreed definition of what constitutes erotic transference. Some authors draw a line between frankly malignant erotisations of the transference and developmentally compatible manifestations, the intensity of which depends on the degree of resolution of underlying Oedipal conflicts. The terms used to define these differences vary according to authors: erotised versus erotic (Blum 1973), sexual versus generative erotic (Bollas 1994) and erotised/erotic versus loving/affectionate (Bolognini 1994). Other authors broaden the concept of erotic transference to include dynamics brought about by some narcissistic patients who create an atmosphere infiltrated with subtle erotic features, as a way to try to seduce the analyst into becoming emotionally involved with them and enter into a collusive relationship in order to avoid painful analytic work (Joseph 1993).

In this chapter I will confine my discussion to the overt presentation of erotic/sexual involvement in the analytic encounter (erotised transference) in order to illustrate the complexity both of the underlying dynamics regarding its onset and of the technical difficulties involved. In addition I will illustrate the role played by denial and dissociation when erotic feelings set in the transference.

OVERT EXPRESSION OF EROTIC TRANSFERENCE

Some patients develop an intense and persistent erotic preoccupation for their analyst in the course of treatment. Typically the onset is early on in therapy, becomes the central feature, and at times finds no resolution. These cases are to be distinguished from those in which more benign, episodic and self-limiting erotic transferences emerge at particular points during therapy, which should be considered as the manifestation of the ubiquitous nature of erotic elements, part of our psychological make-up. The challenges posed by full-blown erotised transferences are both conceptual and technical. What are the environmental early experiences and internal dynamics, which predispose some patients to develop a fully blown, egosyntonic erotised transference? The growing literature on this subject has given interesting and convincing contributions, but many questions remain unanswered. Most of the genetic and structural hypothesis brought forward do not seem specifically confined to these patients – for example, a history of childhood seduction, of parental tolerance of incestuous/sexualised behaviour within the household, or of early sexualisation of the relationship with caregivers – as in other cases which do not develop erotic transferences similar experiences or internal dynamics may also be found. It is likely that the overt phenomenon of erotised transference is multi-determined and that each patient has to be evaluated in terms of the individual/idiosyncratic effect which a specific blend and cluster of events, experiences and internal states of mind has on psychic development. Trying to find a universally causal explanation may prove elusive as it has been the case for most emotional disorders. From the point of view of technique the understanding and management of transference–countertransference dynamics is crucial if the analytic encounter is to continue on solid and therapeutic ground. Therapy can otherwise easily enter into an irreversible impasse or worse falls prey to boundary violations.

Although there may be several common grounds across cases, transference–countertransference interactions take on specific features between a particular patient and a particular therapist. The way in which the therapist understands and responds to transference manifestations, based on his awareness and working through of his own countertransference responses, will determine the shape therapy will take. For a variety of reasons the onset of erotised transference has a marked impact on the therapist's emotional state: anxiety, fear, confusion, surprise, gratification, disgust, condemnation, attraction and a wish to reciprocate may all be elicited. Unless we experience the full range of our internal reactions and analyse them within ourselves, we will not be in the right frame of mind for working therapeutically with the patient's emerging transference. When one of my patients developed erotised transference I felt threatened, proceeded to react defensively and, mainly through my tone of voice, I conveyed a critical attitude. The patient felt that I was not ready to 'take in' her emotional state, withdrew from contact, and her erotised state of mind was pushed under ground, which became unavailable for analytic work. It took several weeks of work on that particular session for the patient to feel safe again and to verbalise the erotic feelings, experienced towards me. A therapist, supervised by me in a seminar, spoke in a derisory and dismissive way of her male patient's tentative expression of his feelings of attraction for her. By conveying her contempt the therapist triggered a gratifying sado-masochistic scenario for the patient, who had a pattern of seeking rejection and humiliation from women. The patient, inhibited and dominated by a cruel internal maternal figure, felt that the therapist belittled his expression of love and sexuality, and was kept down in a state of infantile and masochistic dependence.

Unless a therapist becomes aware of what is being enacted and actively interprets what goes on, they will not be able to overcome the impasse therapy may have fallen into. The therapist has to be open to what a patient feels towards them while maintaining a non-judgmental position of technical neutrality, which allows for a partial identification with the patient. In other words, in order to avoid enactment the analyst has to maintain a dual state of awareness in which he or she is both participant in and observer of the immediate experience with the patient (Gabbard 1994). This is a precondition for furthering dynamic understanding of the patient's erotised transference and for obtaining a grasp of the specific functions it serves, in the light of the patient's early experiences and current defensive structure.

Yet it cannot be ignored that the therapist has feelings of their own, still unresolved areas of conflicts in the personality and possible concurrent stress in their personal life, which may colour the way they react to erotic material from the patient. In some cases the therapist may wittingly or unwittingly stimulate a dormant erotic transference or magnify its manifestations by his or her attitude and responsiveness to the patient's own attitude – for example, by conveying too great an interest for the patient through verbal and non-verbal means.

In a version of the first case of erotised transference in the analytic literature, it was said that Breuer became increasingly fascinated with Anna O's treatment, and ignored his wife, evoking her jealousy (Spector-Person 1993). It has to be recognised that as human beings we are not immune to experience attraction, fascination and love for some of our patients; we must be open to experience such feelings, which are part of our intense and long interaction with another human being. However, it is imperative to be aware of these feelings and not be driven by them, and recover to a position of neutrality in order to safeguard the therapeutic setting and to allow us to think as clearly as possible under pressure. In recent years there has been renewed encouragement from some analytic quarters for an attitude of greater openness towards patients, including self-disclosure of sexual feelings, and for a more 'physical' contact with the patient, including holding and touching. These practices are put forward in the name of 'spontaneity', of the 'human aspect of therapy' or of the 'real relationship' between therapist and patient. Freud's warning against such practices (Freud 1912, 1915), however, written in response to Jung's affair with one of his patients, and to Ferenczi's increasingly advocating use of physical closeness towards patients as a way to make up for early parental failings, still holds true.

A case in my own psychoanalytic practice highlights some of the aforementioned transference–countertransference dynamics, as well as showing that positive aspects intertwine with defensive and destructive functions. Ms A, a 21-year-old woman, developed strong erotised feelings towards me after a few therapy sessions, which constituted a salient feature throughout her therapy and beyond.[2] Her frequent sexual fantasies about myself were matched by her intense hope that one day they would come true. The blow inflicted by the realisation that being her therapist was incompatible with me becoming her lover was softened by her belief that we could then make love once therapy had finished! Romantic and affectionate feelings were mixed with more overt sexual strivings, on the whole contained within the verbal domain, although I suspect they would not have remained that way had I given her any opening. She came into treatment following a disturbed adolescence, which culminated into two attempts to take her life. Her short-lived depressive episodes were superimposed on a character disorder with borderline features, which included intense and unstable relationships, periods of promiscuity, episodic substance abuse and suicide attempts. At the peak of her disturbance Ms A had been admitted to a psychiatric unit and a subsequent attempt at therapy failed.

She settled unexpectedly well into therapy, but the experience of feeling understood by me gave way to a positive, erotised transference. Ms A held that it was my physical attributes, the way I was making her feel during sessions, my kindness and reflective attitude towards her which made her fall in love with me. Although it is possible that the analyst's 'real' characteristics may have a part to play, among other factors, in shaping transference manifestations (Gabbard 1996), Ms A's attraction to me no doubt had deeper determinants. Ms A experienced her mother as a malignant witch-like figure who hated her, while she held a much more benign picture of her father, himself a doctor, towards whom she turned for protection and gratification. Although not overtly erotised, her Oedipal longings for him were strong and unresolved, and were quickly displaced on to me when she started therapy. The erotised transference created a mental space, which protected her from persecutory anxieties deriving from the exposure to a terrifying maternal introject. This intrapsychic process was lived out in the hospital milieu, in which the therapy sessions/father were considered a safe heaven in contrast to the hell of the sociotherapy/mother. This configuration of transference split was subject to quick shifts, as she could not sustain the erotised idealisation of me, when interpretative work broke through her defensive structure. Then for short but intense periods I became a persecutory figure out to harm and damage her. When I became invested with that version of the maternal transference Ms A felt that her 'good' objects had deserted her and she plunged into a mental state of horrors and persecution. This was somatically expressed through flair-up of unpleasant skin problems and through other bodily reactions.

I would like to illustrate how my countertransference may have contributed to shape the patient's transference manifestations. Ms A felt very possessive about me and overtly resented that I saw other patients in psychotherapy within the hospital; in particular, the prospect that I could take on new patients fired her up. In such circumstances acting out was always on the cards, such as Ms A not returning to hospital after a weekend break, threatening self-destructive actions or starting a lesbian affair.

As part of an ongoing research project I had to meet another hospital patient (Ms C) who was at the time the closest friend of my patient. I happened to see Ms C in the hour before Ms A's scheduled therapy session. Ms A came into the session in a vitriolic state of mind and accused me of not being at all interested in her, while devoting my time and attention to Ms C, whom she felt had now become my favourite patient. Ms A could even smell Ms C's perfume; earlier she had seen Ms C taking particular care for her appearance just before coming over to my consulting room. It was obvious that Ms A was consumed with jealousy, that she hated me and that she considered me as responsible for having elicited such feelings in her. She told me that in the morning she had a long and noisy row with Ms C, which required the intervention of nursing staff. After she vented her anger, I pointed out that she was feeling and behaving as a woman who had found out that her lover was betraying her. She seemed to be oblivious to the reality that I was her therapist and had other functions in the hospital other than seeing her. If she was made aware that I had other activities which did not include her, that punctured her hope and belief that we were in an exclusive relationship. This challenge to her 'Oedipal illusion' (Britton 1989) created further disappointment and fury and she stormed out of the session slamming the door.

Ms A came to the next sessions in a somewhat more reflective frame of mind, although still hurt and angry with me, and we could talk over what had been happening with her, with particular reference to the previous session and to her recent behaviour in the hospital setting. Ms A felt that I had set up to meet with Ms C to humiliate and to inflict pain and suffering upon her, since I knew well how she felt about me. Here we could see how I had become in Ms A's mind a sadistic and tantalising couple, whose aim was to exclude her and to feel pleasure at her suffering. I linked her current feelings to her original jealousy for the togetherness of her parents who excluded her and produced a rival in the shape of her eighteen-month younger brother.

Although similar events in the external reality provide the hook upon which specific internal object relationships become manifest, and consequently become available for analysis, with the benefit of hindsight, I suspect that my countertransference played a part in inflaming Ms A's reaction. Psychotherapy was taking place within an institutional setting and Ms A made no secret of her feelings towards me to the rest of the staff. By presenting such an idealised picture of therapy and of me as a therapist, and by contrast conveying quite a dislike and, at times, a sense of contempt for the hospital's other therapeutic activities, Ms A created an atmosphere of suspicion and potential resentment in the sociotherapy staff towards me. In staff meetings, which I attended twice weekly, I often was put on the defensive having to justify the nature of my approach with her, as it was felt that I might collude with Ms A's idealisation and erotisation of her rapport with me. I felt uneasy about the atmosphere which was building up, and started to wonder myself whether there was any way in which I might have encouraged the patient in that direction. These doubts became stronger when I became aware that I did find Ms A attractive and did not feel completely immune to her sensual presentations in the session, and further I had to acknowledge to myself that at times I felt gratified by her longings for me. Although I never deviated from my usual interpretative stance, I felt that an enactment took place. I unconsciously created a situation, which I knew would hurt the patient, as retaliation for the way Ms A was undermining my relationship with the rest of the team. In fact I could have asked a colleague involved in the same research to meet with Ms C, whom I knew was very close to my patient. Certainly I did not need to see Ms C right before Ms A's session, therefore adding insult to injury. Through my behaviour I was also creating a defence against my own feeling of attraction for Ms A by eliciting her jealousy for me, which emphasised that *she* was the one attracted to me. I think that I enacted the scenario of a father struggling with his own incestuous wishes who defensively parades his relationship with his wife in front of his daughter.

DENIAL OF EROTICISM IN THE TRANSFERENCE

At the opposite end of full-blown erotised transference manifestations, with egosyntonic sexual wishes directed towards the analyst, we may find patients who dissociate and deny their sexual feelings in the transference. Here the erotic elements are profoundly egodystonic and they emerge in dream material or free associations, without the patient seeming aware of them under the influence of denial. These patients may react with surprise or even indignation when interpretations of the erotic wishes present in the material are offered. It is not unusual to find that these patients received a puritanical education regarding sexual matters, and have introjected strict and prohibitive parental objects. In patients with more severe psychopathology the denied, split-off erotic transference is not expressed as disguised verbal material as in the previous case but it becomes evident from the patient's actions. I would like to illustrate these features by presenting extracts of material from the analysis of two patients.

In the few occasions sexual matters were raised in the analysis, Mrs G spoke of them in a factual and emotionally distant fashion. The erotic material was usually embedded within a narrative with a different focus, such as more general difficulties in her relationships with others. Overt sexual material was slipped in almost casually, in a way that should not be too noticeable, as if to convey the message that it was rather unimportant. Mrs G expressed genuine surprise that these rather private issues should in fact be part of the analytic work. Dual and discrepant trends became manifest: on the one hand the emergence of material which indicated possible erotic preoccupation in the transference, while Mrs G held a parallel position which regarded such a possibility as erroneous. For example, she became preoccupied and guilty that her involvement in the analysis made her withdraw from contact, including sexual, with her husband, since she found it difficult to open up to two men at the same time. She could do it with me in sessions but not with her husband: this made her feel very uneasy, as though she was in a situation in which she was betraying him. Yet she would express total surprise and disbelief that her attachment to me might include erotic elements, which needed to be understood.

Two dreams help to illustrate the degree of internal dissociation and denial of erotic strivings. In the first dream she came to a session, opened the door leading to a bedroom, which was where the session was to take place. I was inside the bed and invited her to join me under the duvet. She declined to do so but lay down at the bottom of the bed instead and started to talk to me from there. She found the situation very odd and wondered why I had decided to have a session in my bedroom. When I commented on her silence after recounting the dream, Mrs G spoke about one of her cats having gone missing for the whole day, and having returned injured after a fight. As she elaborated on the subject, I interrupted her by pointing out that any wish to work on the meaning of her dream also seemed to have gone missing. Mrs G answered, 'What else is there to say. . . . I don't know what to make of it,' and then proceeded to say that the duvet on the bed was made of very nice material, and had beautiful colour. As winter was approaching she thought she needed to buy a good quality duvet, and started to speculate which department store she might visit to find one. Again when I interpreted her evasiveness and blanking out of the main content of the dream, Mrs G rather reluctantly conveyed her puzzlement that I should hold a session in the bedroom, and said that she could not understand the reasons why I invited her to join me in the bed. I pointed out that the dream was being enacted in the session: Mrs G felt suspicious of the motives I had for inviting her to join me in understanding the dream she brought, which seemingly had now become my concern.

In the second dream reported in a subsequent session Mrs G was in a bedroom with Robert (an old boyfriend). Suddenly somebody knocked at the door; she put her dressing-gown on and went to open the door. It was James (Mrs G's husband) alongside another woman, who wanted to see Robert. This other woman stormed into the bedroom slamming the door behind her. Mrs G and James looked at each other in puzzlement, without saying anything: the understanding was that 'if you are not going to say anything then I am not going to say anything either'. Mrs G commented that the dream was very strange and shrugged her shoulders. She stressed that she had never seen this woman, that she was sure that she was not sexually involved with Robert, but that she went to see him for different reasons. No other association was forthcoming. In the light of previous material this dream had several themes and meanings, the illustration of which goes beyond the scope of this chapter. What I wish to emphasise here is the patient's refusal to enquire into the evident sexual details of the dream, for instance that Mrs G must have been undressed in the presence of Robert if she needed to put her dressing-gown on. In the same vein one might ask what she was doing in the same bedroom as Robert. Mrs G cut off all her curiosity and interest in the material she produced in the sessions. If I did pursue the matter, then it was perceived as though the interest belonged solely to me, and consequently my interpretations were experienced as intrusive and related to what goes on in my mind rather than to what she herself brought.

The second case pertains to a disturbed young woman (Mrs B) who came into analysis following a series of serious suicide attempts and long periods of hospitalisation. She had been suffering continuously from severe depression for several years. Mrs B presented in a semi-mute state, holding that she was puzzled as to why her treating psychiatrist sent her to me and why her husband insisted that she should come. Given these premises the treatment alliance was very weak. She did not know why she was coming and spent most of the first week in silence. She found the unstructured nature of therapy extremely painful and difficult. Over two consecutive sessions she spoke of the death of her parents and of her brother's suicide, which occurred a few years earlier, for which there was some evidence that she felt unconsciously responsible. It seems that the impact of those deaths, the defences against their mourning and working through were central to her recurrent depression. Although Mrs B experienced some relief, those two sessions had been extremely painful and she felt she could not possibly continue with treatment.

The following week she came to the sessions wearing fashionable but audacious and revealing outfits. Her posture on the chair, although not overtly provocative, exposed sensitive areas of her (pleasant looking) body allowing me a full view, which was impossible to avoid. Her mostly silent attitude was interrupted by complaints that 'therapy is very static, nothing happens here'; 'I am a doer, I find inactivity difficult'; 'I expect more feedback from you but you just sit there in silence'. I found these remarks as unconscious reference to my lack of response to her erotic presentation, expressions of an unconscious sexualisation of 'doing', 'happening' and 'feedback'. They were unconscious because I have no doubt that Mrs B was not aware of her seductiveness and erotic posture. This dissociated ego state allowed her in turn to split off and distance herself from the disturbing affects connected with the memories of her parents' death and brother's suicide, the implications of which were felt to be catastrophic for Mrs B who found no alternative but to retreat. This double dissociation created a challenge, which I found very difficult to address. At the time I decided not to comment on the erotised presentation, but implicitly I interpreted its defensive function by addressing how Mrs B had been moving away from the pain and discomfort generated by the previous sessions, which she seemed to have completely blanked out. As the splitting became bridged she could verbalise the suffering which the memories of those difficult years marked by these tragic events had brought her. However, she did not think this was healthy; she felt that she should be helped to forget and move forward in her life and leave all that weight behind her.

CONCLUDING REMARKS

In this chapter I have described some of the ways in which erotic transference can become manifest in analytic practice, and influence the analyst's countertransference. As emphasised elsewhere (Chiesa 1994), erotic transference is a complex phenomenon, which subsumes several determinants. It is by no means a homogeneous clinical entity and each manifestation in the therapeutic setting has to be approached with an open mind with regard to its dynamic significance. Some authors have stressed different aspects of the same problem, and have created a typology according to the way erotic transference presents itself in the analytic situation (Blum 1973; Bollas 1994; Bolognini 1994; Gabbard 1994; Hill 1994). I consider the various forms on a continuum between love and affectionate transferences at one extreme and erotised transferences at the other extreme. Detailed analysis will reveal that several aspects and functions operate at different degrees in the same patient: for instance, defensive, destructive and regressive elements were present in Ms A, who sought to ward off terrifying persecutory maternal and early Oedipal object representations, while seeking to destroy her therapy by seducing me. At the same time important dynamic work was achieved following analysis of her erotic feelings, enabled by the emergence of undisguised object relationships, which in turn recreated in the transference with me and the whole institution early experiences within her own family. Although her erotic transference continued through to the end of therapy, she made significant improvements in her life, which continued several years after the end of therapy. This case may add to the evidence brought by other authors (Bollas 1994; Lachmann 1994; Hill 1994; Kavaler-Adler 1992) who have stressed that the emergence of erotic transference, if properly handled, has facilitating, restorative, generative and therapeutic potential.

NOTES

1 Figures based on a PsycLIT database literature search which included the following journals: *International Journal of Psychoanalysis, Psychoanalytic Inquiry, Journal of the American Psychoanalytic Association, Psychoanalytic Psychotherapy, Psychoanalytic Review, Psychoanalytic Psychology, British Journal of Medical Psychology, International Journal of Psychoanalytic Psychotherapy, Journal of the American Academy of Psychoanalysis, Contemporary Psychoanalysis, Journal of Analytic Psychology,* and *Journal of Analytic Social Work.*
2 The therapy took place while Ms A was an in-patient in a London psychotherapy hospital.

REFERENCES

Blum, H.P. (1973) 'The concept of erotized transference', *Journal of the American Psychoanalytic Association* 21: 61–76.
Bollas, C. (1994) 'Aspects of the erotic transference', *Psychoanalytic Inquiry* 14: 572–90.
Bolognini, S. (1994) 'Transference: erotised, erotic, loving, affectionate', *International Journal of Psychoanalysis* 75: 73–86.
Britton, R. (1989) 'The missing link: parental sexuality in the Oedipus complex', in J. Steiner (ed.), *The Oedipus Complex Today*, London: Karnac.
Chiesa, M. (1994) 'Some thoughts on erotic transference', *Psychoanalytic Psychotherapy* 8: 37–48.

Freud, S. (1912) 'Recommendations to physicians practising psychoanalysis', *Standard Edition* 12, London: Hogarth Press.

—— (1915) 'Observation on transference love', *Standard Edition* 12, London: Hogarth Press.

Gabbard, G. (1994) 'On love and lust in erotic transference', *Journal of the American Psychoanalytic Association* 42: 385–403.

—— (1995) 'The early history of boundary violations', *Journal of the American Psychoanalytic Association* 43: 1115–36.

—— (1996) 'The analyst's contribution to the erotic transference', *Contemporary Psychoanalysis* 32: 249–73.

Gabbard, G. and Lester, E.P. (1995) *Boundaries and Boundary Violations in Psychoanalysis*, New York: Basic Books.

Hill, D. (1994) 'The special place of the erotic transference in psychoanalysis', *Psychoanalytic Inquiry* 14: 483–98.

Joseph, B. (1993) 'On transference love: some current observations', in E. Spector-Person, A. Hagelin and P. Fonagy (eds), *On Freud's Observations on Transference Love*, New Haven, CT: Yale University Press.

Kavaler-Adler, S. (1992) 'Mourning and erotic transference', *International Journal of Psychoanalysis* 73: 527–39.

Lachmann, F.M. (1994) 'How can I eroticize thee? Let me count the ways', *Psychoanalytic Inquiry* 14: 604–21.

Spector-Person, E., Hagelin, A. and Fonagy, P. (eds) (1993) *On Freud's Observations on Transference Love*, New Haven, CT: Yale University Press.

Part III

Sexual abuse and its impact on psychotherapy

9   A sense of all conditions

Fiona Gardner

This chapter explores the erotic transference and countertransference in psychotherapy with patients who were sexually abused as children. Child sexual abuse causes pathogenic and distressing effects and in the first section of the chapter the outer and inner disorder is considered. In the second section aspects of the erotic transference and countertransference are discussed and then five key aspects are highlighted and illustrated through clinical material. In the final section it is suggested that the analytic setting provides a structure for transformation of what previously may have been felt as perverse and abusive into something more creative and potentially healing.

The title of this chapter is taken from the Journal of George Fox, the founder of the Society of Friends, who in 1647 described his developing awareness of all aspects of the human condition, including what he experienced as the most depraved, within himself. Despairing of why he needed to know about such terrible feelings, he reached an understanding that it was only with 'a sense of all conditions' that he would be able to 'speak to all conditions', and that this was the path for potential healing and transformation. This process of deeply examining our own personal experience and responses is an integral part of the construction and validation of psychoanalytic meaning with the patient; we can understand what we know something about.

THE PSYCHOLOGICAL AFTER-EFFECTS OF SEXUAL ABUSE

A comprehensive summary of the after-effects of sexual abuse is an extremely complex task because of the variety of factors to be included: for instance, the age of the child, the life circumstances, the frequency of the abuse, and the degree of aggression and physical damage involved. There is a high likelihood of depression, suicide attempts, low self-esteem, alienation, distrust, sexual acting out, problems with sex and self-destructive behaviours. The need is to know how the abusive event(s) are taken up into the patient's imaginative life, the psychological significance. The inner disorder may be reflected through some of the following: dissociation or split-off parts of the person, altered states of consciousness, repeated highly emotional relivings of the trauma, and the somatic manifestations of the repressed traumatic memories (Gardner 1990).

There would appear to be a correlation between the depth of the trauma and the degree of powerlessness experienced by the child during the sexual acts. It has been found that one of the most frequent complaints of survivors entering therapy is a sense of feeling different and distant from others. This sense of an absence of feeling is most marked in sexual relationships. In some cases this psychic closing off is clearly a defence against the feelings aroused by the molester during the childhood experience. Passive resistance and dissociation of feeling appear to be among the few defences available in an overwhelming situation. Later it carries over into relationships with others. The real-life abuse is not itself part of the patient's psychological world: it is part of reality, or what Lear (1996) refers to as 'objective space-time' which has helped to shape the psychological world. The experience and interpretation of the abuse are internalised at least partly in unconscious form and repetitiously evoked, though not necessarily recollected in conscious life; for example, through later relationships including the psychotherapeutic relationship.

The dissociation and inability to remember the abuse paradoxically reflect a disordered inner preoccupation with it and relate to the fact that no child could integrate such a mind/body assault. The child is unable to integrate the abuse adequately at the level of its whole psychosomato-affective existence. The trauma may be grasped and interpreted by the child some time later than his or her original observation of it, by 'after-revision' or 'deferred action' at a time when he or she can put it into words. However, in the inner world of the child the trauma may remain 'thing-like' with little room for the use of fantasy and for metaphorisation.

The physical concrete nature of the actual abuse appears to extinguish all but the echo of sexual fantasy and leave behind the accompanying guilt. The echo of the fantasy is replicated within the body if there is a body response whispering of a sort of gratification. For if the child experienced any erotic or sexual pleasure during the abuse there may be an idea about the 'betrayal of or by the body'. If the child knows then or later that this should not be something to be enjoyed, there is a sense of the body colluding with the aggressor and in conflict with the child's own mind. Inevitably this effects the experience of the erotic transference in the therapeutic relationship.

The after-effects of this mind/body assault involve mind and body memories and resonance. The abuse is about inappropriate touching and intrusion of both mind and body, and the child's sexuality in part fantasy and in part unknown and repressed is pushed into prominence. The child becomes fearful of their own desires and of the desires of others, and fearful of further attack on mind and body, and these fears tend to be active when later the survivor enters psychotherapy (Gardner 1993).

TRANSFERENCE AND COUNTERTRANSFERENCE ISSUES

One of the aims in psychoanalytic psychotherapy is to encourage and develop, partly through interpretation, the manifestation of the transference as one aspect of the interpersonal relationship with the therapist. The therapist is able better to understand the compromise formations, the solutions to conflicts at various stages of development that continue into adult life as fantasies, symptoms, character traits or adaptations. Both patient and therapist bring to the interactional process their own set of unconscious needs and expectations and this process is utilised to study the patient's intrapsychic externalisations (Loewald 1970).

Transference as an interpersonal phenomenon attempts to create an idiosyncratic world of meaning, a private version of shared cultural values (Lear 1993). In the transference relationship the patient endows the therapist with meaning and expects the therapist to behave accordingly. The present immediacy of the transference relationship is a microcosm, a world of present unconscious fantasy shaped by past internalised relationships. Transference can be seen as a dialectical term, taking the form of either a fully experienced relationship between patient and psychotherapist or as a structured conflict among intrapsychic forces.

Freud (1920: 19) wrote about the inevitable characteristic of repressed material to break through 'the pressure weighing down on it and force its way either to consciousness or to a discharge through some real action'. The transference is activated into intrapsychic conflict within the patient and so into a fantasy about the interpersonal relationship with the therapist, there is a shift towards fulfilment of that fantasy, a movement from thought to action, and from the unconscious into the potential for conscious recognition. The patient is searching for a relationship with the therapist that repeats and so confirms the patient's fantasy expectations, but also for a new love object that might heal and gratify. At the same time the therapist has their transference, the externalisation of their own internal conflicts, and their countertransference, their own emotional reaction towards the patient's projected transference. In turn the patient has their countertransference towards the therapist's transference and behaviour, and all these erotic energies contribute to the interactional field and what White (1996) describes as 'a feedback loop' between patient and therapist.

However, there needs to be a level of difference in the psychological organisation of the therapist and that of the patient whereby the therapist can communicate meaning and thereby facilitate order for the patient. In the therapeutic work with people who have been sexually abused, as distinct from those who have not, there often appear to be five key aspects that permeate the erotic transference both in the sense of the interpersonal relationship and through intrapsychic conflict within the patient. The first is the traumatic sexualisation of dependent behaviours; second, the sense of the betrayal of trust and responsibility by a significant adult; third, the sense of powerlessness; fourth, a sense of guilt; and finally, a sense of the mind of the abuser as experienced by the child. All five aspects are intertwined but I shall separate them to discuss the issues raised in the context of the transference and countertransference and use clinical examples from work with both adults and older adolescents.

In their widest sense all therapeutic transfers of energies are erotic and therefore the erotic aspects of the transference are present always. However, the psychological significance of the actual abuse may lead to transference manifestations that appear erotic but perversely so. As child sexual abuse is a perverse form of relationship based on the gratification of an adult's desire at the expense of the child's needs so such an experience can contaminate future relationships. To some extent this is encouraged in the analytic relationship so that such manifestations of the transference may be brought to consciousness, broken through interpretation, and some insight and relief from past trauma gained by the patient. The perverse erotic transference based on the abusive relationship is brought to the therapy alongside other transference relationships, and in the countertransference the therapist can gain a sense of the trauma alongside other aspects of the patient's inner world, for it is possible to feel that the actual trauma can dominate the therapy and this may be linked to the actual intrusion into the fantasy life of the child.

The sense of the sexualisation of dependent behaviours

The erotically charged energies of the transference and countertransference are present and potentially felt within the psyche and the bodies of both therapist and patient, as well as in the field between and around the analytic couple. Donleavy (1995) writes of the erotic desire for merger as a demonstration of a psychic split that needs to be healed and a desire for wholeness. This is not for physical merger, rather for a form of psychic resonance which leads to new intrapsychic wholeness and is a possible opening for psychic transformation. Nevertheless in work with patients abused as children the erotic energies that initially emerge into consciousness appear to be more complex.

Aspects of the psychological significance of the abuse are repeated in the transference to the therapist and there are different thoughts on the meaning behind this need. One is that the repetition is a way of mastering the earlier trauma by a working through via an emotional experience; another is that the repetition is related to the most instinctual parts of our unconscious, a form of sado-masochism. In therapeutic work there is a chance to explore the unconscious need to repeat as transformational and/or as self-defeating for both elements may be blended in a given action or exchange. It is sometimes possible to make out the construction of a script, the main aim of which is to undo childhood traumas and conflicts by converting these earlier abusive experiences to present (fantasised) triumphs.

The sexualisation of dependent behaviour may be overt to the therapist and yet unconscious in the patient, as in psychotherapy with a middle-aged female patient who sometimes sat with her legs apart, revealing her underwear, once removing her trousers ostensibly to dry them from the rain and in the process, half pulling off her pants. On the couch she lay for a while 'the wrong way round' with her legs apart and skirt ruffled up. As the therapy progressed this patient felt increasingly young, vulnerable and dependent, she would sit on the floor, or on the couch, legs apart, sucking her thumb, and call me 'my love' and 'darling'. The patient appeared to have been deprived of appropriate affection and these demonstrations felt uncomfortable and not erotic. The transference elicited was a maternal non-intrusive and non-abusive one, and I was left with a sense of her need for protection.

One dilemma for the therapist lies in working with the identification in the transference as abuser, and therefore the patient's experience of psychotherapy as associated with molestation or intrusive attack. This is a perverse variant of the erotic transference and countertransference. A young female patient found it very hard to talk about herself. She could tell me about other people or events, but interpretations linking such descriptions to her own state were denied. Over the months the patient slowly withdrew, becoming increasingly uncomfortable and uneasy in my presence. The tension increased with bursts of self-deprecation and despair. She said: 'It's only when I'm here that I think of my father'. In the transference I brought to mind her abusive father, and her defence throughout was against experiencing any therapeutic intercourse with me. Fusion with the abuser/therapist implied disintegration and the threatening of her very being. Her dislike of my transference interpretations compared with her self-deprecating masturbatory use of the sessions. Excluding me emphasised her sense of personal autonomy and mastering of events. These defensive manoeuvres had to be used in an attempt to abreact the abuse and in a sense emotionally survive the assault as she re-experienced it in the therapy. The confusion and sexualisation of the relationship with her father were repeated in the transference, and there seemed no way to reach her. She needed to disregard what was happening between us in order to preserve a precarious and predominantly defensive psychic equilibrium, and eventually chose to finish the sessions finding it too painful to continue. Her strong transference response made all interpretative work and attempts to break the transference through emphasis on the working alliance difficult. In the countertransference I experienced feelings of hopelessness and despair of ever reaching the patient, but also a determination to try and understand the dynamic so as to help break it. The consolation seemed only that the patient had been able to deny me the intimacy forced on her by her father.

The sense of betrayal

Psychotherapy with an 18-year-old girl showed that the betrayal of family trust was the most hurtful aspect of her abusive experiences and this in turn had serious implications in the transference relationship.

The patient was aged 9 when over a three-day period she was seriously abused by a much older stepbrother (then a man in his late 20s). He had told her that her father with whom she was then living knew and approved of what was happening, and indeed when all appeared normal at breakfast the next morning the girl took this as confirmation. This belief remained for many years, and the sense of betrayal was compounded when she later disclosed the abuse to a therapist at a residential unit. Despite the girl's pleas not to do anything the therapist had to follow guidelines and involve the father, stepmother, social services and the police. The ramifications were extensive and disturbing. When I began to see the patient a few months later her confidence and trust in adults was low and her anxiety during the session high. It seemed that I was to be regularly tested and the slightest slip felt as an enormous betrayal.

Three years into the twice-weekly treatment a serious incident occurred. The stepmother allowed her abusive son into the flat when the patient was visiting (he had been banned for many years). The patient was terrified by the experience which again felt as a betrayal, and this seemed to evoke the betrayal by the first therapist. A similar dynamic was re-enacted within the sessions and became actualised when she began to misuse her antidepressant medication and told me about this, at the same time forbidding me to say anything to the psychiatrist involved in prescribing. I understood that the betrayal by the first therapist represented the greater betrayal by the family at the time of the trauma, and that I was being tested to see if I too would repeat this experience. The difficulty was to hold her self-destructive behaviour until she could accept my understanding and interpretation of what was happening between us.

In the interpersonal transference was the expectation that I would betray her confidence as she had experienced with her first therapist and stepmother, but also the expectation that I would, like her father, collude with the abuse she was perpetrating on herself. The intrapsychic conflict was between the internalised experience of the abuser and the abused. In my countertransference I felt unaffected by the danger of the drug misuse and, even when the danger was pointed out to me by the very concerned psychiatrist, this seemed to reflect the patient's own dissociation both from the abuse and other self-destructive behaviours. Later I allowed feelings of anger and hopelessness to surface, along with a sense of feeling trapped by the patient's resistance. This again demonstrated a perverse aspect to the erotic transference and countertransference.

The sense of powerlessness

Issues of power and control are fundamental in the abusive relationship and as pertinent in the therapeutic relationship. Technical issues of lying on the couch and payment always require awareness but take on further implications in this situation. The way interpretations are heard and incorporated may also reflect the effect of the abuse. Dorey (1986) in his analysis of 'mastery' defines it as a tendency to neutralise the wish of the other using a technique involving seduction. The victim will experience being both the dominator and the dominated. Dorey suggests that in relationships the victim feels that he or she is really threatened in their autonomy and their very identity is being denied. Re-enacted in the transference this may lead to the therapist experiencing in the countertransference the anxiety of the threat of obliteration, as well as the experience of both helplessness and violence commensurate with the degree felt and inflicted on the child.

In psychotherapy with a female patient the issue of her powerlessness to effect her own will emerged in the transference. She would come to sessions saying that she had nothing to talk about and felt terrible, and in the countertransference I experienced a sense of immense and exciting power. Despite interpreting what I thought was going on, the projection was diffused only when the patient herself took physical control and left the room during a session. I remained seated explaining that I would stay until the end of the session time. Although the patient left the building, she returned after ten minutes, explaining that she could not return to the room. I suggested that we sit in another room which was free and where we would be undisturbed. This felt less tense and the patient was able to understand and speak about what she felt was happening. She had physically mastered her earlier paralysis and done what she needed to do to prevent a repetition of the experience of powerlessness. Although the experience became actualised and enacted it was possible then to link the actions with thoughts and words. The energies in the transference and countertransference that had felt perverse and negative became less so.

The sense of guilt

The sense of guilt can be conscious, partly conscious or repressed and not accessible. Children usually feel that things are their fault, so it is not unexpected that there is a sense of guilt around the idea that something wrong and secret happened, and that if the child were part of it then it must be their fault. The child as innocent often carries the guilt of the adult abuser, and this may be manifested via masochism and a need for punishment. One aspect of the guilt is a feeling that somehow as a child they could have stopped the repetition of the abuse and not returned to the abusive situation.

In psychotherapy with a male patient this issue emerged very quickly. He was sexually abused from the age of 6 to 9 by a family friend. As an adult he described the abuse as brutal, sordid and often very painful. He had to dress in girls' clothing and elaborate rituals proceeded the actual abuse. His mother failed to comment on what he now thought must have been obvious physical injuries. In the countertransference my feeling of being abused and my sense of guilt and confusion about the way he responded to me became the most important clues to understanding his inner state of intrapsychic conflict and terror. He left me feeling that I had to respond directly to the fear and terror of the abuse that he described, while he remained low in affect and matter of fact about the experiences. My guilt became that of doing further violence to him as a patient alongside the violence he had experienced as a boy. I was also left feeling physically sick, resentful and desperate to speak to any available colleague to help me make sense of my experience.

The sessions were always about the abusive events, it seemed as if he spoke as the abuser and the abused. He wanted to know why he kept going back, and his own answer was that he must have enjoyed it. In the countertransference I experienced painful and uneasy feelings. The words did not fit the feelings in me and the lack of feelings in the patient. It seemed that his voice was the voice of the abuser who had been sexually gratified and excited, and I did note some sexual anticipation in myself when he described the rituals involved. The voice also explained 'how' he as a small child had survived the abuse. It emerged that he was told by the abuser to go off and play and forget about what was happening until the next time. As a child the patient had split off his feelings, and it was this dissociation that he brought to the sessions. In his transference to me as the abuser he forgot about what he was saying and spoke 'as if' nothing had happened, while unconsciously projecting his unwanted feelings of pain and fear.

I understood his return in the therapy to the painful details of the abuse as a defence against the terrible chaos and disintegration inside. The words describing the abuse within the therapy had become a denial of his deadness and feelings of non-existence other than as an object. He also needed me to respond to his injury in the way that his mother denied, and for me to have some sense of the scale of the abuse he had experienced. This patient showed that to survive you identify with the abuser and with the crime becoming one with the perpetrator. The price was carrying the guilt, the abuser's guilt and the child's own guilt through identification with the role assigned as the seductive child. The abusive relationship is usually a secret one that carries stigmatisation and it is this aspect of guilt in holding the secret that the abuser passes on to the abused, which is then brought to the therapeutic relationship.

A sense of the mind of the abuser

In each of these aspects already described it is apparent that because the experience of the abuse was perverse, a perverse variant of the erotic transference is brought to the therapy, although often alongside a positive transference to the therapist as a potential new love object. Each patient brings their experience of the mind of the abuser to the therapist either through conscious memory or unconscious communication and fantasy. In the countertransference this may require separation from the therapist's own sexuality and erotic imagination, and requires more than an analysis of incestuous desire. The shadow aspect of work with survivors is a recognition of the abuser's perverse sexual feelings towards children and his sense of their complicity in the act. For example, following work with an abused girl my feelings of horror became interwoven with an awareness of shameful excitement at the images of physical pain and intrusion on a small child. Discussion with a colleague helped me to separate the girl's internalised experience of the abuser and his pleasure from the horror of her pain and humiliation. Such a recognition can be repressed or denied, but is diffused of its power once it is understood and brought to consciousness. It is also possible to feel genital sexual excitement in the sessions, and again this needs careful analysis to separate out the therapist's externalisation of their own internal conflicts from projective identification. Stringent self-analysis needs to occur to recognise any unresolved incestuous desires, repressed experiences of sexual abuse, sexual fantasies or memories, and so to leave the therapist clearer to understand what the patient is bringing to the sessions. Supervision or consultation may be essential at times so as to bring a third party into what may feel an over-secretive dyad.

The mind of the abuser may be brought to the therapeutic relationship through the defence of identification with the aggressor, so that what was passive becomes active in an attempt to gain mastery over fear and boost self-esteem. It may be that aggression by the patient in a session can be a way of dealing with humiliation. One characteristic of a sense of the mind of the abuser is when the erotic excitement is permeated by a sense of humiliation. Stoller (1985: 31) writes of humiliation as a hidden presence in the erotic moment and the mechanism that makes up the excitement of revenge – humiliating another as payment for others having humiliated one. He suggests that humiliation is at work 'wherever sadism and masochism appear – for example, in paranoid (sadistic) or depressive (masochistic) responses . . . and shapes erotic life only when the attack is aimed at those parts of the body/psyche concerned with erotic or gender behaviour'. The abuser dehumanises his object in order to feel safe enough to get excited, and to avoid genuine intimacy, but in the process dehumanises himself. This process may become conscious in the therapeutic relationship through spoken responses or through recognition of feelings in either patient or therapist.

A STRUCTURE FOR TRANSFORMATION

The erotic energies that permeate the psychotherapy are often seen as reflecting the perverse nature of the trauma and while that is true there is also the sense in which the analytic setting can provide a safely structured environment where the abusive experiences can be isolated, held and understood, and potentially transformed. Without such transformation creativity is stultified and, though the patient may gain temporary relief, at a deeper level may be left compulsively to repeat their behaviour. The perverse erotic transference can be reduced and neutralised through the exploration of other aspects of the transference when the therapist is experienced as a benign and enabling object.

In psychotherapy with a woman who had been subjected to anal abuse as a child a series of dreams took her back to a state where she had control over her body. She reported a dream: 'I am lying in my bed and am beginning to feel uncomfortable. I think I'd like to shit, but I can then feel something coming out of my bottom. I can't see but when I look down I can see insects, spiders and cockroaches; they have come out of me. They are black and scuttle away'. A year later, a different sort of dream was brought to a session: 'I am at a meeting, people have been talking together and I've been taking part. As I point to some words on a piece of paper I look down and see that my index finger is sore at the cuticle. Instead of pus out of it pours sunflower seeds'.

The patient's associations to both dreams were that they were about the therapy. In her association to the second dream she linked it back to the first. A year on the therapy felt like something that she was taking part in, not something that was being done to her. The index finger reminded her of the gesture 'up yours', while the sunflower seeds she liked to eat and grow. The patient was able to see the painful part of her body that had become accessible to her. The outpouring of seeds implied a sexual aspect but had a pleasurable association. The first dream signalled the emergence of humiliating and sadistic elements of the abuse into the transference. As control became the issue in our relationship, so the patient regressed to a stage where she felt some mastery of her anus, as represented in the 'seeing' and the pleasurable outpouring of good stuff.

If the erotic transference is to emerge as with other patients, there has to be recognition of the incest taboo – the boundaries between parent and child need to be understood and kept. Once 'known' the taboo is repressed, and this potentially allows the fantasy of incestuous desires to be brought to consciousness. Wrye and Welles (1989) write that the erotic transference, if it is understood, can be potentially creative and transformational, although it can be defensively employed. They explore this through the maternal erotic transference and three dynamic aspects. The first is the rich sensuality of the mother–baby relationship; the second is the transformation from pre-Oedipal to Oedipal issues in the therapeutic relationship; the third is the adaptive aspect which represents a creative transformational attempt to make the therapist/mother into a living, more dimensionally integrated whole object. By such a route a healthy sense of 'adult' identification and adult sexual needs is reached.

Psychotherapy with patients sexually abused as children necessarily involves taking on perverse aspects in the transference and countertransference, and if these manifestations from the patient can be held and understood alongside the therapist's personal experiences, then it is possible further to expand awareness of the erotic transference as a way of creating a possibility for healing, creativity and increased spontaneity. By gaining this 'sense of all conditions' we relinquish both our fear and ignorance, and from that position are available to work with and respond to the deeply traumatised child in the patient. The erotic transference is a structure for transformation as the analytic relation is a re-creation of the early parent–infant relation and opens up the possibility of further re-creations both from the past and in the future. Loewald (1970: 297) writes of eros as constituting a field across which psychological contents and organisation may flow. And because the psychotherapist's communications tend to facilitate psychological growth in the patient there is reason to conceive of eros as developmental, and in that sense the analytic process can be seen as a manifestation of love. 'In our work it can be truly said that in our best moments of dispassionate and objective analysing we love our object, the patient, more than at any other times and are compassionate with his own being.'

REFERENCES

Donleavy, P. (1995) 'Analysis and erotic energies', in Murray Stein (ed.), *The Interactive Field in Analysis*, Illinois: Chiron Publications.

Dorey, R. (1986) 'The relationship of mastery', *International Review of Psychoanalysis* 13: 323.

Freud, S. (1920) 'Beyond the pleasure principle', *Standard Edition* 18, London: Hogarth Press.

Gardner, F. (1990) 'Psychotherapy with adult survivors of child sexual abuse', *British Journal of Psychotherapy* 6(3): 285.

—— (1993) 'Creating order out of abuse', *British Journal of Psychotherapy* 10(2): 159.

Lear, J. (1993) 'An interpretation of transference', *International Journal of Psychoanalysis* 74: 739.

—— (1996) 'The introduction of eros', *Journal of the American Psychoanalytic Association* 14(3): 673.

Loewald, H. (1970) 'Psychoanalytic theory and the psychoanalytic process', in *Papers on Psychoanalysis*, New Haven, CT: Yale University Press.

Stoller, R. (1985) *Observing the Erotic Imagination*, New Haven, CT: Yale University Press.

White, R. (1996) 'Psychoanalytic process and interactive phenomena', *Journal of the American Psychoanalytic Association* 14(3): 699.

Wrye, H. and Welles, J. (1989) 'The maternal erotic transference', *International Journal of Psychoanalysis* 70: 673.

10 From sexual misconduct to social justice

Andrew Samuels

Psychotherapy is a field that is divided about almost everything. We analysts just do not get along, whether in clinic, professional organization or academy. But one theoretical, practical and moral thing on which we all seem to agree is that sexual activity taking place in analysis and therapy is a profound abuse of power, is hence wrong, and therefore liable for punishment when discovered. It is one of the supreme values of psychotherapy. Another is that we should try to understand a problem, not merely seek to suppress or eliminate it.

What we know from the psychological study of incest is that when one meets a universal moral taboo with which everyone in a culture seems to agree, one is probably also in the presence of a universal impulse. No need for taboo without impulse. Therefore, the common view, that sexual behaviour in analysis and therapy is damaging to the patient or client – with which I am in total agreement – stems in part from a universal impulse and desire in therapists and analysts to engage in sexual behaviour in the session (Stein 1974).

On this issue, the public is right! The public is right to focus on sexual misconduct by practitioners of analysis and psychotherapy. As our social critic – perhaps even the term 'analyst' would be fitting – the public is having an empathically attuned response (which we could even call a 'countertransference') to our difficulties when it, the public, focuses on the question of sexual misconduct by practitioners. Of course, one could at this point cite the statistics and refer to the empirical research into sexual misconduct. But this is not the path taken by this essay. It is by now common ground that a significant amount of sexual and other misconduct by practitioners (mostly but not all male) is going on. The point I want to make is that we should not dismiss the public's concern as misinformed or as energized by its supposed unconscious conflicts or complexes. Outrageous as it sounds to say it, the public is a better analyst than that. (The best literature review that I know is by Schaverien (1995).)

The public has understood very well that intimacy between practitioner and patient or client may be the most important part of the process of analysis and psychotherapy. Maybe the public has grasped, if not yet articulated, the necessity of there being a sexual tone to analysis. Can psychotherapy respond to the concerns being expressed by its analyst, the public? I want to discuss certain issues that, in my view, will determine whether or not psychotherapy will respond positively and constructively. Taken together, these contentious issues enable us to make a move from the problem of sexual misconduct to matters of social justice. For I see public concern over sexual misconduct as providing a stimulus and an opportunity, not only to address the problem itself but also, on the basis of an engagement with sexual misconduct, for analysts to go on to make a contribution to several key issues of social justice.

SOCIAL JUSTICE

Social justice is, of course, a familiar term from politics and social science. As used here, the reference is not only to a set of abstract principles that might govern the formation of a 'good' or 'just' society. Following current usage in the United Kingdom, the idea of social justice also encompasses the organizational and cultural changes necessary to fashion such a society. Thus discussions about measures to alleviate poverty increasingly are not divorced from questions of constitutional change – for example, to a less rigid electoral and parliamentary system incorporating proportional representation, devolved government and a bill of rights. The Labour Party, prior to its election victory in 1997, set up a Commission on Social Justice to explore these issues and publish a report on them, so this kind of thinking is by no means a fringe phenomenon.

Gender issues are prominent when social justice is under consideration, and that is one reason why what might be thought of as the microcosmic phenomenon of sexual misconduct by analysts and other professionals is useful as both a symbolic and an intellectual entrée to social and political concerns. But there is also a wider background to my introduction of politics at this point.

In my book *The Political Psyche* (1993a), I suggest that politics in the West is experiencing a paradigm shift in which old definitions, assumptions and values are being transformed. Whereas politics will always be about struggles for power and the control of resources, a new understanding of all that is political has evolved since feminism introduced the phrase 'the personal is political'. This new kind of politics is often a feeling-level politics, or a politics of subjectivity, that encompasses a key interplay between the public and private dimensions of power. For political power is also manifested in family organization, gender and race relations, connections between wealth and health, control of information, and in religion and art. Hence, together with abstract principles of social justice and the organizational changes that are inspired by such principles we can add a frank recognition of psychology's role in political analysis – an awareness that there is something like a 'political psyche' to factor into political discourse.

It is the tragicomic crisis of our *fin de siècle* civilization that incites analysts to challenge some boundaries at the same moment that they reinforce others.

Conventional boundaries that might be challenged include those between the public and the private, the political and the personal, the external world and the internal world, life and reflection, being and doing, extraversion and introversion, politics and psychology; between the fantasies of the political world and the politics of the fantasy world. If we mount this challenge, then it is easier to accept that subjectivity and intersubjectivity have political roots. Constructed as they are, subjectivity and intersubjectivity are not nearly as private as they seem.

Psychology and the therapies can fill crucial roles in this late modern world we have made. Not only in the rich countries of the West, but also in Russia, Eastern Europe and the developing countries, politics and questions of psychological identity are linked as never before. This is because of myriad other minglings: ethnic, national, socioeconomic, ideological. The whole 'mongrel' picture is made more intricate by the exciting and rapid course of events in the coruscating realms of sexuality and gender.

Gender is *the* gateway or threshold between the public and the private dimensions of experience. Gender is an exceedingly private story we tell ourselves about ourselves; gender is also a set of socioeconomic and cultural realities. Recently I carried out an international survey into what therapists and analysts do when their clients bring overtly political material to the clinical setting (Samuels 1993a). Among the questions asked were some designed to find out which political issues or themes were most commonly introduced by clients. This survey went to two thousand practitioners from fourteen organizations of differing theoretical orientation in seven countries. Nearly seven hundred replied. In a worldwide table of issues, 'gender issues for women' came out highest for every group except German Jungian analysts. For their clients, the number one issue was the environment and gender issues for women came second. 'Gender issues for men' came fourth worldwide. The American groups that I surveyed, two well-established psychoanalytic organizations and three Jungian analytic societies, produced results broadly along these lines. The point here is not that these findings are surprising – they are not, given the liminality of gender referred to above. What is highlighted is that gender issues, which must include desire itself, and sociopolitical issues have become completely intertwined.

Taken overall, the responses to the survey suggest that the clinical office can be a bridge between the inner world and the political world as well as being the source of a divorce of the two worlds. This is why I do not support calls for the ending of the project of therapy and analysis. Clinical practice has been accused of being a bastion of possessive individualism and narcissistic introspection for a hundred years; it is not a new criticism. And it is right to criticize greedy and myopic clinicians who cannot perceive that their work has a political and cultural location and implication. But it is not right to indulge in simplistic, populist rhetoric that would do away with the entire clinical project. Without their connection to a clinical core, why should anyone in the world of politics listen to therapists and analysts at all?

The huff-and-puff rejection of the clinical forecloses what is, for me, a central issue: the relations between the private and the public realms of life. The funny thing about this foreclosure is that it mimics the attitude of the most conservative, dyed-in-the-wool clinicians and mental health professionals – the keep-politics-out-of-the-office types. As I see it, the high-profile apostates and renegades of therapy and analysis are as terrified and perhaps as incapable of exploring the relations between the personal and the political as are the fanatical adherents of therapy and analysis.

In this chapter I will first discuss the growing practice of what I call 'safe analysis,' meaning a style of analysis in which the exploration of sexual desire is repressed by the institutions of analysis themselves. It is a misplaced response to the problem of sexual misconduct which brings a whole new set of power problems with it. Second, I will try to show that a fresh look at the theme of incestuous sexual fantasy in family process is urgently needed. This would provide a broader theoretical base for the exploration of sexual desire in analysis. Third, I will attempt a retheorizing of the father in general and paternal sexuality in particular. The father is important here because more subtle understandings of his sexuality will benefit male and female individual practitioners when they become the father in the erotic transference and countertransference. Such understandings will also help our thinking and training about what Rutter (1989) calls 'forbidden zone relationships'. Moreover, new psychological thinking about fathers and the sexuality of men will have many sociopolitical implications (as I shall show later).

'SAFE' ANALYSIS

There is a consensus among practitioners that sexual desire in analysis is not what it seems. Sexual desire in analysis may be interpreted as transference, a defence, an infantile wish, a replication or recapitulation of a real event in the patient's past life, a zonal displacement (what is sought is not genital but oral or anal gratification), or there may be a narcissistic problem in the analyst. Relationship not orgasm is the secret goal of the sexually aroused patient. Power not orgasm is the secret goal of the sexually active male analyst as he replicates the power relations between men and women in our culture.

All of us who have practised or been in analysis know about the deliteralization of sexual desire by interpretation of it. In fact, without interpretation couched in the metaphorical language of deliteralization of desire, one might even ask if the work is psychological at all. But this leads us to a formidable problem. How are analysts to make interpretations about the metaphorical and symbolic dimensions of sexual desire in the analysis, how are they to explore sexual imagery and sexualized emotions, how can the myriad styles of object relating be revealed within monolithic sexual excitement, without there being something literal, actual, concrete, corporeal, real, experiential in either or both of the participants in the first place? But a reluctance to stay on or with this level, a reluctance presented now as a feature of much contemporary analysis, later as something to explore in family process, is a background part of the problem of sexual misconduct by practitioners. An analyst cannot make a symbolic interpretation of nothing without identifying that nothing; they cannot say much about the significance of a desire that is not, or not yet, embodied without apprehending that desire; they cannot respond to, say, the homosexuality within the relationship of a non-homosexual analysing couple without its being experienced in soma as well as in psyche. An analyst can certainly interpret the patient's reluctance to enter into the sexual material, but analysis of what is apparently absent or unthought is a different line of exploration altogether, depending even more than usual on a set of expectations about what should be there to be analysed. As my first training patient put it, when referring to her reluctance to meet the expectations of her analyst: 'An orgasm a day keeps the analyst at bay'.

The problem of safe analysis cannot be solved merely by noting the emergence of sexual arousal in the analytical relationship, for that state brings with it its own conundrum: how, when it is all so real, so infused with *physical* reality, are the analysing couple going to reach the very symbols and metaphors they are hoping to work with?

I do not think we can solve the problem by opting for certitudes: *this* sexuality is literal, *this* sexuality is metaphorical, *this* sexuality is both literal and metaphorical. The matter may be undecidable and resist foreclosure. A comparison may be drawn with the difficulty in maintaining a hard and fast line between images of literal and images of metaphorical parents in analytic material . . . *that* father literal, *that* father metaphorical. In and out of analysis, I have come to see that a new category is needed and is hard to name – a take on sexuality that is neither literal and hence prone to being acted upon, nor metaphorical and hence prone to abstraction and denial, nor both, which is the easy way out. *Neither* literal *nor* metaphorical as well as *either* literal *or* metaphorical: that is the new category.

The problem of safe analysis stems from and is exacerbated by the evolution of a style of analysis mainly based on object relations theory but practised by many analysts using a variety of appellations designed to distinguish the practitioner from adherents of the drive/structure models of classical psycho-analysis. It is analysis that has become dominated by the numinous power of the very mother-and-baby imagery it often sets out to explicate: analysis that gets into a panic over incestuous sexuality and flees into a milky *Weltan-schauung*. No ethics problem there. Now I do not expect any reader readily to own this style of analysis as theirs, and I am sure my racy depiction truly is, to some extent, a distortion, for some distortion of the views of others is inevitable in psychological dispute (see Samuels 1989, 1993b). But that does not mean that what I am saying is a lie as well! The style of analysis to which I am referring (which is increasingly influential worldwide) makes entry into the metaphorical and symbolic aspects of the sexual virtually impossible. In 'safe analysis', there is no sexual prima materia for the necessary symbolic work of the analytical opus. (See Samuels 1989: 175–93 for a fuller discussion of the use of the alchemical metaphor in relation to these matters.)

INCESTUOUS FANTASY IN FAMILY PROCESS

In examining the role of incestuous fantasy in family process, I think it is worth looking at a slightly different set of questions than are usually asked by psychoanalysts concerning sexuality in general and incestuous sexuality in particular. Different, I mean, from the questions on a Freudian agenda, crucial though that listing has been. Perhaps, following Jung's example, we should begin to explore once more the why and the whither of sexuality, as well as the what and the whence of it (Jung 1912). We might even overcome intellectual embarrassment to ask what is the psychological 'function' of incestuous sexual fantasy: what is it *for* beyond reproduction, why do we suffer and enjoy it, why is it as universal as the universal taboos suggest it is? What is the *telos*, the goal, the aim, the magnet, the aspiration, the prospect, the dream of human incestuous sexual fantasy? Where does human incestuous sexual fantasy lead – and do we need human incestuous sexual fantasy to get us there? Why is human incestuous sexual fantasy *constructed* by culture in the way it is? Let us make judicious use of teleology, of final causes. Perhaps Jung's teleology and phenomenology's stress on affective embodiment and lived experience will turn out to be compatible.

I want now to write directly about incestuous sexuality in the family. I will try to do it without idealizing either incestuous sexuality or the family. The central question, it seems to me, is, how do we grow? Or, put differently, how do personality structures become or *seem* to become more extended and encompassing over time? We may reply to the question, 'How do we grow?' by saying that it is all the outcome of psychological, biological and cultural interactions, or something anodyne like that. But insatiable curiosity continues to make me ask, *exactly* how does it happen, how does it work? One often invoked answer focuses on relationships in general and relationships with parents in particular. We can unpack certain implications of this. Getting really close to someone who is more developed than you are psychologically (whatever that 'more developed' might mean) leads to some kind of enhancement or enrichment or expansion of the personality by virtue of the extreme closeness. The idea that a person grows *inside* by relating to people *outside* who have qualities that he or she has not yet manifested is at the heart of all the depth psychologies.

We have to ask, then, what in our general human make-up enables us to get that close in the first place? If you are a parent and I am your child, and I need to be close to you to grow, close enough to internalize you, something other than my mere dependence on you is needed to make it happen. We cannot do it by willpower. It happens (and this is my point) by way of a variety of psychological processes, such as the build up of trust, the vicissitudes of ambivalence, mutual recognition and so forth; and these are, to a degree, held together and organized by ordinary human sexuality. The psychological function of fantasies of incestuous sexuality is to inspire and facilitate that multi-layered closeness we call love. This means that incestuous sexuality and the social bond are also interrelated just as pleasure and power are interrelated. Experientially, as parents know, sexual desire between parent and child means that neither of them can ignore the other. Is not that what adult sexual experience also suggests? When one is aroused, it has to be that individual, that precise one – a permitted, humane fetishism. Desire in a relationship guarantees the importance of that relationship, guarantees the *regenerative* importance of that relationship to both participants. It can and does go horribly wrong. It can and does get enacted and embodied. It can and does possess generation after generation. But incestuous sexual desire also has the function, the goal, the telos of providing the fuel for the means by which we get close to other people and hence grow. Then we can get into the early object relations algebra of projection, introjection, identification and internalization.

Physical incest results from incest fantasies that have, for whatever reasons, become enacted. We know that a child's fantasies cannot be adequately understood as the child wishing for intercourse with the parent. A response on that level is totally inappropriate. Adults who take their own incestuous fantasies or what are deemed or theorized to be those of children as such are mistaken and destructive. But I think that alongside a stress on the many adults who deliver excesses of sexual communication and attention to children, we should also try to explore the less apparent forms of abuse and deprivation in what could be called sexual deficit. Quite understandable and necessary concentration on sexual excess has made it very hard to speak of sexual deficit without being misunderstood as advocating incest or being indifferent to it.

At the height of the Cleveland crisis (a child sexual abuse episode in Great Britain), my then next-door neighbour, a man I do not like, confessed to me that he was frightened to cuddle his 2-year-old daughter in public. Media discussion of child sexual abuse was reinforcing difficulties that many fathers (in particular) have over physical aspects of their relationship with their children (not just with daughters, though we see it more clearly with daughters). Years later, when some daughters enter analysis, past inhibitions about bodily contact and apparent failure to establish a warm, shared physical rapport with the father turn out to have been very wounding. In a sense, these wounds are at the opposite extreme from the wounds caused by actual incest, but they generate their own brand of profound psychic pain. The understandable, appropriate and vital stress on the avoidance and detection of actual incest can mask this other problem.

I hope it is clear that I see similarities between this problem of sexual deficit in the family and the problem of safe analysis. Let us now consider the problem in terms of a retheorization of the father.

RETHEORIZING THE FATHER

Before developing my argument in detail, I want to mention a few important themes that I have omitted from this essay for reasons of space.

The father is not the only parent implicated in sexual deficit, any more than he is the only parent implicated in sexual excess; maternal sexuality has its own vicissitudes. Nor is some temporary and much-needed concentration on the psychology of the father relation an ignoring or depreciation of the mother. Nor are daughters the only victims. Mine is not a heterosexist text. Nor do single-parent families suffer in any inevitable and predictable way in regard to sexual deficit. On the basis of twenty years' research work with single parents, I maintain that the main deficit single-parent families suffer from is a deficit of money. The more work you do on the father, the more qualified your enthusiasm for him becomes – hence my coining of the term 'the father of whatever sex' (Samuels 1993a: 125–35). Nor is there any reason why two homosexual women or two homosexual men bringing up children together would be more likely inevitably to get it 'wrong' than so-called ordinary families. (And this may be the moment to say in print once again that no analytical or psychotherapeutic training programme that bars persons of homosexual orientation can ever be considered a good training, no matter how prestigious and productive the training appears to be. (See Samuels 1993b for a fuller account.))

Finally, in this list of necessary omissions, let me say that I do not deny the existence of different clinical dynamics according to the sexual combination and sexual orientation combination of the analysing couple. A great many papers claim to know the specific features of each combination (see Schaverien 1995). But let us be careful before indulging too freely in specificity here lest it lead to an omniscient efflorescence of new essentialisms: for example, the sexual transference–countertransference of female analyst and female patient is such and such; the sexual transference–countertransference of female analyst and male patient is such and such; homosexual orientation on the part of one or both participants in analysis does such and such to the sexual transference–countertransference. These differences need for the moment to be spoken with more diffidence, and it may be better to say 'We don't really know'. One thing we do not really know much about yet – not even what the terms of reference might be – is sexual misconduct by female practitioners. Female practitioners may sleep with their patients and they certainly experience sexual fantasies about patients of both sexes in the countertransference. But there may also be a kind of misconduct that we have not yet learned to recognize as such.

This would be a sort of maternal abuse, taking the form of overinvolvement with the patient and resulting in gratification of power urges in the analyst. Indeed, male analysts could also be guilty of such maternal abuse. These thoughts raise all kinds of questions about the relations between gender and power, which are surely a key element in any discussion about sexual misconduct. One thing that does seem clear about sexual misconduct on the part of female practitioners is that people are quite shocked and outraged to hear of it. This point emerges clearly in Eileen McNamara's (1994) account of the celebrated case in which the suicide of her patient led to charges of sexual misconduct being brought against a psychoanalyst.

At present I am in the middle of a small-scale informal research project in which, having elicited the sexual fantasies in relation to their clients of analysts of both sexes, the material is presented to a panel of experienced clinicians for review. The object of the exercise is to see whether or not there are specific styles of countertransferential sexual fantasy according to the practitioner's sex. A second panel examines the same material, but this time the material is doctored to remove indications as to the practitioner's sex. Both panels reach a broadly similar and unexpected conclusion, namely, that it is extremely difficult to put into words what, if anything, divides the male and female fantasies. The problem seems insuperable when the doctored version is under consideration. At the moment, the data are insufficient to permit more than anecdotal reportage, but it strikes me as an extremely interesting phenomenon.

Now back to the father. When Winnicott coined the phrase 'the good-enough mother' he had a number of aims in mind. Undoubtedly, he wanted to highlight the undesirability of either idealizing or denigrating the mother. He wanted to make sure that his ideas about mother–baby relating did not become some sort of persecuting ideal for mothers. He also sought to introduce the notion that a kind of graduated failure of mothering, leading to the possibility of there being feelings of hate between mother and baby, was a good thing. Mutual hate was a vital step on the road to achieving what Winnicott called 'unit status'. To be good enough, a mother had to be able to fail, to become a very bad mother indeed, and to hate her baby as much and as thoroughly as her baby fantasized she did. The good enough *father* has not been written about very much. Why not? Why do we prefer either to idealize or to denigrate the father? What would graduated failure of fathering look like? What can psychology say about the nature and quality of the relationships in which the good enough father participates? He only exists in relationship, after all.

Retheorizing the father is necessary for psychoanalysis in particular because it is becoming clearer that psychoanalysis has introjected an image of the father that is politically biased, reflecting a specific historical and social moment in Western culture. When Winnicott (1968) disputes the seriousness for a small baby of having a psychotic father (as opposed to a psychotic mother) or when he speaks of the father showing his gun to the children as a way of explaining what the outer world is like in 1944, it reeks of cultural and historical contingency. Yet psychoanalysis worldwide continues to offer what I call the 'insertion metaphor' as the penetrative unwavering root image of the father's psychological role in early life. The pre-Oedipal father is supposed to insert himself, like a giant depriving and separating penis, between mother and baby who would otherwise stay locked in a psychosis-inducing and phase-inappropriate symbiosis. In fact, the distinction between Oedipal and pre-Oedipal begins to look increasingly artificial and defensive. In Margaret Mahler's amazing language, the father awakens a 2-year-old from sleep and turns that child towards the (or is it his?) world (Mahler 1971). This comforting but reactionary story about fathers – father holding mother who holds baby – with its third-term denial of the detail of a more direct relationship with children is one that urgently requires critique, not least because of the appalling insult to mothers and to babies contained in the notion that they have no commitment and no capacities in themselves to becoming separate. Do mothers and babies really want to be psychotic? Moreover, what is so wonderful about the rapture of psychoanalytic separateness, rapture over the strong ego, a question well posed by feminist theorists (e.g. Jordan *et al.* 1991) on both sides of the Atlantic?

And what if Lacan's father turned out to be – well – Lacan's father, Lacan's Dad, Lacan's old man, Lacan's pater, a French pre-First World War bourgeois father, and not a metaphor at all? It would be ironic if the 'third-termism' of Lacanian psychoanalysis itself turned out to be a culturally and historically contingent production, a highly conventional developmental psychology. Unlike some, I do not look to France for a solution of what is often presented as an Anglo-American problem over the father. (See Samuels 1993a: 138–42 for a fuller discussion.)

Retheorizing the father will have profound sociopolitical implications in the long term. But there are also some shorter term gains to be made. We can achieve a more subtle understanding of paternal erotics and even of male sexuality, understanding these as historical constructs and hence relative and mutable. Such understandings would dispute Klein's locus for the father's penis, moving it from inside the mother's body and reattaching it to the father's body.

'What of Jung?' readers will ask. Because of the absence of a coherent developmental psychology in Jung's own writings, the post-Jungians have had to be in close attendance on psychoanalysis here (see Samuels 1985: 133–72). And, as we have seen, today's psychoanalysis is mother centred. Crucially, Jung overlooks the way in which father–child relationships are built up as he seeks to identify the essential and invariant features of such relationships. But if we do explore the father–child relation, we see that, in most cultures, it is made up out of the interaction of two other relationships – between mother and child, and then between woman and man. A man does not become a father in any formal sense unless something happens between these two other relationships. What that 'something' is and what the father does varies from culture to culture and across time. Nevertheless, to be a father in a full emotional sense a man needs to have a connection to the woman and for her to have a connection to the child. It is still a direct, primary relationship, still passionate and intense, but it is a constructed, discovered relationship. Actually that makes the father–child relationship no different from the mother–child relationship, which, as many writers have shown, is not as natural, biological, innate and given as we used to think. Motherhood has a history; it changes over time (see Badinger 1981).

Realizing that the father himself is a culturally constructed creature of relationship leads to all kinds of rather exciting possibilities. If the father relation is always a product of two other relationships, and hence of culture, then it cannot be approached via absolute definition; it is a situational and relative matter. If we can face this, then we will sense that a new judgment is required on our part towards what seem like hopelessly idealistic and Utopian attempts to change the norms of father's role. The father's role *can* change because written into father's role is the refusal of an absolute definition of it. This refusal is made possible, not to put too fine a point on it, because of male power and because of the historical and cultural mutability of the father relation that I have just described. Hence, in one sense of the word, the only 'archetypal' element in connection with the father is that there is no archetypal element in connection with the father. In full paradoxical form: the archetypal thing about the father is that he is culturally constructed.

Let me ground this outrage at once with something from empirical research. It has been generally agreed that fathers and mothers universally play very differently with their children and that these differences can be clearly seen on videos. Fathers are more physical, outgoing and so forth. Mothers are quieter and encourage more reflective play. The picture seems logical and eternal. But if we observe videos of the play of fathers who, for whatever reason, are the sole or primary caretakers of the children, their play resembles that of mothers (see Raphael-Leff 1991: 372, 533). Fathers can change. Maybe men can change. Moreover, the lesson we learn from multicultural experience, that differing cultures do the family thing differently, not always along nuclear lines, reinforces this challenge to the conservative deployment of archetypal theory.

If fathers can change in principle, and if there is no father archetype of the kind that would hold us back here, then what can we do to help the process along? For bringing the good enough father into existence would truly mean the dismantling of the patriarchy we all say we want. We can learn a good deal from crosscultural studies of fathering patterns and practices that make it difficult to hold to 'archetypal' certitudes.

It is not enough to set up a nostalgia game in which the traditional family is portrayed as that which can salve all, but especially male, wounds. Anyway, what was this 'traditional family'? It is becoming ever more apparent that the so-called traditional family, the one politicians and some leaders of the men's movement encourage and exhort us to get back to, with its clear demarcation of roles on the basis of gender, is not really the 'traditional' family at all (Seccombe 1993). The stable family unit in the Western countries between 1850 and 1950 was only one step in the ever-changing trajectory of the family in our culture. If we glance back to 1780, in the early days of industrialization in Europe, we find a very different kind of 'traditional' family. For one thing, it was positively crawling with children, all of whom would be in work, whether at home or in a factory, from the earliest age. Married women too were working women in this traditional family. As the social historian Roy Porter points out, the move from the disorderly working family of the late eighteenth century to the sober, respectable unit that we see between 1850 and 1950 was mainly a response to economic change (Porter 1993). The family has always mutated in a duct with economic and industrial organization. That is one reason why it is so important not to fall for the temptations of underclass theory (see, e.g., Murray 1990) and pillory today's lone parents and their families. It is supine, ridiculous and nasty for analysts to fall in with the dominant ideology that yearns with scarcely disguised racism for yesterday's model family in today's marketplace. (I wrote this last sentence well before the publication of the underclass theorist Charles Murray's latest offering on race and intelligence – Hermstein and Murray 1994.) We merely contribute to an undermining of the levels of self-esteem in lone parent families.

Researching the depth psychological literature, it is still hard to find texts of paternal sexuality that depict its benevolent aspects as opposed to seizing on its undeniably malevolent ones. To the contrary, in my vision of it, the father's body may turn out to resist censure and to contain a hidden sanctioning of the cultural diversity and political emancipation of others, particularly his children. It has become common to note the mobility, enfranchisement and emancipation of men in contrast to the oppression and subordination of women. But very little has been said about the father's potential to carry a positive attitude towards the mobility, enfranchisement and emancipation of others. Perhaps some will feel that there isn't anything to say about it! It is certainly not something we can exhort or force fathers to do. Nevertheless, I suggest that images and experiences of paternal sexuality often carry a secret symbolism for social and political change. Regeneration and renewal stand alongside the far better known symbolism of an oppressive, repressive and static political order. This would be a far more radical argument than seeing the penis merely as a useful weapon for beating the mother back (a point Jessica Benjamin makes independently of my work in one of the very few psychoanalytic books to address any of these issues – Benjamin 1988).

But we cannot make use of a text or testimony that tells of the father's progressive reinforcement of political and social change until we acknowledge the potential existence of such a text, protect it from the vicissitudes of sexual deficit, try to avoid idealization, and then raise it to a level of consciousness that allows for entry into cultural discourse. The fact is, we still do not really know what fathers do or could do. If we did, then we could get on with the business of finding out how much or how little of fathering has to do with maleness.

THE FATHER AND SOCIAL JUSTICE

To put my various suggestions in a necessarily abbreviated form, mutual sexual communication that is not acted out – what I have called 'erotic play-back' – between father and daughter cannot be understood primarily as free-ing the daughter from symbiosis with her mother (see Samuels 1989: 77–91 and 1993a: 125–75 for fuller versions of these ideas). Rather, what flows from erotic playback is the daughter's own recognition of her erotic viability; an inner as well as an outer recognition. This helps to shatter the equation in her mind that woman equals nothing but mother. That, in turn, opens up the possibility of a simultaneous exploration and filling-out of psychosocial pathways in addition to motherhood: a spiritual path, a work path, a path that integrates her aggressive side, a path of sexual expression, maybe a path of celibacy. Crucially, there also have to be paths that are not male-oriented, that involve movement away from the father – for example, a path of solidarity and community with other women. Here, the mother's con-scious and unconscious attitudes to the psychosocial tensions within her own self come into the picture, but the present cultural reality is that there are limits to a mother's capacity to point to other ways of being a woman as alternatives to the singularity of motherhood.

Most fathers and most daughters know already that some kind of mutual renunciation of the hell of actual incest is going to have to happen. Provide we scan it with a politicized eye, such renunciation may be read as a negotia-tion by both daughter and father of what Judith Butler (1990) calls the 'heterosexual matrix' itself. And *both* (not just the daughter) benefit from this partnership. Safe analysis, no; safe incest, yes (to use Emmanuel Ghent's (1995) epigram).

My point is not that the father simply liberates the daughter or permits her to take up different psychosocial roles, including maternity if she desires it. No, the father–daughter relationship has something to do with the special contemporary problem of the plurality of differing psychosocial roles, the ways in which all those paths mentioned do or do not shake down for women into a workable inner and outer blend of oneness and manyness. Who can doubt that this will be one of the key sociopolitical issues of the next century? This psychological pluralism facilitates the daughter when she says to us 'Don't ask me to stay the same' and when she says to herself 'I'm me'. Nowadays, men are starting to speak in the same way.

For the son, erotic playback from the good enough father helps to lead to the growth of what I want to call 'homosociality'. (I am grateful to Sonu Shamdasani for pointing out this term to me; see also Sedgwick 1985.) It means a recognition that community-mindedness and non-hierarchical relating between males can exist alongside the pecking order and the rat race. Men can learn from other men and homosociality is illustrated by the ways in which the gay community has responded to AIDS, particularly at the time when AIDS was thought to be a problem only for homosexuals. Here we have practical and inspiring models for different variants of masculinity: love between men, as between father and son, as a kind of political praxis. Notice the paradox: many among the group of men regarded by Western culture as the least 'manly' have become the pioneers, the frontiersmen, the leaders in forging a fraternal way through a huge and hostile territory. What is pointed up here, of course, is the enormous diversity within the term 'men', and what is emerging from gay life and endeavour today may be reframed as the political telos or goal or end product of erotic playback between the good enough father and his son. In saying this, I have not forgotten that the category of homosexual is of relatively recent origin (Weeks 1985) and, as time passes, has less and less of a precise meaning. Indeed, the category of homosexual should really be abandoned. And I certainly have not forgotten what we learned from Foucault (1979–88) and others about homosexuality as the means by which our culture has sought to regulate everyone's sexual and social behaviour.

Specifically, dominant heterosexual culture has employed a fear and loathing of homosexuality in order to frighten men so that a man will be tied into the role of provider in the family, the one who must remain emotionally distant. The payoff for men has been access to economic and political power – though gay men, or groups of men living in poverty and homelessness, or physically challenged men, or African American men, or men in countries that have been invaded would certainly dispute that they possess effective political or economic power. We do have to take care when generalizing about men (see Dollimore 1991). In my thinking about the good enough father, I have come to see that a tremendous fear that the ordinary, devoted, good enough father will somehow be effeminate (which means homosexual) is perhaps the most difficult obstacle to overcome.

Father–son homosociality is a striking illustration of the upsidedownness of 'sexual dissidence' (Dollimore 1991). For daughters and for sons, the relationship they have with the body of their good enough father has implications far beyond the individual and private spheres. There is also the part such relationships play in the formation of social organizations in the public sphere. Erotic playback – not sex itself – can inspire cooperative activity in the political world. Is not desire also a social phenomenon? There are special bonds shared by those who share the same bondage (again, the use of this imagery evolved independently of Benjamin's pathbreaking work).

For sexual desire is primarily constructed. There is no unsocialized and ahistorical essential sexuality, no 'archetypal' sexuality that is innocent and individual prior to its acceptance of the role of serving society's economic, political and reproductive needs. In my view, sexuality is itself manipulated by gender, class, ethnicity and history. Heterosexual relationships are themselves rarely if ever relationships of mutuality and equality to the extent claimed (or promised). Many homosexual relationships, despite being marginalized and condemned, have this secret, dissident, queer power to destabilize and interrogate the so-called 'normal' at the centre.

THE GOOD ENOUGH FATHER OF WHATEVER SEX

When the father's body, and the penis, are the foci of attention the question of literalism cannot be avoided. Is the penis an anatomic organ in this context or a metaphor, a *signifier* of difference, a phallus? Or is it a bit of both? Or, as I hinted earlier, something in another category altogether? I want to turn to the social realm for a possible elucidation of this seemingly psychoanalytic problem (a nice reversal of so much depth psychological critique of culture, my own included).

Scanning the huge and passionate debate about lone parenthood in most Western countries leads to the suggestion that there is both more and less to fathers than the moral panic of such debate suggests there is. In many Western countries, as I pointed out earlier, we are witnessing a damaging and misleading idealization of fathers and the roles men play in families. It would be folly to base policy on this idealization. But the fact that there is an idealization is giving today's political debate about lone parenthood a marked psychological character: the politics are psychological and the psychology is highly political.

At the same time, we are witnessing the emergence of many new ideas about fatherhood that depict and sometimes advocate a father's active, direct emotional involvement with his children from the earliest age. The new models of fatherhood support an egalitarian, cooperative, non-hierarchical family, rather than just seeking a pointless restoration of father and his authority as the (flawed) source of rules and regulations – not to mention his role as the source of sexual and physical abuse of women and children.

As I see it, there are two crucial psychocultural implications of these new approaches to fathering. The first has to do with the debate that rages over the consequences (or lack of them) of lone parenthood for child development, especially or even exclusively when the lone parent is a woman. We could call this for convenience the 'lone mother question'. The second implication has to do with the equally tempestuous debate over what fathering is these days, even when it is done by men. We could call this the 'crisis in fatherhood question'.

The insight I want to share is that these two apparently different questions – the lone mother question and the crisis in fatherhood question – lead us in a surprisingly similar direction. Addressing one question helps us in engaging with the other. Both questions stimulate responses based on the same search, which is to find out what fathers do, or can do, that is life-affirming and related, beyond being at best a sort of 'moral presence' in the family (to use a phrase from the London *Times* of 19 November 1993).

If we do this, then I think we can begin to create and assemble a sort of psychological information pool or resource both for women bringing up children either on their own or together with other women, and for men contemplating or engaged in fathering. Such women are truly fathers of whatever sex when the father is revisioned as being able to be less like a patriarch. In saying this, we immediately undermine everything that our society assigns or wishes to assign to men. Anatomy would cease to determine parental destiny and the lone mother question would be thereby completely reframed.

There is a crucial sequence in which this project has to be carried out. Initially, we have to find out more about fathers, then move on to see if we can depict the father in a less hypermasculine way, and then finally address women. Can women do these things that male fathers do? Do they want to do them? The invitation is for women to assert their capacities to be fathers of whatever sex, which would make them good enough fathers, rather than setting them up to fail as phony ideal fathers. Men fail to be ideal fathers, too. I am not anticipating that women would choose to perform all of our list of fatherly functions, nor would they necessarily perform these functions (including erotic playback) in precisely the same way that men might perform them. But would that matter? Some may say that might be a pretty good thing! Difference does not mean deficit.

Gathering enough information about the father might enable women to decide how much of it they could do themselves. This is why I give twists to the usual formulations and propose that we perceive women who parent alone as good enough fathers. I am sure that many women who parent alone or parent together with other women are doing a lot of being a good enough father of whatever sex without naming it as such. This group of women represents an incalculably valuable resource. We need educational campaigns fuelled by some of these thoughts about gender politics and organized in some way around the images of the good enough father and the father of whatever sex. This could herald a whole new approach to parenting that taps into the fluidity in gender roles that has evolved since the Second World War and that is not going to be wished or legislated away by governments. You cannot pass Acts of Parliament that control what people feel and experience: that is what the collapsed totalitarian regimes in the East learned the hard way.

To those who have a negative gut reaction to the idea that women can be good enough fathers and play the father's role, I say: men, too, only *play* the father's role. Fathering does not come 'naturally' to men, along with penises and stubble; it has to be learned and every new father finds there are rules in our society about how to do it. There is a masquerade of manliness, a male masquerade (Riviere 1929). Women who father as good enough fathers of whatever sex may teach a thing or two to men who father, who knows?

I remember my daughter setting up a game with me by saying 'You be the daddy, Daddy' – and then, at some point in our family play, announcing 'Now I'll be the daddy, Daddy'.

This is the fundamental lived-experience point arising from all the academic work on the cultural construction of gender and its roles (see, e.g., Foucault 1979–88; Weeks 1985). Men already play the role of fathers as much as women will come to play the role of fathers. It is surely significant how much we all use this word 'role'. So, for the sake of completeness, I want to reverse what I have been saying. Men who look after very small children are not playing at being mothers one jot or tittle more than women who mother play the role of mother. Motherhood, too, is not as 'natural' as some people continue delusively to think it is. Maternity and paternity have evolving histories.

What of the question of the crisis in fatherhood, what fatherhood is and means for men? Let us see what happens if we make use of the same words and images but this time with a focus on fatherhood and men. We certainly need to make the role of the male parent more interesting and meaningful for our younger men who have, quite rightly in my view, started to reject a dictatorial, Jurassic style of fathering – even if their female partners are prepared for them to be like that, which, by and large, they are not. This refusal of male dominance by women, coupled with men's beginning to search for inspiring ideas about manhood and fatherhood, are crucial social and psychological changes on which the debate about fathers should be focusing. There is scarcely a social critic (feminist or non-feminist) who has not explored the question of what would happen if fathers were to become more active parents of very small children. Would such fathers eventually be able to present themselves as more 'sexy' than many 'new men' manage to do?

Men are being scrutinized nowadays in ways that hitherto they have scrutinized everyone and everything else. 'Men' has become a category, one of many, and not some sort of privileged vantage point. This huge change in Western consciousness does not mean that men and women now have identical agendas; I have become suspicious of simplistic calls for partnership between the sexes. Men will not give up their power that easily, and there is a lot of making up to be done. But the notion of partnership between the sexes in pursuit of social justice remains as an ideal to aim at.

Lone parent families need more resources, support and approval from the community and not less. In addition, we need to work out strategies for making sure that lone parents and their children are not simply seen as victims, deserving of the ministrations of well-meaning folk like me. Writing as a man, a father, an analyst and one who has researched into lone parenthood and fathering for nearly twenty years, I have come to see that, strange as it may seem, it is not the actual maleness of the person from whom we obtain fathering that is the key issue. Saying this does not mean that I deny difference between the sexes when it comes to parenting; I have already said that women and men might not do it in precisely the same way but that this might not matter very much. The main thing is that what happens in the relationship between the father of whatever sex and her or his children be good enough.

In this chapter, I have been trying to sketch out some of my ideas about what fathers do do, or can do, that go beyond discipline, order, morality and so forth. The essay is supposed to work on two levels, both derived from the focus on sexual misconduct: as a resource for women who parent alone, and as an agenda for contemporary men who want to father in a new way that is psychologically realistic. If some readers cannot agree with me, if the idea of a father of whatever sex being good enough just goes against everything they believe, I would ask merely that they note that it is possible to say it: it is *possible* to depict the father of whatever sex as a good enough father, it is possible to challenge the assumption that only a male can do 'fatherly' things. I would urge sceptical readers not to forget how many men do not or cannot do them before it is regarded as impossible for a woman to do them.

One way in which men in general are changing is that they are becoming more aware of a deal that they have made with our society. In this deal, the male child, at around 4 or 5 years old, agrees to repudiate all that is soft, vulnerable, playful, maternal and 'feminine' by hardening himself against these traits. In return, he gets special access to all the desire-fulfilling goodies that Western capitalism seems able to provide. Increasingly, and especially in midlife, men (including analysts and therapists) are becoming aware that the deal was not altogether a good one from their point of view. Among many experiences that are denied them by the deal, the experience of being a hands-on, actively involved father of very small children is the one that is most relevant.

I have always urged caution in relation to men changing. The parallel some men's movement leaders make with feminism and the women's movement is a fallacious one because of male possession of power and resources. (Also, to refer to the sobbing little boy inside every powerful man as 'feminine' is highly sexist.) We should certainly listen to what the empirical social scientists tell us about the unchanging picture in most households with men not looking after children, not doing their share of the chores, and being responsible for most of the sexual and physical abuse that is perpetrated.

But something is changing: the 'aspirational atmosphere' is changing. This is very hard to measure empirically, and the intuition of a depth psychologist sometimes does not pass muster when compared with 'real' social science. What we can say is that if men are changing, if we are about to see good enough fathers in larger numbers, then the very existence of male power takes on a new significance. The existence of male power means that if changes are taking place in the world of men and fathers there will be immense political and social effects in the not-too-distant future.

This is almost the key background political issue of our times and is certainly something mainstream politicians should pay attention to. I was in the United States at the time of the Anita Hill-Clarence Thomas congressional hearings (on the question of his sexual harassment of her and its impact on his nomination to the Supreme Court), and the implications of those events changed the American political scene. I think the attack on lone parent families and its aftermath are having a similar effect on politics in several Western countries. As I mentioned earlier, gender issues are especially important because gender is something that sits midway between the outer world and the inner world. Our subjective and public lives are riddled with gender issues (see Butler 1990). Indeed, one way of understanding the never-ending sex scandals in British and American politics is to see them as highlighting how shaky and shifting are our present images of masculinity and how problematic we are finding it to work out what are and are not acceptable modes of behaviour for men.

FROM SEXUAL MISCONDUCT TO SOCIAL JUSTICE

This is a list of the sociopolitical themes to which our exploration of sexual misconduct has led us:

1   Changing the pattern in which only women look after small babies;
2   Fostering a culture in which parenthood and work may coexist;
3   Working towards more cooperative and less hierarchical forms of social organization;
4   Getting a clearer understanding of male sexuality in general and paternal sexuality in particular so as to work better with the problem of child sexual abuse;
5   Changing how we define and what we expect from good enough families to include lone parent families and other transgressive modes of family life.

A sixth theme affects analysts and their clients. When supervising, I have found these ideas to be helpful in expanding the clinical repertoire, of analysts as fathers in the transference, especially female analysts.

To conclude: in spite of having written a good deal on many of these topics I felt more anxious about submitting this essay for publication than I can recall ever feeling before. I think this is because raising the issues involved in the problem of sexual misconduct is rather confidence-sapping. I do not want to be heard as saying that psychic pain is caused (in a positivistic sense) exclusively by sexual deficits in inner world, family or society. Nor do I want to be understood as saying that the mere overcoming of such deficit in analysis would be some kind of personal or social panacea, or would stop sexual misconduct by practitioners.

The difficult thing to do is to move from a consensus about ethical ideals to a consensus about ethical practices when sexual (or other) misconduct takes place. From a British perspective, it long ago became clear that the private psychotherapy organizations (including the psychoanalytical ones) are not adequate for the self-policing of the professional practitioners they have produced. Other European countries report the same difficulty, as meetings of the European Association for Psychotherapy have demonstrated. The cross-profession organizations that have emerged in many countries must take on a role in this area. It follows that any cross-profession organization worth its salt should equip itself with powers to intervene or function as a court of appeal in relation to complaints. What this would mean for the United States is a national psychotherapy umbrella organization covering all the therapies, not just psychoanalysis. Such a body might itself have to be organized along 'federal' lines, with each professional orientation having some (but not unlimited) 'state's rights' and the federal part having equally limited and clearly defined powers.

We need to talk more about the nuts and bolts of 'worst case scenarios'. For example, what kind of procedures will be needed if an analyst and client decide that they want to convert their relationship into a non-professional relationship – get married, say? What do we think about cooling-off periods? Or should there be an absolute ban as there is now in California? And how much (if any) of this should apply to supervisor and supervisee? Another crucial question concerns what to do about perpetrators. Can they ever be rehabilitated? Under what conditions? Can treatment of the perpetrator ever be true analytic psychotherapy given its manifest agenda of rehabilitation?

The way I see it, the exposition and development of new and better theory – what I have been trying to achieve in this essay – is a central and pressing requirement. New theory inspires and is inspired by new moral and ethical attitudes leading to changes in practice. We can, however, reframe this question of theory by saying that in the public expressions of concern over sexual misconduct by analysts and therapists (concern, that is, over sexuality in analysis), collective awareness has provided all of us in depth psychology – clinicians, patients, academics – with a marvellous stimulus. Responding to the stimulus is more than having to put our house in order. It is more than an exercise in discipline and regulation, absolutely vital though that is. It is more than an attempt to refresh our theories and ideas about sexuality. It is more than a matter of trying to heal, or at least to ease, the crisis of our incurably wounded profession, because some sexual misconduct is always going to occur. Above all, responding to the stimulus provided by the public in its role of 'analyst of the analysts' might give us a slightly better basis from which to make a contribution on the levels of social and political justice.

SUMMARY

Sexual misconduct by analysts and psychotherapists is a topic that causes great public concern. The profession should certainly respond to this concern. But the problem of sexual misconduct also provides a stimulus to new theorizing leading to an engagement with issues of social justice. I argue that there are three contentious issues. First, I criticize the growing practice of 'safe analysis', seen as a misplaced response to the problem of sexual misconduct. Second, I urge a fresh look at the theme of incestuous sexual fantasy in family process: this would provide a broader theoretical base for the exploration of sexual desire in analysis. Third, I seek to retheorize the father in general and paternal sexuality in particular. New thinking about paternal erotics turns out to have many sociopolitical implications.

REFERENCES

Badinger, E. (1981) *The Myth of Motherhood*, London: Souvenir Press.

Benjamin, J. (1988) *The Bonds of Love*, London: Virago.

Butler, J. (1990) *Gender Trouble*, London and New York: Routledge.

Dollimore, J. (1991) *Sexual Dissidence*, Oxford: Oxford University Press.

Foucault, M. (1979–88) *The History of Sexuality*, London: Allen Lane.

Ghent, E. (1995) Personal communcation.

Hermstein, R. and Murray, C. (1994) *The Bell Curve*, New York: Free Press.

Jordan, J. *et al.* (1991) *Women's Growth in Connection*, New York: Guilford.

Jung, C.G. (1912) 'Symbols of transformation', *Collected Works* 5, London: Routledge & Kegan Paul.

Mahler, M. (1971) 'A study of the separation-individuation process: and its possible application to borderline phenomena in the psychoanalytic situation', *The Psychoanalytic Study of the Child* 26, New Haven, CT: Yale University Press: 403–27.

McNamara, E. (1994) *Breakdown*, New York: Simon & Schuster.

Murray, C. (1990) 'Underclass', in D. Anderson and G. Dawson (eds), *Family Portraits*, London: Social Affairs Unit: 2–29.

Porter, R. (1993) 'Review of *Weathering the Storm* by W. Seccombe', *London Sunday Times*, 8 August 1993.

Raphael-Leff, J. (1991) *Psychological Processes of Childbearing*, London: Chapman & Hall.

Riviere, J. (1929) 'Womanliness as a masquerade', *International Journal of Psychoanalysis* 10: 303–13.

Rutter, M. (1989) *Sex in the Forbidden Zone*, London: Mandala, 1990.

Samuels, A. (1985) *Jung and the Post-Jungians*, London and Boston: Routledge & Kegan Paul.

—— (1989) *The Plural Psyche*, London and New York: Routledge.

—— (1993a) *The Political Psyche*, London and New York: Routledge.

—— (1993b) 'What is a good training?', *British Journal of Psychotherapy* 9: 317–23.

Schaverien, J. (1995) *Desire and the Female Therapist*, London and New York: Routledge.

Seccombe, W. (1993) *Weathering the Storm: The History of Working Class Families*, London: Verso.

Sedgwick, E. (1985) *Between Men: English literature and Male Homosocial Desire*, New York: Columbia University Press, 1992.

Stein, P. (1974) *Incest and Human Love*, New York: Penguin.

Weeks, J. (1985) *Sexuality and Its Discontents*, London: Routledge & Kegan Paul.

Winnicott, D.W. (1944) 'What about father?', in *Getting to Know Your Baby*, London: William Heinemann: 160–74.

—— (1968) 'The effect of psychotic parents on the emotional development of the child', in *The Family and Individual Development*, London: Tavistock Publications: 125–42.

Cupid's myriad arrows

An afterword

David Mann

At the beginning of this book I quoted the opening line of a poem by Elizabeth Barrett Browning:

How do I love thee? Let me count the ways.

I have left it until now to comment on this quote. If the reader has read the discussion of the literature in the Introduction and all the subsequent chapters of this book it is obvious that counting the number of ways of love seems almost infinite, many more than even the poetess imagined. For me this conjures up a puzzling thought: whence did Eros/Cupid get all these arrows? Either he has a very large quiver or the arrows magically replace themselves when fired. Clearly, ancient mythologists seldom bothered themselves about practical details!

The authors included in this volume have interpreted the ideas about love and the sexual in their own personal ways. The chapters by Gerrard, Gordon and Field place more emphasis on love as something distinct from the sexual. Conversely, the chapters by Thomson, Mann, Doctor, Stanton, Chiesa, Gardner and Samuels speak more of the sexual side of the erotic. Such demarcations are artificial but inevitable: love and sex, while not the same thing, clearly have an indeterminate area of overlap. Occasionally in the literature (Ireland 1988) an author seeks to clarify this distinction as agape and sexual love, usually with the assumption that platonic, agape love is purer or superior to sexual love. However, such a split is a fabricated theoretical device. This is a further reason for describing such processes under the umbrella term 'erotic'. The erotic, therefore, needs to be a fairly loose term. Consequently, discussion of the erotic will always be closer to poetry than science. Perhaps the erotic can only be spoken of with all the uniqueness that characterises individual lovers. In the analytic couple, as with love-making itself, each couple discovers desire in a unique way. With the exception of perverse states of mind, no person loves two people in quite the same way.

The difference in understandings of the erotic transference and counter-transference can partly be considered by regarding how each author thinks about the analyst/therapist, as either object or subject, that is to say, whether they are merely responding to the patient's desire or are seen as having desires of their own. The chapters by Thomson, Doctor and Stanton seem to emphasise the role of analyst as sexual object: an object used by the patient's desires. The chapters by Gordon, Mann, Chiesa, Field, Gardner and Samuels draw attention to the role of the analyst as sexual subject with desires of his or her own. While stating the former, Gerrard's chapter seems to emphasise the latter. In fairness to all the authors, all ten chapters draw attention to the analyst as erotic object and subject but differ in where they place the emphasis.

The difference is also apparent between authors with the same theoretical starting point. This is most striking in the chapters by Thomson, Field and Samuels (Chapters 3, 6 and 10). Although they are all Jungians they approach the erotic transference and countertransference in very different manners. While the three chapters by writers influenced by the independent group – Gerrard, Mann and Gardner (Chapters 1, 4 and 9) arrive at similar conclusions about the need of the therapist to find or reach some authentic subjectivity in themselves, they take very different theoretical journeys. The Kleinian chapters by Doctor and Chiesa (Chapters 5 and 8) are more cohesive, but still illustrate a different emphasis. Altogether, there is a conscious diversity within particular psychoanalytic groups as well as between them.

It is difficult not to fall into what I would consider a defensive position when writing about the erotic transference. We can see this in the patterns of all ten chapters as a whole. By and large, a pattern of difference emerges between the male and female authors. The female authors (Gerrard, Gordon, Thomson and Gardner) tend to cite work mostly with female patients, the exceptions being that Gardner describes one male patient and Thomson cites the male patient of a female supervisee. Apart from Gardner the female writers focus more on the loving rather than the sexual aspects of the erotic. Amongst the men writing in this book we see a different trend. With the exception of Mann and Doctor, all the authors (Field, Stanton, Chiesa, Samuels) cite material exclusively with female patients; with the exception of Field, all the men have written about the sexual rather than the loving aspects of the erotic.

If we place these various observations together we note that, by and large, the women are describing issues about love in the homoerotic transference. The overtly sexual, especially with men, is conspicuously absent. The male writers are primarily focusing on the sexual aspect of the heteroerotic transference. Issues about love and homoerotic material are not generally mentioned. A similar pattern is discernible in the literature generally about the erotic transference and countertransference. There are probably individual and cultural (and biological?) reasons for such a split. Writing about all aspects of the erotic transference and countertransference certainly creates difficulties that are hard to overcome.

This book also needs to be seen as part of a developmental process. In the twenty years from 1980 more books and papers have been written about the erotic transference and countertransference than in the previous eighty years of psychoanalysis. This explosion of interest is partly the result of social trends that have led to more open discussion about the erotic, and partly due to processes within psychoanalysis itself. I outlined this in the Introduction, referring to the changing nature of the understanding about the transference and particularly the countertransference, bringing into the light erotic processes that had previously not been articulated.

Does this burgeoning discussion lead to greater clarity about the erotic transference and countertransference? I would suggest that this is not necessarily so. However, the growing discussion at least represents a willingness to find expression to thoughts and a climate of reduced anxiety makes conversation possible. If we remain confused about the erotic this is perhaps inevitable, though hopefully we reach a higher level of confusion.

Hamilton (1996) seems to suggest that the erotic sows confusion in the minds of psychoanalysts. She conducted a large-scale research project using questionnaires and interviews with analysts in the UK and USA to determine how analysts preconsciously use theory. In the chapter 'Do patients *really* love their analysts?' she notes that, in general, positive feelings towards the analyst by the patient are met with distrust on the part of the analyst and that attitudes of love, especially passionate, erotic love have changed little in the last hundred years of psychoanalysis. (Actually, as I demonstrated in the Introduction, attitudes have been slowly changing, at least among some practitioners since the 1980s.) Yet she notes that love is an 'irreducible ingredient in the patient's search for cure and in sticking with analysis' (Hamilton 1996: 165). However, contemporary psychoanalysts' views about the erotic transference (with reference to the 'positive unobjectionable transference', idealisation and narcissism) tend towards attitudes that are 'complex and contradictory' and many British analysts were 'unable to give a clear response' (p. 172), with many saying they had not come across an erotic transference. This latter point contrasts quite sharply with my experience: most of the psychotherapists I know and most of those who have attended my workshop on 'Working with the erotic transference and countertransference' have encountered the erotic transference, though there is a considerable amount of uncertainty about how to approach the material clinically. The observation remains, none the less, that understanding clinical approaches to the erotic transference and countertransference is perplexing. As the chapters in this book demonstrate, there are some areas of widespread agreement as well as divergence about what constitutes the erotic and how best it should be addressed.

This brings me to the final strand of the erotic narrative: the reader's transference (or would it be more appropriately considered as a countertransference?) to the subject of this book – the erotic transference and countertransference. My love of the tradition of British humour nearly led me to entitle this Epilogue 'And how was it for you?' I assume a counter-transference simply because I cannot imagine an absence of countertransference to erotic material. How this book is understood, what chapters appeal to or disagree with the reader's digestion will introduce yet another strand in the myriad arrows that permeate this subject. In this respect the reader's process of understanding will be adding further erotic narratives in what seems to me to be an inexhaustible volley of Cupid's arrows.

REFERENCES

Hamilton, V. (1996) *The Analyst's Preconscious*, Hillsdale, NJ/London: The Analytic Press.
Ireland, W. (1988) 'Eros, agape, amor, libido: concepts in the history of love', in J. Lasky and H. Silverman (eds), *Love: Psychoanalytic Perspectives*, New York and London: New York University Press.

Index